Millennium Folk

Millennium

The University of Georgia Press

Athens and London

AMERICAN

FOLK MUSIC

SINCE

THE SIXTIES

THOMAS R. GRUNING

© 2006 by the University of Georgia Press

Athens, Georgia 30602

Set in Minion and Scala Sans by Bookcomp, Inc.

Printed and bound by Maple-Vail

The paper in this book meets the guidelines for
permanence and durability of the Committee on
Production Guidelines for Book Longevity of the
Council on Library Resources.

Printed in the United States of America

10   09   08   07   06   c   5   4   3   2   1

10   09   08   07   06   p   5   4   3   2   1

Library of Congress Cataloging-in-Publication Data

Gruning, Tom.

Millennium folk : American folk music since the sixties /
by Thomas R. Gruning.

p. cm.

Includes bibliographical references (p.), discography (p.),
and index.

ISBN-13: 978-0-8203-2829-4 (cloth : alk. paper)

ISBN-10: 0-8203-2829-4 (cloth : alk. paper)

ISBN-13: 978-0-8203-2830-0 (pbk. : alk. paper)

ISBN-10: 0-8203-2830-8 (pbk. : alk. paper)

1. Folk music—United States—20th century—History and criticism.

2. Folk music—Social aspects—United States—History—20th century.

I. Title.

ML3551.5.G7 2006

781.62'13009045—dc22   2006005467

British Library Cataloging-in-Publication Data available

This project is dedicated to my wife Jo-Anne,
my son Anton (Tabo),
my mother-in-law Vera Shaul,
and my parents Rolf and Pat,
all of whom contributed in so many ways.
Your support and encouragement has been invaluable
and I am eternally grateful to you all.

CONTENTS

ACKNOWLEDGMENTS

Thanks to my friends, colleagues, and mentors from the University of Texas at Austin whose encouragement, help, and critical eyes made this book a reality. I owe a special debt of gratitude to Gerard Behágue, who passed away during the prepublication phase of this work. It was through his help and encouragement that I came to study ethnomusicology, which subsequently became my chosen field. Gerard always seemed to enjoy it when composers or theorists "saw the light" and turned into "ethnoids." He will be missed. Veit Erlmann's assistance with this project was incalculable. I continue to appreciate his friendship, support, and thoughtful, if occasionally scathing (and usually well-deserved), criticisms. Andrew Dell'Antonio, Ward Keeler, and Bob Fernea also deserve my profound appreciation for their encouragement and patience with my occasional stodginess. You have all changed my life. I would be remiss if I did not also mention all the new and old friends—folkies—who helped to make the work involved in this project a pleasure rather than a burden. The list is long, and you have all helped beyond measure. Special thanks to Alan Whitney, who always seemed to call when I was puzzling over particularly thorny issues: those conversations invariably helped me sort out and organize my thoughts. Finally, thanks to everyone at the University of Georgia Press, particularly Andrew Berzanskis for tracking me down and believing in my work and Jennifer Reichlin for her patience and guidance throughout the process of turning this project into a book.

Introduction
Folk at the Crossroads of the Ordinary

When I began this work, my intent was to produce an ethnography of contemporary singer/songwriters loosely categorized under the umbrella of folk music. In the course of researching and then writing about that research, it became, on one hand, a larger and broader account of the American folk's history, its present, and its potential future. In another sense it became a personalized account of the current folk music scene, one that is necessarily colored by my own subjective perceptions as a participant/observer.

To the reader involved in the contemporary folk community, my observations may at times seem incomplete. For a number of reasons I chose not to discuss various traditional and popular styles often subsumed under the rubric of folk: sacred harp singing, old-time string band music, and so forth. Generally these styles have their own, often limited but very specific, audiences. Bluegrass is also conspicuously absent from the text. The literature concerning bluegrass is voluminous, with hundreds of books and articles on the topic published by popular and academic presses. There are several well known and well attended bluegrass festivals. It is unquestionably a popular music on many levels, yet in terms of commercial and stylistic lineage, it seems to be situated more on the fringes of the country music scene than immediately akin to this ambiguous thing called "folk."

If I don't mention your favorite artist, style, venue, or folk-related activity, I apologize. However, while I attempt to provide an overview of the folk "industry" as it currently exists, my primary goal is to address conceptual issues that came into play in constructions of notions of "folk" in the latter half of the twentieth century and the beginning of the new millennium. For the folk, neither the past nor the present is free from a deep sense of paradox that pervades multiple levels of what has become an increasingly active community of musicians, fans, and entrepreneurs. This book is about the complicated and sometimes convoluted ways in which today's folk communities negotiate the paradoxical terrain of modernity and the past.

Folk music has changed. In the process of traversing the technologized present, many of the folk's past ideological precepts have metamorphosed, keeping pace with and mirroring the development of Internet communication technologies that have served to galvanize contemporary folk communities. The fictions of the folk as rural, working-class, "just plain folk" have given way to a new "common man": one whose position of privilege is marked by a decidedly middle-class nature.

Throughout this text the word "folk"[1] occurs in a variety of contexts. This is not meant to confuse the reader. Rather, in its common usage, the term is mired in ambiguity. "Folk" has become the repository for a surfeit of musical/cultural phenomena. The old-time fiddler, the pop influenced singer/songwriter, the West African drummer, the street poet, and the fingerstyle guitarist, among others, meet under the folk umbrella. "Authenticity," specifically in claims to folkness, has become a multifarious idea in the postrevival world of Folk music.

For today's folk singer/songwriters, indexes of authenticity have changed, sometimes dramatically and sometimes subtly, since the 1960s folk revival. The anonymous author of folk's past has given way to a revival of authorship and ownership in which a politics of experience plays fundamental roles in constructions of authenticity. Folk's traditionally contested relationship with the popular has become less so as stylistic distinctions between them become more ambiguous. I will explore the fundamentally paradoxical nature of contemporary folk idealism as it regards constructed histories and imagined pasts within the context of an increasingly globalized present. Additionally I will suggest that various issues regarding gender, sexuality, and race operate both explicitly and implicitly at multiple levels in today's folk community, reflecting a paradox of exclusion and inclusion that at once reinforces folk idealism and exposes its darker side.

My interest in folk music began as a child. My father, a career army officer, has been interested in folk at least since the 1940s when he and my mother lived in Greenwich Village and would listen to people like Richard Dyer-Bennet, Burl Ives, and Pete Seeger sing in various area venues.[2] I remember singing folk songs with my parents and siblings, reading the lyrics from collections such as *The Fireside Book of Favorite American Songs* or *The Burl Ives Songbook*. My father played a baritone ukulele during these sing-alongs and my mother would play melody lines on an old bowl back mandolin. While these occasions were infrequent, they were nonetheless memorable. As an American child living in Germany, songs like "Red River Valley" and "Clementine" inspired a certain nationalistic pride and imagined connection with my country's rural history.

Around 1963, I saw a movie called *Hootenanny Hoot* at the army post theater in Nürnberg, Germany, where my father was stationed. The movie, not an artistic tour de force by any stretch of the imagination, nonetheless convinced me that the life of a folksinger had to be the most fulfilling path a person could possibly follow. To an impressionable ten-year-old, folk music appeared to be a surefire road to public adulation, general popularity, and romance. What could be better? I immediately began saving my weekly allowance to buy a flattop folk guitar. A few months later I went to the post exchange and came home with a shiny new twenty-dollar Framus guitar. I was hooked.

By the age of sixteen, then living in San Antonio, Texas, I began playing in coffeehouses and bars and for private parties. While some of the music I was playing fit neatly into the traditional folk genre as defined by the folk revivalists of the late 1950s and early 1960s, music written by the next wave of folk and folk-rock performers—Bob Dylan; James Taylor; Arlo Guthrie; Crosby, Stills, and Nash; and others—began to occupy my attention. Many of these songs were characterized by a certain pop sensibility and their texts addressed topical concerns that I found more relevant and appealing than a great deal of the traditional folk song repertory. If as a child folk songs helped me to imagine a rural past, as an adolescent they enabled me to imagine an active and engaging present.

Throughout the next two decades I continued to play music professionally in various contexts, many having little to do with folk music specifically. As folk declined in its mass popular appeal, the economics of music led me to explore jazz, rock, country, and assorted combinations thereof. Yet by the early 1990s it appeared that folk music, and the singer/songwriter phenomenon particularly, was experiencing a resurgence of public interest.

Where there were comparatively few folk music venues during the 1970s and 80s (the ones that survived folk's lean years were, for the most part, halls associated with previous folk revivals), the 1990s saw an unprecedented number of new folk music oriented venues opening throughout the United States.[3] Prior to the 1990s, the big names in folk music, most of whom had been folk's "stars" during the 1940s through the 1960s, dominated the limited folk marketplace provided by the venerated music halls.[4] By 1992 new "stars" were emerging, the folk landscape was becoming stylistically less homogeneous than it had ever been, and new venues sprang up in response to increasing audience demand. While traditional folk musics continued to occupy players within folk communities, the singer/songwriter became the dominant feature on the folk landscape in the last decade of the twentieth century (much to the chagrin of many traditional "folkies"). If folk already carried with it a somewhat ambiguous notion of musical style, the new legions of singer/songwriters, whose early musical inspiration often came from Beatles records and other popular music of the 60s and 70s, took it to new levels of ambiguity. Ambiguous or not, today's folk singer/songwriters are finding a growing national and international audience of listeners whose interest in music and lyrics often borders on the passionate.

Alongside this increasing audience for folk songs, my own involvement, both as a songwriter and a performer, was rekindled. Eventually I became interested in exploring the social and cultural implications of the new folk phenomenon, and my position as a performer offered certain advantageous possibilities for conducting research. In some ways I have been (and continue to be) considered an insider within the folk community. However, as an academic and a composer,[5] a somewhat tenacious and common anti-intellectualism occasionally drives a wedge between the "folk" and me. Yet unquestionably I am involved in the study of what Philip Brett, in referring to the subjects of his research, has called "the music of my own tribes" ("Musicality, Essentialism, and the Closet," 15). As such, some of the problems inherent to ethnography are considerably less problematic than if this project concerned a tribe other than my own.

As a musician and performer with long-standing associations in the American folk community, the possibility of "exoticizing" the folk—a familiar topic in anthropological and ethnomusicological literature—is unlikely to present itself as a serious concern within the context of this project. Yet general problems of ethnography must, by their very nature, lead to a degree of skepticism. The ambiguity that characterizes all ethnography lies in the fallibility of comparisons and the haziness between fact and allegory that cannot help but color the interpretive process (see, for example, Clifford, "On Ethnographic Allegory";

Erlmann, *Nightsong: Performance, Power, and Practice in South Africa*). Likewise my own experiences as a folk insider/outsider (my position as "ethnographer" marks me as an outsider despite my participation as a performer) and the periodic autobiographical inclusions in the following pages may further blur borders between fact and fiction.

This project will not attempt to offer an encyclopedic catalog of American folk singer/songwriters. Others have made that attempt only to produce snapshots of a rapidly changing landscape. Further, I am less interested in folk music's "stars"—a notion that seems antithetical to the popular perception of the egalitarian folk—than I am in rank-and-file singer/songwriters who travel the country entertaining today's folk audiences and in weekend players who bring their guitars to festival campgrounds and eagerly play their songs for anyone who will listen. The music that these people make may be technically complicated or quite simple (I use these terms in their conventional Western sense), may serve to inform and/or to entertain, may carry apparently innocent celebrations of life and love, or may be constituted by a jaded worldliness. These surface characteristics do little to differentiate today's folk music from that of the past. The marked differences lie in the socially grounded discourses of the "new folk" within the context of a global ecumene characterized by changing and increasingly interconnected modes of cultural production. The contemporary American singer/songwriter is, to borrow a phrase from an ad slogan of the late 1980s, not your father's folk.[6]

Folk music has changed. In the past decade or two public perceptions of folk music have changed; the ways in which music is disseminated and consumed have changed; many of the faces have changed; and in subtle and not so subtle ways, the signs, symbols, and messages of folk are different today than they were even twenty years ago.

Folk music, like all music, is a discursive vehicle through which public and private issues are expressed and shared. Yet the meanings of folk's familiar thematic material have become more fluid for today's performers and listeners. The exoticism of the primitive that marked folk's early entrée into "polite society" has shifted to "world music." Folk's "exotic" has moved to the crossroads of the ordinary: an "Ordinary" in which interrelationships of image and meaning are entrenched in complex webs of signification.

In some respects the contemporary American folk music landscape lends itself well to a postmodern reading. The notion of pastiche and the sometimes ambiguous referential positions enacted in contemporary folk performances may suggest that approach. To be sure, popular dissatisfaction with the global and the return to a secondary localism resonates in terms of today's folk "community." The complexities of global interaction and interconnectedness that may seem to overwhelm local attachments to commodity and cultural production are reactive elements in the process of embracing this secondary localism. Where complexity reigns, simplicity exerts a strong appeal. However, attachments to the simplicity of a folk community and localisms that emerge in the context of the postmodern moment are constituted by convoluted connections between past and present, the old and the new. A communal sense of nostalgia for the local accompanies the fragmentation of center/periphery relationships endemic to post-structuralism, yet this new localism inextricably intertwines with the global. While various notions of the postmodern can be useful in coming to grips with diverse levels of human activity and interaction, they cannot in and of themselves dictate an exclusively postmodern reading of the "folk." Clearly a strictly postmodern approach risks being unable to reconcile the theoretical with the lives of very real people.

I will argue that images—signifiers and chains of signifiers—are anything but empty; that for the "folk" each image and the relationship of one signifier to the next may be endowed with meaning; that the signifier (or the interrelationships of multiple signifiers) is no less meaningful due to the absence of a signified; that interpretive strategies are operating on different levels than in the past.[7] Fredric Jameson suggests that "depthlessness" is one characteristic of postmodernity. I will argue that the notion of "depth" has changed and that claims of a lack of depth constitute a peculiar sort of modernist nostalgia.[8] The American folk, like everyone else (whether we like it or not), are situated within what Caren Kaplan has called the "postmodern moment." What that may mean in terms of a changing aesthetics of interpretation and how it ultimately affects our work and our lives remains to be seen. According to Kaplan in *Questions of Travel: Postmodern Discourses of Displacement,* "Just as the concepts of colonial and postcolonial must be grounded in material specificity, poststructuralism can no longer be generalized as a monolithic entity but must be studied as immensely complicated and varied versions" (6). Like notions of the "folk," postmodernism refuses to be easily categorized as a fixed set of ideological precepts. The world is rarely a simple place.

In the context of the comparatively recent phenomenon of the "singer/songwriter" as a reasonably distinct (and sometimes disdained) subgenre of "real" folk, I will argue that changing modes of interpretation for contemporary folk musicians and audiences mirror larger and more far-reaching changes in modes of cultural production both at local and global levels, at the same time offering discourses of resistance to those changes: a dialectics of folk. Yet the dialectical relationships that mark folk's present and past extend beyond an obvious politics of power and resistance or, to use Michel Foucault's terminology, an "employment of power."

Like Foucault's notion of power as "the multiplicity of force relations imma-nent in the sphere in which they operate and which constitute their organiza-tion" (*The History of Sexuality*, 93), folk's production of "truth" is thoroughly imbued with subtly nuanced aspects of power. Through power relations and employments of power, the cultural and musical landscapes of folk are contin-ually constructed, reconstructed, recalled, and reconfigured. Gage Averill in *A Day for the Hunter, a Day for the Prey: Popular Music and Power in Haiti* (1997) suggests that music is more than simply an "instrument of resistance," although he shows it to be quite effective in that regard; it is also "a medium of the nego-tiation and communication of power" (Averill 1997: 210). Taken in the light of Foucault's idea of power, Averill endows music with a particularly potent role, one in which power is negotiated at multiple levels and degrees and through which the potential for equity exists alongside the potential for terror.

This notion of the dialectics of power relations in music communities and in folk music specifically, draws heavily on the work of Theodor Adorno and Max Horkheimer, whose responses to the rise of National Socialism in pre–World War II Germany adeptly demonstrate the Janus face of reason and ter-ror. Following the Frankfurt School, Veit Erlmann has suggested, "Music everywhere says yes and no at the same time" (*Nightsong*, xx). Music can prom-ise redemption and come up short on delivery. It can be a potent vehicle in struggles for social change and at the same time reinforce the power relations that undermine that change. It can be highly referential, evoking profound emotional responses, while at the same time being strikingly superficial: an art of the surface. The evocative imagery of love and loss, rural pasts, and a chang-ing sense of the authenticity of experience—folk music "texts"—can appear to be a continual reprocessing of nostalgic fictions. Without question the politics of image plays a powerful role in the aesthetic production of contemporary folk music.

Yet these texts with their particular signs and symbolic codes—the references to imagined pasts, idealized interpersonal relationships, and the artist as the au-thentic subject—have taken on a referential life of their own. Each participant in the performative experience becomes an active agent in the interpretation of the text. Aesthetic value can be determined by its efficacy in exciting these imaginative processes, which in turn is linked to personal experience in nec-essarily complex and convoluted webs of symbolic interaction. The imaginary and the experiential "authentic" are inexorably intertwined within folk's discur-sive fields. Indeed, suggesting that the experiential authentic has referential sig-nification beyond the imaginary—beyond the chain of empty signifiers—will have my postmodernist colleagues hurling accusations of blatant modernism. However, like the politician walking the fence of moderation, I will continue to suggest that some aspects of postmodern critical analysis are necessary to explain contemporary lives, while others, which may present fascinating philosophical conundrums, are less useful.[9]

From a folkie perspective, the heady and ethereal conundrums of the postmodern condition are the stuff of intellectual engagement, but what you take home at the end of the day are the things that determine engagement with the experiential "Ordinary": the condition through which the potential negation of an idea or ideology is intentionally subverted before it approaches its dialectic extreme and the phantom signified is unnecessary, the signifier(s) generating its own meaning.

The multiple and sometimes conflicting (and conflicted) meanings implied by the "folk music" label are perhaps the most problematic aspect of this or any other work concerning contemporary notions of the folk. What does it mean to say, "I am a folksinger," in the information age? Is it simply a label through which commercial value as a commodity can be determined, as critics such as Charles Keil have repeatedly suggested? Is "folk" itself an empty signifier for which there is no signified: another third-order simulacrum, as Jean Baudrillard might suggest? Yes and no. There is an element of smoke and mirrors in current claims to "folkness," and the retrospective imagination plays a critical role in shaping social behaviors and aesthetic choices.[10] However, notwithstanding the basis of these behaviors and choices, their effects are very real and can have profound consequences for people's lives.

From time to time I will have to address the ongoing debates regarding definition of the term "folk," regardless of the fact that I find these the least interesting aspect of this broad and multilayered musical culture. In these definitional skirmishes lie clues to some of the more subterranean cultural codings through which people define themselves as individual subjects and members of larger social groups. It is partially through self-labeling that people's claims to authenticity are exerted and contested.

In the United States and Europe, the need to define folk in terms of oral transmission and traditional practices, for example, is a product of a long history of fetishizing authenticity. With regard to various folk arts, we in the West have cultivated an obsession with imagined and real rural heritages: what Eric Hobsbawm has called " 'invented tradition,' whereby present interests construct a cohesive past to establish or legitimate present-day institutions or social relations" (quoted in Walser, *Running with the Devil*, 60). The proclivity for categorization—which is undoubtedly linked to exchange value as well as notions of "high" and "low" cultural hierarchies—takes shape in a sort of aesthetic Darwinism through which we can make claims to the presumed primacy of our highly evolved musical expressions and at the same time organize the constructed histories that help to define our social and cultural identities.

Throughout this work the term "culture" is used in a variety of contexts: culture of the campground, popular culture, cultural imperialism, and so forth. The fluidity with which the term winds its way through this and many other texts suggests common, if perhaps crude, interpretations or characteristics. Immanuel Wallerstein situates culture within the context of two "tonalities" (Roy Boyne's term). The first of these explains culture as "a way of summarizing the ways in which groups distinguish themselves from other groups. It represents what is shared within the group, and presumably simultaneously not shared (or not entirely shared) outside it" ("Culture as the Ideological Battleground of the Modern World-System," 31–32). The second interpretation asserts "culture is also used to signify not the totality of the specificity of one group against another but instead certain characteristics *within* the group, as opposed to other characteristics within the same group" (32). While Wallerstein's tonalities of culture are arguable—for example, Boyne rightly suggests they do not fully account for *all* contingencies of culture—they are nonetheless serviceable, providing general and easily accessible terminological and behavioral contexts. Wallerstein is too astute a scholar not to see the difficulties in defining the criteria for "group" claims to a culture (in the first sense of the term). The question of "who or what has a culture" (33) can be superficially explained through common group characteristics, beliefs, and behaviors, but as Wallerstein points out, "behavior or value-preferences or however one defines culture is of course an evolving phenomenon" (34). Yet, acknowledging the changes that occur over time and therefore the somewhat fluid nature of the first designation, his dualistic model provides a relatively simple tool for interpreting culture in general terms. In this text the uses of the term should be readily apparent as applying either to the tonality of the group—those who count themselves as part of a folk music community—or "certain characteristics *within* the group" that account for notions of value and categorization: high, low, or popular culture, for example.

While the notion of high/low culture has been laid bare in recent years,[11] leaving scholars considerable latitude for institutionally sanctioned popular music studies, few are concerned with what has come to be known as American folk music. In chapter 1, I will discuss how the notion of high/low culture has metamorphosed for the folk in the past few decades. The high/low dichotomy has turned in upon itself in recent years exacerbating the sense of contest with folk's longtime nemesis and frequent consort, the popular. In the process of a rapidly changing folk landscape, the folk/popular relationship has contributed to a reconfiguration of authorial roles and "authority."

In the past few years popular music scholars have applied current conceptual trends in philosophy and literary criticism to rock music and various pop-oriented local and world musics, yet there seems to be a certain reluctance to apply those same concepts to folk music research. Perhaps the reason for this lack of attention is that because of its nostalgic content, folk music is an easy target, and therefore subtle aspects of its cultural production and dissemination are overlooked in favor of studies concerning more popular "popular" musics. Maybe it is because folk music is considered by many to be boring: another notion with which I will grapple in chapter 1. In any case, most academics have ignored folk music in the last decade or two. There are notable exceptions: Robert Cantwell's book *When We Were Good: The Folk Revival* (1996) and Ronald Cohen's more recent *Rainbow Quest: The Folk Music Revival and American Society, 1940–1970* (2002) present retrospectives of the 1960s "folk scare"; Charles Wolfe and Kip Lornell's *The Life and Legend of Leadbelly* (1992), offers an engaging history minus the celebratory mythology that so often accompanies biographic accounts of "great men"; and Benjamin Filene's *Romancing the Folk: Public Memory and American Roots Music* (2000), which begins to account for the cultural construction of a folk "authentic" in twentieth-century America. In chapter 2 the notion of authenticity and its shifting referents will be discussed in terms of its past construction and the sometimes subtle, sometimes explicit reconfigurations within the contemporary folk landscape.

Wolfe and Lornell's and Filene's studies have proven useful in terms of their historical content. However, neither of them is specifically concerned with the present-day folk music landscape and its ties to the past, its disjunctures from that past, and the increasing ambiguities that arise in light of those relationships. This leads me to what is perhaps the most fundamental point of my analysis: what singer/songwriters as a music culture have left behind and, more importantly, what they hold on to and why. Through an interrogation of folk's real and imagined ties with the past, I hope to facilitate a broader understanding of the conflicted and often ambiguous nature of this genre. My project is not to debunk or discredit. Rather it is to explore music, social processes, and cultural constructions through which these people (and I include myself) make sense of the world: to traverse musical landscapes of contemporary singer/songwriters whose work resonates for a broad audience—the "community" of folk—in profound and meaningful ways.

This project will not provide a definition of folk music. Defining folk music is a task that is hopelessly entrenched in various and subjective perspectives. Scholars and lay people alike have been wrestling with that one for well over a hundred years. As time passes it becomes increasingly difficult to settle on a definition that everyone involved can live with. Rather than attempting to define, I will investigate underlying factors behind those difficulties. The ambiguities in terminology, or more precisely the multiple meanings of "folk" in the United States, are ultimately and intimately linked to larger social and cultural developments that have occurred since the beginning of the twentieth century. The world is a very different place today than it once was. To rely solely on historical precedent in any analysis of contemporary culture is to engage in folly. The ways in which much popular music is learned, transmitted, commodified, marketed, authenticated, and legitimized are different today than in the past. The dynamic nature of these processes is, most often, directly connected to advances in mass mediation and technology and is critical in coming to grips with the multiple roles of music in modernity. For a musical genre historically associated with notions of tradition, the rural, egalitarianism, and populist idealism, the dialectics of this relationship are unavoidable. But to consider technology and the "folk" as incongruous ignores the long history of that relationship.

Chapter 3 concerns folk's historical relationship with technology, the contradictions of that association, and recent manifestations that have proven fundamental to the grassroots revival of folk in the past decade. Technology, in the context of the recording, reproduction, and broadcasting industries as well as in mass communication and marketing, has played a pivotal role in the development of folk music and most other popular musics in the twentieth century and is an issue that will wind its way throughout this text. The availability of inexpensive high quality recording equipment in the past few decades has provided what Peter Manuel, in describing India's cassette culture, calls a "democratic-participant media" (*Cassette Culture*, 3). However, to blindly celebrate this technology's potential for redemption is to ignore the warnings of earlier critical thinkers.[12]

In very direct ways, new information and communication technologies increase the sense of social and economic division within American society. In other ways, they make the world a smaller and more understandable place. Those who can afford to take advantage of technological advances have access to a vast volume of information, and the availability of information technology is increasing. However, like those who owned television sets in the 1950s and early 1960s, personal computer owners are a minority of the world's population. Computer literacy remains by and large a condition of social privilege. The demographics of today's folk community bear this out and will be discussed at length in chapter 4.

In the past ten years the "business of folk" has become increasingly dependent upon Internet communication. For today's folk singer/songwriters Web presence has become unavoidable. Booking information, biographical information, tour schedules, artist promotional material, and recorded musical selections

can all be had at the click of a mouse. While access to and training in this technology is becoming more available to greater numbers of people, it continues to
delineate a metaphorical line in the sand between the haves and the have-nots.
The interrelationships of new technologies and the demographics of the "folk"
bring to bear issues of race, class, and economics. These issues are addressed
explicitly in this study, but are also located in the interstices between other aspects of the project. Social and cultural inequities notwithstanding, modern
recording and communication technologies have irrevocably altered the face of
global and local music industries.

Chapter 4 concerns the developing industry of folk. Due in no small part to
general dissatisfaction with the mainstream music industry's corporate control
of aesthetic production, contemporary folk musicians have created a microindustry that appears to be independent of the mainstream but is tied to it in more
ways than most participants care to acknowledge. Connections are apparent at
conceptual, aesthetic, and practical levels. I will describe the various primary
aspects of the industry as well as the central roles technology has played in the
folk microindustry's inception and development. Working singer/songwriters
have directly and indirectly embraced many recent advances in technology: the
resulting conflicting ideological associations between "authentic" folk pasts (albeit pasts that may be largely based on fiction) and the present are usually either not acknowledged as being incongruous or are begrudgingly accepted as a
practical necessity. The invention or fragmentation of traditions—an increasing
fluidity of "acceptable" musical conventions—mirrors a sometimes contested,
but ubiquitous confluence of current and traditional performance practice.

Through necessity the venues in which folk music is presented will occupy
chapters 5 and 6. Chapter 5 details the emergence of the house concert, concert
series, and changing notions of the coffeehouse. The increasing number of professional and semiprofessional folk singer/songwriters who have begun touring
in the past ten to fifteen years, and the audiences whose newfound reclamation
of folk music has affirmed the practicality of those projects, have collectively increased the demand for venues. However, the nature of the venues has changed,
again in both tacit and explicit ways, mirroring larger and more generalized
changes in the nature of the audience. The expression of those changes and
of a certain unwillingness to discard the baggage of folk's past is most clearly
demonstrated in the folk festival.

Chapter 6 interrogates the folk music festival as a microcosm of the contemporary folk landscape. This chapter is not intended to be a comprehensive
description of all, or even a great number of festivals. Rather it addresses generalized notions of festival "cultures" and deals with issues that became apparent

to me over a period of several years attendance at the Kerrville Folk Festival, the Falcon Ridge Folk Festival, and others. Generally, these festivals lean more toward presenting contemporary singer/songwriters than traditional folk music performers. I focus on venues that highlight the changing nature of the contemporary folk landscape rather than on those at which traditional musics are primary.

Through participant observation my experiences at numerous festivals serve to document cultural, musical, and social processes through which countless facets of the contemporary folk scene are enacted. The festival is a site where folk's egalitarian idealism, hierarchical social strata, economy, and racial imagination converge in a paradoxical spectacle of community interaction.

Chapter 7 explores the seemingly unlikely association between the recent fascination with and popularity of so-called "world music" and the folk. Within the past decade folk music organizations, publications, and venues have increasingly featured non-Western performers alongside the conventional American singer/songwriter, espousing the universality of folkness: "It's all folk music." Folk's historical association with non-Western musics is well documented and recently has been soundly criticized. A brief foray into the contested realm of those arguments is followed by an analysis of the role of the contemporary singer/songwriter in global contexts.

Chapter 8 concerns attitudes, roles, and actors at the forefront of rapidly changing ideas about and perceptions of gender and sexuality. For most of the twentieth century folk music has been, at least in its public face, a primarily male, heterosexual pursuit. The idea of the common man, with which folk music is usually aligned, left little room for obvious allusion to anything other than confident heterosexuality. Women have played important, if subordinate, roles in folk's past, but homosexuality was rarely a topic for public consumption. However, along with a relatively widespread public acceptance of homosexuality over the past decade,[13] the folk landscape has proven to be fertile ground for the expression of sexual freedom. A number of openly gay artists have brought the politics of sexuality into the folk limelight and have received varying degrees of popular acceptance. Reconciling folk's past and present through the lens of sexuality presents folk communities and musicians with the potential for new readings of traditional texts and a rich source of topical compositional material.

Chapter 9 explores the directions that folk singer/songwriters have taken in presenting their material and offers general observations regarding the present trajectory of the folk community at large, the incorporation of diverse artistic influences, and the potential for future development, or for disenchantment and subsequent decline of folk's current popularity.

My Folk

In the last decades of the twentieth century the crucible of American folk music changed hands. A new generation of folksingers began to mature. The old guard, those who remain of the generations who took folk music from the 1930s bourgeois drawing rooms and 1960s college campuses and situated it in the commercial mainstream (if only for moments), have become icons of folk's commercial "glory days." Where folk music was once a reasonably and usually well-defined category of American music,[14] it has become considerably less so for today's folk music communities. Having been actively involved in the American folk music community for some thirty years, I will find it necessary to include brief autobiographical sketches of that involvement in order to provide a sense of context for describing the changes that have occurred in the folk landscape over the past decades. Clearly this is a risky project in a number of ways. My account must certainly betray a vested interest in its own outcome. As a member of this tribe, my objectivity must be called into question. However, the truth of objectivity, even under the most ideal ethnographic circumstances, has proven to be a myth.[15] Additionally the very nature of historicity and particularly of personal histories have repeatedly come under fire in recent years.

Vincent Crapanzano has suggested that "historical texts resemble rather more often the fairytale than history" (*Tuhami*, 7). In the process of conducting interviews, often with the same actors over several years, Crapanzano's observation seems particularly insightful. As a narrator I can aspire to present an account that corresponds to past experience. However, in the final analysis my account, like all historicity, is necessarily suspicious due in part to the multiple reconstructions and reconfigurations of the past that occur in the processes of remembering. In light of recent scholarship regarding memory, it seems clear that history is often as much a process of forgetting as of remembering (see Schacter, *Searching for Memory*).

Millennium Folk

They built a house two stories high

And realized before the paint was dry

If it's not being built

It's falling down

If it's not being born

It's passing on

And all that remains the same

Is change

—Michael Jerling, "All That Remains the Same,"

    from *New Suit of Clothes*

 Folk Music Has Changed
The Author(ity), the Popular, and the
"What Is Folk?" Debates

"Hi, you can call me Bugkiller." The weathered middle-aged man, wearing a baby-blue jumpsuit and a bone-white Panama hat, began his litany about anything and everything but killing bugs. His poetry was either well rehearsed or, as seemed more the case, a rhetorical patchwork arising from a well of personal experience: both general life experience and, more specifically, performative experience. Clearly he had done this before. The relentless delivery of verses concerning his sexual prowess, working for a living, politics, women, television, and south Texas landscapes—each verse ending with some reference to bugs—went on for about twenty minutes before he tipped his hat, left the stage, and wandered out the door as casually as he had wandered in.

The year was 1972. I was playing an acoustic guitar/vocal gig in a bar in Dallas when the Bugkiller's uninvited appearance amused, annoyed, and most certainly took me by surprise. Granted, the peanut shells that littered the floor of the north

Texas beer joint didn't exactly delineate the space as a bastion of high culture. Still, where did this guy get off interrupting my set with his rambling narrative? I was engaged in my "Art" when this grizzled old fellow with an acre or two of South Texas grit under his fingernails grabbed my vocal microphone and began his extended monologue. At first I supposed that my role was to provide background music for his poetry—in much the same way as I imagined the beatnik model of poet accompanied by jazz musicians or bongo players—and played some unobtrusive accompaniment until it became obvious that my participation was superfluous. At that point I stopped playing, trying not to appear annoyed, but hoping to disassociate myself from the spectacle in the eyes of the audience. His words poured out, sometimes in a singsong fashion, sometimes in a quiet almost intimate poetics, the tempo and dynamics changing without apparent reason but somehow complimenting the fragmented thematic content of the piece. Certain words were sustained for dramatic or humorous effect and the inflections of his vocal delivery accentuated the musical characteristics of speech. There was a sense of organization—the nature of which escaped me—and a method behind the madness.

The most troubling and, in retrospect, the most memorable aspect of this chance encounter with Bugkiller was that it revealed some of the ambiguities of the "folk," which had until then, in my mind, been completely unproblematic. The ideas of art, artistic value, and the stylistic autonomy of what I thought of as folk music (or classical or jazz or rock) had reasonably solid bases within the context of my brief experience as a professional musician. Bugkiller's performance, as strange as it seemed on one level, was somehow connected to my limited notion of a folk aesthetic. There was something oddly compelling about it, an elusive perception of commonality between his and my performances. Perhaps the rural authenticity of his persona was what the audience (and I include myself regardless of the fact that I was at times involved in the performance) found intriguing. At that time the rural folk ideal and its connection with American folk music was unmistakable.[1] For young, middle-class, suburban American folksingers (once again I include myself), imagining a folk identity—a rural past that in most cases never existed—had become a full-time occupation. Bugkiller was heavily endowed with the appearance of rural authenticity. Further, the textual content and delivery of Bugkiller's monologue revealed him as the ideal hayseed whose intelligence transcended the obvious limitations of the collectively imagined rural past. Bugkiller seemed to possess some mystical insight, an awareness impenetrable to the uninitiated. At the same time, his performance was perceived as a bit weird, and the audience reacted with increasingly nervous laughter as the apparently disconnected narrative unfolded. My own reaction, to distance myself from this man through body language, rolling eyes, and knowing glances, was even at the moment tempered with a peculiar fascination, not unlike the sense of mixed attraction and revulsion that causes people to slow down to observe a car wreck. The casualty of this wreck was to be my paradigmatic notion of folk music.

While neither Bugkiller nor I realized it at the time, his performance planted a seed of change in my aesthetic worldview. Twenty-eight years later that night remains among a handful of turning points in my musical life: not as a momentous cathartic event, but more as a point at which I could have turned one way or the other at an intersection with no apparent advantage to either. Turning in the direction I eventually chose led to unexpected and serendipitous consequences that may or may not have occurred had I turned a different way. I could have forgotten about Bugkiller and his poetic and certainly "musical" performance. Rather, with the advantage of almost three decades of retrospection, the experience has taken on the patina of an old photograph, slightly browned around the edges and instilled with a sense of authenticity that can be claimed only through the gauze of the historical imagination. Through the imperfect lens of memory, Bugkiller marks a point at which the "folk" and "folk music" became ambiguous, amorphous, and consequently much more intriguing.

However, for most scholars and folk music aficionados, the general cultural attributes ascribed to the genre were, and in many cases continue to be, somewhat more distinct. As Simon Frith suggests in *Performing Rites: On the Value of Popular Music* (1996),

> Now it's easy enough to be cynical about folk discourse, which seems to rest on an essential self-deception—that which is worked hard for is presented as coming naturally, that which is commodified is presented as communal. But this is not to say that folk ideology isn't (perhaps for just this reason) rhetorically very persuasive, and there are two further reasons for this. First, the folk world, like the classical world, in preserving its ideals puts a central emphasis on tradition. It has its own archives and archivists, its own scholars and scholarly magazines, its own instructive use of liner notes ("the record as teaching device"). The emphasis, though, is less on history and the accumulation of knowledge than on "purity" and the correct (traditional) way of doing things. Folk music is thus evaluated (and condemned—Dylan going electric) according to concepts of unchanging musical "truth." (40)

The suggestion that folk ideology can be easily compartmentalized as a fixed set of assumptions presents a particularly superficial perception of the folk as a homogeneous community of style. It implies a static concept of folk that relies on scholarly and popular notions inscribed in public memory during and immediately following the 1960s folk revival. Much has changed since the 1960s, and even then the generalized ideological precepts assigned to the folk by scholarly analysts failed to extract the fine gradations of personal, individual, and group investment in those notions. Further, by asserting that folk's "central emphasis on tradition," "purity," and "unchanging musical 'truth'" is part of that fixed ideology, Frith assumes a monolithic and inflexible notion of tradition. Clearly, certain folk ideals are drawn from the ideological wellspring Frith mentions, but even the most basic of those assumptions are far from being universally accepted paradigms. The popular perceptions of those paradigms are what Frith, and other scholars who look at folk communities from an etic perspective, assume to be fixed characteristics of a generally accepted ideology, an ideological trend that was perhaps more accurate forty years ago than it is today. The archetypal ideological bent Frith describes is simply the easiest cultural starting point from which to provide an analysis of the folk. Like most stereotypes, Frith's folk ideology has some basis in the popular imagination. Like any generalization, it is an unfortunate analytical stopping point.

Individuals and groups have often made imitation of particular older folk music styles their forte, thus creating museum piece performances. Many of these practitioners compulsively adhere to "traditional" performance practices as prescribed by historical precedents. For these groups of performance historians, Frith's assertion of a folk ideology that makes claims to purity and unchanging truth is on point. However, in today's folk landscape these purists are in the minority.

In *When We Were Good: The Folk Revival* (1996), Robert Cantwell, while acknowledging the complexity of the relationships between folk pasts and their adaptation by 1960s revivalists, quotes Paul Nelson to describe the same sort of characteristic folk ideological archetypes.

> By 1965, as Paul Nelson noted, the folksinger's persona had evolved into a loosely conventional form, that of the "casually road-weary" traveler in jeans and boots or peasant frocks, "clothes as rumpled as parents would allow," "erratic" hair, one who speaks a pidgin idiom neither south nor west but vaguely regional and proletarian, "that non-regional dialect of the Shangri-La West that Bob Dylan and Jack Elliott hailed from, that mythical nowhere where all men talk like Woody Guthrie and are recorded by Moses Asch." (328–329)

Where Frith's account is merely an excerpt from a work not specific to folk music, Cantwell's book presents a detailed social history of the revival. Yet in both cases the paradigms of what Robert Lumer calls "the grass roots movement of amateurs" (56) continue to be the most obvious surface elements of folk's engagements with modernity. Through the late nineteenth century and continuing into the first half of the twentieth century, folk music scholarship laid a conceptual groundwork for constructions of folk's lingering archetypal narratives.

It was Francis James Child who set the standard for the epistemological trajectory of folk music scholarship in the late nineteenth and early twentieth centuries. Generally ballad collecting and classification with regard to specific European origins and details of song texts loosely marked the boundaries of scholarly research, a trend that shifted slowly. This is not to say that all folk music scholarship of the period followed the strict constraints of collection and classification. For some regional archivists, particularly those who collected work songs, social contexts and functions within those contexts were fruitful areas of inquiry. By midcentury, context became a central focus.

In his classic book *Anglo-American Folksong Scholarship Since 1898* (1959), D. K. Wilgus suggests, "The study of folksong is becoming no longer a comparison of ballad texts, but a study of what people sing in their daily lives, a study including the singer as well as the song" (242). The same year Alan Lomax's essay "Folk Song Style" outlined a framework for his immanent "cantometrics" project. [2] Lomax asserted, "The study of musical style should embrace the total human situation which produces the music" (929). A wider interest in musical accompaniment paralleled the apparent paradigm shift toward studying folk music in culture. Where earlier scholars were concerned primarily with folk song texts—the music playing a secondary role—for Lomax and others writing in the 1950s, music and text were equally important. However, beyond the initial and primary interest in text and finally in music *and* text, constructions of folk ideology have provided a backdrop for scholarly literature. From Johann Gottfried von Herder's notions of folk purity by which Child determined which songs were "real" folk songs—and therefore worthy of inclusion in his collection—to Alan Lomax's contextual approach and the subsequent/simultaneous glorification of a folk authentic, much early (pre-1960s) scholarship reinforced what have become conventional myths of folkness.

During folk music's commercial glory days in the 1960s and after, a great deal of research concerned folk music's association with what are generally considered liberal political causes. R. Serge Denisoff wrote extensively and articulately on protest songs, highlighting the sometimes conflicting messages of various political/folk texts in the context of their role in the commercial limelight of the revival. Like the earliest examples of folk music scholarship, Denisoff's work is more concerned with song texts than with music. However, central to his work are the messages and meanings of songs within the milieu of the American social landscape. Where folk music as social protest and resistance was most prominently theorized during and after the 1960s revival, the association continues to inculcate contemporary notions of the folk.

By the time Denisoff published his seminal *Sing a Song of Social Significance* in 1972, various generalized folk paradigms (including the notion of folk as a vehicle for political expression and, not coincidentally, its association with the Communist Party) were already firmly embedded in the American popular imaginary. Many, if not all, aspects of the American folk's cultural construction achieved paradigmatic status through longevity, repetition, and perhaps also intent. Benjamin Filene suggests that notions of the constituent elements of "authentic" folk music and performance were delineated, defined, and inscribed in American popular consciousness by various scholars and ideologues in the early twentieth century: folk's "power brokers."

If It's Got an Author, It Ain't Folk

The idea of anonymous authorship of folk songs, one of folk's grand narratives, presents a peculiar set of problems: in the process of recycling claims to particular attributes of an imagined folk "authentic," the authorial specificity of the original claim to folkness is obscured by its continual reinscription over time, and thus the claim itself is legitimized, becoming part and parcel of its own romantic mythology. Authorial anonymity suggests a number of additional problems in light of folk music's engagements with capitalism—music as commodity—or Roland Barthes's less prosaic, and befuddling to many, pronouncement of the death of the author. Folk and its relationships with capitalism will wind its way throughout this text. Barthes's ideas, delineated in his 1968 essay "The Death of the Author," while conceptually intriguing, provide little practical insight into current evocations of the anonymous author as a claim to folkness.

According to Pete Seeger, the term "folk music" was coined by "nineteenth-century scholars to describe the music of the peasantry, age-old and anonymous" (*The Incompleat Folksinger*, 5). This requirement for achieving folk status has served to standardize various descriptions or definitions of folk music through academic and popular accounts since the nineteenth century and continues to resonate today (although the sort of prescriptive dogma has become less prevalent in recent years). However, while popular definitive notions regarding the nature of folk song have become less rigid in the past few decades, any song attributed to an anonymous author unquestionably fits the folk mold: authenticity through anonymity.

The apparent oxymoronic nature of this relationship between authenticity and anonymity has, at its root, two epistemological threads. First, it underlies a distinctly anti-Enlightenment ideology embedded specifically in such early nineteenth-century notions as Herder's theory of culture and, more directly, his aggrandizement of the *volk*. While the cultural relativism that marked his work asserted that all cultures were equal but different and that each was endowed with its own authenticity, Herder's glorification of the special character of the common German volk (at the expense of the general humanism that formed the foundation of European Enlightenment thought) eventually sowed the seeds for the particularly virulent and tenacious nationalism that, in the twentieth century, played a pivotal role in the rise of Nazism. Yet the glorification of the folk and, specifically for the American folk, the persistent currency of the anonymous author confirms the legacy of Herder's ideological perspective. The second, equally persistent idea, which presents a peculiar contradiction to the volk ideal, concerns what Steven Connor in his essay "The Ethics of the Voice" calls "proprietary voice":

> During the course of the seventeenth and eighteenth centuries in Europe, the operations of the voice became powerfully politicized. The agency of this change is the formation of an ethics of property, which put into place a concept of self related to itself in terms of ownership and possession, and worked to fix and assign the discourse of the self (for example in the coming into being of the idea of authorship), and to textualize voice. The politics of voice is inseparable from this phonographic hunger. The ethical injunction against the reduction of others to the condition of objects suggests the injunction against the theft or misuse of the attributes of the other, and especially of their voice. But it is only as a result of having been thus construed as a possessable and therefore alienable kind of object, that the voice can appear vulnerable to such illegitimate appropriation. (226)

The eighteenth-century discovery of voice as a subjective property, as belonging to each individual, foreshadowed the immanently contested issue of ownership as it applies not only to the voice per se, but to music generally, and eventually even to the anonymous folk song. In the twentieth century, the notion of the anonymous author, as well as the idea of an idealized folk reinforced Charles Seeger's (Pete's father) model of communal interaction in the evolution of folk songs. The elder Seeger's famous idea of "Folk Process" has become an oft-quoted argument for legitimizing or disputing claims to folkness as well as claims to authorship.

In the early twentieth century—the germinal age of copyright, performing rights organizations, and music as commodity (specifically the recording industry)—the notion of "authorship" began to take on a broader meaning than simply a product of the composer. The assignment of ownership and the potential for substantial income derived as a result of that ownership has often blurred the distinction between the composer and the collector, and between the composer or collector and any number of subsequent interpreters. The latter is apparent in Christopher A. Waterman's chronology of "Corrine, Corrina" and its various incarnations, each carrying "additional words and music by . . ." on the copyright.[3] The issue has become more complicated and more contested in recent decades as musical appropriation of non-Western musics by Western popular music stars has become commonplace.

Yet apart from legal claims to publication and performance rights, the development of the song in terms of musical and lyric rearrangements that occurred over time by numerous authors, mirrors Seeger's exploration of some thirty versions of the song "Barbara Allen." Seeger's observations of these diverse versions of the song, which he collected between 1933 and 1954, led to his process-driven model of folk song development. Each of the thirty different examples of "Barbara Allen" is imprinted with characteristics reflecting the transmission of the song from one source to another over extended generational periods. Seeger's notion certainly resonates in terms of long-term changes in songs passed through generations in an oral tradition. However, Seeger attempted to translate this idea of aggregate song development from its decidedly premodern context into a context in which folk music's engagement with capitalism changed the nature of the playing field. In doing so he suggested that folk songs are by nature products of plagiarism. By making such a claim Seeger limits his criteria for defining "folk song" to an oral tradition that, in the age of mechanical reproduction, widespread radio and television broadcasting, and a burgeoning recording industry, has limited currency and whose mere existence has become a rarity in the industrialized West. Carrying the failed argument to its extreme, he uses it to espouse the absurdity of copyright as applied to folk songs. The elder Seeger's comments are quoted in the younger's *Incompleat Folksinger:*

> Perhaps the Russians have done the right thing, after all, in abolishing copyright. It is well known that conscious and unconscious appropriation, borrowing, adapting, plagiarizing, and plain stealing are variously, and always have been, part and parcel of the process of artistic creation. The attempt to make sense out of copyright law reaches its limit in folk song. For here is the illustration par excellence of the Law of Plagiarism. The folk song is, by definition and, as far as we can tell, by reality, entirely a product of plagiarism. (450)

The idea of the collective long-term authorship of folk (or any style) songs generally, by the late twentieth and early twenty-first century, seems more an exercise in greed than a matter of aesthetics. Changing the song makes for fresh opportunities to claim incomes derived from the machinations of the industry. The chronological accounts of "Mbube/Wimoweh" and "Corrine, Corrina" bear witness to the fact that authorship and ownership may be quite different matters (see Erlmann, *Music, Modernity, and the Global Imagination* and Waterman, "Race Music").

Folk and the Popular

The long history of legitimizing claims to folkness through authorial anonymity underlies folk's historically dichotomous relationship to the popular. In the case of folk music, authenticity was most often claimed through its opposition to popular music. Folk music was determined by what it was not: popular music. While this dialectic was much more pronounced in the first half of the twentieth century than it is today, the notion still resonates for some of today's folk community. However, once again the stakes have changed. For contemporary folkies the distinctions between folk and popular are considerably more flexible than they once were. The oppositional relationship of folk and popular is a timeworn idea initiated by nineteenth-century scholars and ideologues and has been a matter of more general concern only since the 1920s.[4]

The valorization of a folk authentic cast in a dualistic opposition to the urban popular was, perhaps, first elucidated by Hubert Parry in 1899 at the inauguration of the English Folk Song Society.

In true folk songs there is no show, no got-up glitter, and no vulgarity . . . and the pity of it is that these treasures of humanity are getting rare, for they are written in characters the most evanescent you can imagine, upon the sensitive brain fibers of those who learn them, and have but little idea of their value. Moreover, there is an enemy at the door of folk music which is driving it out, namely, the common popular songs of the day; and this enemy is one of the most repulsive and most insidious. If one thinks of the outer circumference of our terribly overgrown towns, where the jerry-builder holds sway; where one sees all around the tawdriness of sham jewellery [sic] and shoddy clothes, pawn-shops and flaming gin-palaces; where stale fish and the miserable piles of Covent Garden refuse which pass for vegetables are offered for food—all such things suggest to one's mind the boundless regions of sham. It is for the people who live in such unhealthy regions—people who, for the most part, have the most false ideals, or none at all—who are always struggling for existence, who think that the commonest rowdyism is the highest expression of human emotion; it is for them that the modern popular music is made, and it is made with a commercial intention out of snippets of musical slang. And this product it is which will drive out folk music if we do not save it. (quoted in Middleton, "Editor's Introduction," 4–5)

In addition to a marked disdain for the popular, Parry's comments illustrate the historically hazy nature of the semantic and conceptual project of definition. In 1954 the International Folk Music Council (IFMC), apparently feeling the need to more adequately address the ambiguities in terminology, posited the following definition:

Folk music is the product of a musical tradition that has been evolved through a process of oral transmission. The factors that shape the tradition are: (1) continuity which links the present with the past; (2) variation which springs from the creative impulse of the individual or the group; and (3) selection by the community which determines the form or forms in which the music survives. The term does not cover composed popular music that has been taken over ready-made by a community and remains unchanged, for it is the refashioning and recreation of the music by the community that gives it its folk character (quoted in Middleton, 3).

The IFMC's definition, while less extreme than Parry's, still falls short of being satisfactory with regard to the current argument in that the reference to oral transmission is, as discussed previously, simply no longer reliable in a discussion of present-day American folk music.

In the early 1920s radio changed the way Americans listened to music or, more precisely, how music was received. The increasing popularity of broadcast music and availability of affordable radios, rapid industrialization and urban growth in the early twentieth century, and the accompanying access to geographic mobility as a result of a concerted effort to expand the nation's highway systems were all intimately linked to changing modes of dissemination for folk and popular musics. Along with the demographic and cultural effects of industrialization and the subsequent increase in markets for mass-mediated entertainment, the borders between rural folk and urban popular became less distinct and therefore more contested. One way this occurred was, in effect, a colonization of rural styles by the urban-based music industry.[5]

This sort of aesthetic colonization eventually—by the 1960s, and increasingly in the 1990s—led to a backlash among various groups of musical "purists" openly and actively disdaining popular music and reclaiming and/or reinventing "traditional" folk musics. Since the late 1960s, I had been aware of various folk cliques whose disdain for my "more popular folk music" was sometimes pronounced. Yet it wasn't until recently that I recognized how deeply these feelings could run.

March 1997: Fieldwork 101

A friend and fellow ethnomusicologist, Ron Emoff, invited me to a "music party" that was occurring as an unofficial adjunct to the South by Southwest Music Conference, an annual music industry event in Austin, Texas. We arrived at the nicely renovated Victorian house in an affluent older Austin neighborhood in the late afternoon on a Sunday. As we walked up the sidewalk to the house we heard the sound of old-time string band music. I was glad that I had decided to bring my 1930s Hawaiian resonator guitar.[6] After being introduced to the hosts and exchanging pleasantries I proceeded to the living room and the source of the music. A group of young instrumentalists, including a guitarist, banjo player, fiddle player, and up-right bass player, were playing energetically in an old-time string band style that predates bluegrass.

In my mind, the music lent itself well to a dobro[7] accompaniment. I took my instrument out of its case and began playing with the group. Moments later the guitarist turned and looked at me in disgust. As a professional musician and a reasonably competent dobro player with nationally released recordings, I thought my participation was adding something musical to the piece. So why was this fellow looking at me as if I had some virulent disease? The group en masse cranked up the dynamic level, drowning out my playing. After a few minutes of this, I retreated to the kitchen for some Irish whiskey.

From the kitchen I heard group singing coming from a behind a closed door in what turned out to be a formal dining area. It sounded like early Anglo-American gospel music, and when I entered the room, dobro in hand, I discovered a group of ten or twelve singers gathered around a large table. After my living room experience I was leery of uninvited participation, so I stood quietly until the song ended—a good decision. During a break I was politely informed that guitars and guitarists were not welcome. The group was an organization of men and women, lawyers, doctors, secretaries, housewives, carpenters, and others who gathered weekly to sing "traditional mountain gospel music." Any accompaniment was considered an incongruous "popular" element. After listening to a few more songs, I again retreated to the safety of the kitchen.

As a fledgling ethnomusicologist, I had committed one of the cardinal sins of fieldwork: not understanding the customs and mores of the community. My experience at the party brought to bear issues I had been thinking about with regard to singer/songwriters and their relationships with "real" folk music. It also situated the specific case of musical preservationism in a context of intersecting fields of revivalism, reconstruction, and reinvention. The us-versus-them nature of the experience was unmistakable and troubling, clearly positioning an imagined folk paradigm on one hand and a reviled popular on the other: the latter threatening to defile the former. As Richard Middleton suggests, "On a historical level it is widely assumed that folk music gives way to, is destroyed by, develops into, at any rate precedes, in some sense, popular music: a simple matter of successive stages in social evolution. Within both theory and history is usually hidden the threat of popular music" (3).

A growing ambiguity that surrounds notions of the folk in twentieth-century America is, as many scholars suggest, at least partially due to the seemingly paradoxical relationship between folk's rural populist ideals— determined largely by nostalgia and the retrospective imagination—and the logic of exchange value. Charles Keil states:

> [T]here never were any "folk" except in the minds of the bourgeoisie. The entire field is a grim fairy tale. . . . Culture versus counter-culture, "high art" versus "folk art" represents a dialectic that is almost completely contained within bourgeois ideology. One requires the other. . . . Can't we keep "the folk" concept and redeem it? No! and no! again. You can't, because too many Volkswagons have been built, too many folk ballets applauded, too many folksongs used, too much aid and comfort given to the enemy. (quoted in Middleton, 5)

Keil, among others, has criticized the labeling of various musics as being a construction of music retailers attempting to organize the shelves of record stores. However, in doing so he may be neglecting certain aspects of the construction of meaning in people's lives. That is, regardless of the origins of the ideological constructs of the folk, the term itself can and does have powerful and tangible consequences for a great many very real people. Michael Johnathon, a self-proclaimed folksinger and the author of *WoodSongs: A Folksinger's Social Commentary, Cook Manual, and Song Book* (1997/1996), is one of these people for whom "folk" is endowed with fundamental potency. He says, "Folksinger. I love that word," and goes on:

> To me, the most passionate and powerful music in America today is folk music. That one word, *Folk*, absorbs generations of music and lyrical momentum that ignited change in communities, nations and musical styles.
>
> But please don't get confused on me here.
>
> I'm not talking about the modern cliché of folk music, of some singer with a guitar whining away about lost ships, maidens and social ills on a stool in some dark coffeehouse. I'm talking about real *Folk* music.
>
> The F word.
>
> Capital F. (46)

Johnathon's vague conventional usage of the term never fully explains what "real *Folk*" might be. Yet regardless of the romanticized and indistinct character of his explanations, stereotypical cultural constructions of this thing called "folk"—those contained within Keil's "bourgeois ideology"—have significantly determined Johnathon's personal worldview and the construction of a public identity. Is his identification with folk any less *real* than anyone else's identification with any tradition, genre, or other cultural construct?

Clearly Keil and many others take issue with the concept of folk in an oppositional relationship with "high culture." In the first few decades of the twentieth century this bifurcation of folk and serious, low and high, was widely supported by academics and ideologues—Filene's "culture brokers"—intent on making reputations and defining disciplines. This is where many of the common images of "folk" took root in public memory. Yet, even then, sharp divisions between the concepts were occasionally challenged. If Béla Bartók could use eastern European folk melodies as the basis for concert music, could "folk" music be antithetical to "serious" or "Art" music?

Increasing numbers of contemporary folksingers claim extensive training in "serious" music. For many of these performers, musical aspects of their "high cultural" backgrounds are seamlessly integrated in their "folk" compositions. "The Courtship of the Brown Recluse" by Austin singer/songwriter Mary Melena illustrates a musical complexity usually not considered an element of folk composition (see p. 14). However, the piece was recorded on Melena's Waterbug Records release *Something Passing Through* (1997) and has become one of the artist's trademark works for performance at folk festivals and other venues. Melena's piece reflects her classical guitar training, her folkie aesthetic sensibility, and a broad knowledge of American musics. Her formal musical training is apparent primarily in the contrapuntal *guitaristic* texture of the tune. The counterpoint between the bass and soprano voices lends the piece a baroque character, and the specific voice leadings are well suited to the instrument. However, Melena plays the piece with her guitar in a DADGAD tuning with a capo on the second fret.[8] The specific open tuning is quite popular among folkies, certainly in some part due to the easy employment of open strings.[9] The transcription does not illustrate all of the internal voices or some of the frequencies that result from open strings vibrating sympathetically.

So What Is Folk, Anyway?

The blurring of distinctions between musical characteristics once considered high and low is only a minor factor in folk's growing sense of stylistic fragmentation. The diverse genres that have converged under the umbrella of contemporary folk music are part and parcel of ongoing problems with terminology.

"Courtship of the Brown Recluse," by Mary Melena

Within the community of musicians, fans, and impresarios who consider themselves part of the folk scene, debates continue regarding the nature and definition of folk music. The default arguments for claims to musical "folkness" usually include terms indicating an oral tradition, although most folkies learn current repertoires from recordings.[10] Charles Keil's comments regarding mediation in blues and polka music are equally appropriate to folk: "[I]f there hadn't been mediation, if there hadn't been radio and records in the 1920s, there wouldn't be any blues or polka 'tradition.' People's music wouldn't exist without the media suction that forces people to identify themselves with a particular form" (Keil and Feld, *Music Grooves*, 21).

But is it entirely "media suction" that causes people to identify with notions of the folk? And are they really forced into these choices at all? If indeed this were the case, would not the definition of terms—a precise categorical box in which folk music would reside—be considerably less contested than it has become? Rather, people's identification with folk and folk music paints a much more complicated picture than any simple causal relationship between the "media" and the hapless masses. This is not to say that the mainstream media play a minor role in the process of folk identity construction. Obviously, the music and broadcast industries continue to play important roles. However, those roles are no longer concerned with defining folk as a style or genre. That happened in the late 1950s and early 1960s when folk became commercially viable in the American popular music marketplace, and the media had a vested interest in defining folkness in terms of record sales and airplay. During the 1960s folk revival the media on the one hand and tradition on the other came together in ways that have become mythologized in the historical imagination: when the older generation of folk musicians—such as Mississippi John Hurt (1892–1966), Josh White (1915–1969), and Mance Lipscomb (1895–1976)—played to huge crowds of adoring fans at places like the Newport and Philadelphia folk festivals and released albums on major record labels that actually sold reasonably well, at least in comparison to their 1920s and 1930s recordings for various "race" labels. It was a time when such ideas as the "oral tradition" were cornerstones in the construction of a conventional folk ideology.

In the United States, and in industrialized and postindustrial literate societies in general, orally transmitted musical traditions—or more specifically, unmediated musical traditions—are becoming a rarity.[11] Bruno Nettl points out in *The Study of Ethnomusicology: Twenty-nine Issues and Concepts* (1983) that in some previous theses on this subject, " 'Oral' was sometimes changed to 'aural'; people learned not so much what was said or sung to them but what they heard" (187). Nettl's observation plays out in intriguing ways for the contemporary folk, some of whom do not make the distinction between "oral" and "aural."

Aurality and Orality: The Metamorphosis of Folk's Oral Tradition

I ran into Steve Gillette today and we walked down to one of the long-established camps beyond the lower meadow called Camp Coho. The resident celebrity at Coho is a New York City based singer/songwriter named Jack Hardy. Steve and I arrived at Coho where a group of folks were sitting under a tarp shelter, a type common at Kerrville.[12] Gillette introduced me to the group and briefly described my research. Several people made mildly interested comments, which indicated that these people were intelligent, educated, and had at least a rudimentary understanding of

*the sort of things ethnomusicologists do. Answering questions regarding my work, I
mentioned the demise of oral tradition in the wake of mass mediation. To my surprise Jack Hardy argued to the contrary. Jack claimed that he had learned several of
Bob Dylan's songs long before he ever heard them on recordings. A friend of Jack's
had taught him the songs.*

For Hardy the musical exchange was an apparently unproblematic example
of oral tradition. The secondary mediation—that whoever taught him the songs
had almost certainly learned them from a recording—was beside the point. Jack
learned them from a person. This was enough to lay claim to the mantle of folk's
oral tradition.

In contemporary folk circles it is acceptable to consider songs written by
Woody Guthrie, Leadbelly, or, as the aforementioned example illustrates, Bob
Dylan, as folk songs, rationalizing that they are part of what has become a traditional repertory. In 1969, R. Serge Denisoff suggested, "The use of the term 'folk'
is provocative since the 'folk' elements present are manifestations of the revival
interpretation of the idiom as opposed to any traditional genesis" ("Folk-Rock,"
214). Denisoff's comments assume that a "traditional genesis" for folk songs is
uncomplicated and implies the distinction between "real" and popular, high
and low: a common assumption for scholars in the 1960s and one that is still
ubiquitous among contemporary singer/songwriters and folk audiences.

In terms of repertory, however, the question remains of how and when a
piece becomes part of a folk tradition. Veit Erlmann addresses the relationship
between tradition and modernization in the South African urban vocal music
genre *isicathamiya* in his book *African Stars: Studies in Black South African Performance* (1991). Erlmann's analysis suggests that various traditions arise and
are reinscribed through complex webs of social and cultural interaction; that
mythic pasts are reconstructed and reconfigured through the lens of modernity
in present performance practice; that the nostalgic past can be at odds with
modernity on one hand, and complicit with its projects on the other. The same
sort of dialectic is at issue regarding American folk music. It suggests not only
a site of contest between the old and the new, but also a synergic relationship
between the traditional and the innovative. Both perspectives are frequently articulated within the context of the what-is-folk argument.

Frank Hamilton, a longtime folk musician, suggested in a posting on an Internet usergroup for folkies (see chapter 3) that songs are recognized as folk
songs when "large groups of people prefer to sing" them. While somewhat non-
specific, Hamilton's statement implies that mass popularity is a determinant of
a song's folkness. Songs that have become popular pieces within the arbitrary
boundaries of the genre and that are performed frequently by numerous performers become "folk" and, given an equally arbitrary time frame in which the

song continues to be performed, become part of a traditional repertoire. Lacking a specific temporal context, the term "tradition" can be as indefinite as "folk music."

Traditions are all too often perceived as static reproductions of past performances or performance practices. However, examinations of "traditional" folk music often suggest that traditions, and particularly traditional musics, are dynamic. To state emphatically that a specific piece of folk music has been performed the same way for many generations and has therefore remained the same is to negate the individual contributions, deletions, degrees of technical competency, and interpretive quirks of those generations of participants in the creation of the tradition, as it exists in the present. We must always experience the past through the lens of the present, a process that inevitably changes that past (see, for example, Hall, "Who Needs 'Identity'?" and Schacter, *Searching for Memory*).

Indeed association of the terms "tradition" and "folk" is inextricable and often misunderstood. To assume that a historically consistent, replicable performance practice is possible in the context of an orally transmitted music is unrealistic. Songwriters working within the folk genre, however, often write their songs using stylistic characteristics consistent with a traditional approach. While the general musical framework might echo traditional practice, preservationists often argue that these recent additions to the repertoire cannot be considered traditional nor can they be considered folk songs.

Inevitably in the what-is-folk debates, while preservationists posit definitions that validate their position and nontraditionalists rationalize the inclusion of their work in the folk repertory, someone finds it appropriate to postulate the "I ain't never heard no horses singin' it" argument, which has been attributed to dozens of musical/historical figures ranging from Louis Armstrong to Big Bill Broonzy.[13] Whoever first said it, the wry absurdity of the remark—which has since become cliché—nonetheless reflects the subjective problems of defining folk music.

Folk music in America, like the society at large, has changed dramatically in the past four decades: in terms of its subject material, topical colloquialism, and performance practices, and no less in its eclectic musical and stylistic influences. Among the many explanations for changes in the folk genre are widespread dissemination of information, particularly by television and the recording industry (mediation); the questionable democratization of the industry through availability of affordable high-quality recording technology; and (perhaps in part due to the democratizing aspect) the newest wave in the popularization of folk music. That increasing numbers of folk musicians are crossing over into the realm of popular music (Jewel, Shawn Colvin, Patty Larkin, James McMurtry, and others) exacerbates the irresolvability of the what-is-folk debate. The people who do it know what it is . . . don't they?

In one of several Internet usergroups comprised of singer/songwriters, instrumentalists, and others involved with folk music, there are continual debates over questions of definition.[14] In the late 1990s, among a staggering number of comments about the issue, were the likes of these:

> How many folks on here actually believe that the term "folk music" necessarily includes a political stance? How many believe it doesn't have to? I'll even go so far as to ask if anyone thinks it shouldn't. That's a call for a show of hands. I am sincerely curious.[15]

And:

> "Folk music" is any song, played in any style, on any instrument, on any topic, in any language, in any country, by anyone, that has the tenacity, determination, and belief to call him or herself . . . A "Folk Musician."[16]

Still the fetishism of labeling may be largely responsible for the continuation of the debate. Preservationists and songwriters alike might be well advised to consider John Blacking's argument that "over concentration on musical categories obscures the more necessary attention to processes of music making" (paraphrased in Middleton, 6).

Twentieth-century constructions and development of American folk idealism represent attempts to define group interests and activities primarily through music labeled as "folk." For today's folk there is much at stake besides economic and transmission considerations. This is not to say that these are unimportant, but the label signifies more than its role in mass marketing or in delineating folk music as a common interest, and has also become symbolic of a largely middle-class, intellectual dissatisfaction with a perceived rampant consumerism. As such, constructing identities labeled "folk" serves as resistance to unbridled capitalism—while also necessarily being complicit in its development—and provides opportunities to enact reconstructions of imaginary premodern communal experiences.[17] The conflicting discourses of past and present associations with the term shape some of the most tenacious myths of the folk.

Clearly the notion that to carry the label "folk music" it has to be the work of anonymous authors suggests another polemic, one that at least peripherally has to do with high/low determination. Equally clearly these determinations suggest a shifting field of reference. The nineteenth-century constructions of high/low that pit folk and popular musics in opposition to "refined" concert musics have given way to multiple levels of shifting ideas about high and low culture that depend entirely upon perspective: the shape-note chorus member looking down on the bluegrass mandolin player; the old-time folk music purist's disregard of the pop singer; or the poetic songwriter's distaste for heavy metal or rap. The gradations of musical class consciousness mirror a decidedly modernist investment in notions of musical value deeply rooted in themes of the authentic. Authenticity has, like cultural production in general, taken on an assemblage of shifting referents for the contemporary American folk.

In the next chapter I will discuss the emergence and nature of the folk paradigms that became embedded in the American popular imaginary in the mid-twentieth century, the association of folk with the "common man" and the roots of that notion, and the shifting authenticities through which the folk redefined itself at century's end.

Hang down your head Tom Dooley
Hang down your head and cry.
Hang down your head Tom Dooley
Poor boy you're bound to die.
—"Tom Dooley" (Traditional)

 Popular Imagination, the "Common Man," and Shifting Authenticities

The terminology and concepts through which folkness is regularly claimed and "folk" is defined inflect and intersect each aspect of today's folksinger/songwriter landscape. Perhaps through "media suction" or simply through repetition, characteristic attributes of folk music and its performance became embedded in popular perceptions. As discussed previously, many of these commonly perceived folk paradigms had their genesis in the folk revival of the late 1950s and early 1960s.[1]

In *When We Were Good: The Folk Revival* (1996), Robert Cantwell suggests that the post–World War II folk revival began with the Kingston Trio's 1958 recording of "Tom Dooley" and ended with Bob Dylan's controversial performance at the Newport Folk Festival in 1965.[2] The author claims, "These are artificial but not arbitrary points; by general agreement they mark the boundaries between which a longstanding folksong movement, with elaborate political and social affiliations, emerged out of relative obscurity to become an immensely popular commercial fad, only to be swallowed up by a rock-and-roll revolution whose origins, ironically, it shared" (21). Clearly, some of Cantwell's assertions are oversimplified,[3] but it is the folk archetype that crystallized in the popular imaginary between these boundaries of general agreement that is of immediate concern.

The Kingston Trio exemplified a particular folk aesthetic emulated by countless subsequent amateur and professional folk ensembles. They were young, white, well-dressed with casual matching outfits, played "folk instruments" (acoustic guitars and banjo), enunciated lyrics clearly, and sang with mellifluous voices devoid of what Alan Lomax would, in his cantometrics project, describe as vocal rasp. Their vocal harmonies were tight and their phrasing, articulation, and intonation were conventionally unambiguous. In short, they were slick in every way. It was precisely this slickness that created an ideological rift between the "bearers of tradition"—characterized as "the unwashed beatnik folk" (Dick Weissman, personal communication, 9 May 2001) whose claims to being real folk were grounded in earlier folk song revivals—and the popular folksingers of the post–World War II revival.

Despite frequently contested claims to folkness during this period, a number of stylistic paradigms emerged. Many of these conventions became thoroughly inscribed in popular notions of the folk and continue to hold a tenacious grip on contemporary folk music practice and consumption. The archetypal folksinger is male, plays guitar, wears worn blue jeans or corduroy trousers and a flannel shirt, and isn't a technically adept musician. While these criteria are obviously stereotypical, they have become embedded in the American popular imaginary. This paradigm of the generic folksinger and "boring" folk music is an unfortunate element of American popular culture's habitus. Yet the same image—the white male college student in corduroy and flannel, playing acoustic guitar and singing boring folk songs—is still in evidence at every folk festival campground, coffeehouse, open mic, and song circle in America, and quite likely at similar venues in other countries. How have these images become so thoroughly ingrained, and why do they persist with such remarkable tenacity?

In terms of outward appearance as well as general stylistic characteristics, long-standing association of folk music with the "folk"—the working class, the common man—plays an ongoing role in its processes of cultural production. Many historical accounts have considered folk's relationships with organized labor and the Communist Party throughout the twentieth century, and I have no desire to revisit that well-traveled ground (see, for example, Brand, *The Ballad Mongers*; Cantwell, *When We Were Good*; Denisoff, *Sing a Song of Social Significance*; Filene, *Romancing the Folk*; Malone, *Country Music, U.S.A.*;

Porter, "Muddying the Crystal Spring"; Santelli and Davidson, *Hard Travelin'*; and Seeger, *The Incompleat Folksinger*). However, Oscar Brand's suggestion that, "for many experts, a song may be accredited as 'a folk song' if it meets with a specific need of the working classes" (9), implies a similar association in its reference to the working classes, but addresses an issue more fundamental to folk's popular imaginary. Brand's "working class" or "common man" idea is a lingering artifact of American folk music whose referential signification has become increasingly fluid in the late twentieth century and the early twenty-first. Regina Bendix's *In Search of Authenticity: The Formation of Folklore Studies* (1997) suggests that American notions of the "common man" have certain characteristics in common with the nineteenth-century German construction of the *volk*, but differ in fundamental concepts of experiential authenticity:

> The construct of the American "common man" markedly differs, then, from the German *Volk* construct. The *Volk* was rooted in an idealized past, encumbered by the complexities of historical influences, and it could be redeemed only by those who, by virtue of their learning and class, had gained insight into its aesthetic and social value. The American "common man," by contrast, lived authentically out of necessity. In acknowledging the common tasks of all Americans to build a new country and to negate class differences, literate men such as Thoreau felt themselves capable of enacting the lifestyle of the common man. A particular group or way of life was singled out from the larger social landscape in both American and German cases. The virtues of this group—whether common man or *Volk*—were praised, and it was contrasted to the decay threatening the social fabric of the nation. (74)

However, in various accounts of the twentieth-century construction of an American folk "authentic," the German *volk* idea and the American "common man" are not as disparate as Bendix suggests.

In *Romancing the Folk: Public Memory and American Roots Music* (2000), Benjamin Filene's analysis of the construction of an American folk authentic by various "culture brokers" suggests less a difference in the fundamental *volk*/common man concept than a striking similarity in its top-down cultural formation. Yes, the American experience between the late eighteenth and nineteenth centuries was characterized by a popular and conscious severance from European models of social class division. Lawrence Levine asserts in *Highbrow/Lowbrow: The Emergence of Cultural Hierarchy in America* (1988) that antiaristocracy sentiments among the consumers of American popular culture during this period often accounted for the success or failure of individual artists and entire productions. The feelings ran strong enough that theaters were occasionally forced to close because of audience riots during which facilities were heavily damaged and actors whose aristocratic demeanor offended an American populist ideal were threatened with, or actually suffered, physical violence.

In the twentieth-century construction of the American folk, the German idea of "an idealized past, encumbered by the complexities of historical influences," which "could be redeemed only by those who, by virtue of their learning and class, had gained insight into its aesthetic and social value" (Bendix, *In Search of Authenticity*, 74), directly indexes the sort of culture brokering practiced by such luminaries as John and Alan Lomax, among others, whose ideological agendas played central roles in the development of American folk mythology.[4] Indeed the demographics of the 1960s revival, and today's folk as well, suggest that the differences in the German and American models are cursory at most.[5] The German notions of *volk* idealized a past that was fundamentally mythological and was reclaimed or reinvented by the intelligentsia. The American "common man" idea sprang from the reaction against European aristocracy and the subsequent glorification of populist idealism. However, its reclamation for American folk music was—since at least the mid-twentieth century—driven by the same sort of top-down historical imagination that characterized the German *volk* model (see Bendix, *In Search of Authenticity* and Filene, *Romancing the Folk*).

The "common man" long ago abandoned folk music for the more popular popular musics—primarily country-western and rock. College students who appropriated folk music in the 1960s and were instrumental in its commercial revival have grown up. The white, middle-aged suburbanite has, for the folk, become the new common man, and today's reconstitution of folk music reflects a striking dichotomy between the imaginative past and the experiential present. Yet the chasm between imagination and experience that marks the American folk—the common man of the past versus the common experience of the present—is being negotiated in a variety of ways. The past's common man has assumed the role of a phantom escape artist providing nostalgic respite from the complexities of modernity. But, as the following example illustrates, the nostalgic specter of the common man can have a peculiar opacity when it occupies a middle ground between the imaginary and "real life."

Monica Taylor and Patrick Williams play music together as the Farm Couple. The two appear to be in their midthirties and live together on a sixty-acre farm in Grove, Oklahoma, which has been in Patrick's family for four generations— "my great grandma and grandpa's Indian allotment land . . . we still managed to hold onto sixty acres of it. . . . It was 160 acres [originally]" (personal interview, 6 June 1999). They play music for a living, occasionally leaving their local area and touring in surrounding states. These tours may be from three weeks to two months in duration. In addition to a public address system, guitars, and miscellaneous necessities of life, the couple carries commercial window cleaning equipment with which they supplement their music-generated income.

Patrick was born and raised in suburban Tulsa, Oklahoma, but spent a lot of time at the farm when he was growing up. No one in his family played musical instruments or sang, but his parents enjoyed listening and dancing to recordings of Bob Wills and Leon McAuliffe and His Cimmaron Boys. "Old country," including the music of Jack Green, Marty Robbins, Connie Smith, Mel Tillis, and Ernest Tubb, also played a role in defining Patrick's musical worldview. His earliest participatory musical experiences occurred as a nine-year-old in the context of singing in a church choir. When he was sixteen or seventeen, Patrick entered a songwriting contest sponsored by Wal-Mart and won with a Faron Young influenced song called "Pretty Mama." This event marked the beginning of his interest in professional music making.

Like Patrick, Monica said she "grew up singing in a church choir—in a Southern Baptist gospel quartet," and added, "My family always went to the Sanders Family Bluegrass Festival [in McAlester, Oklahoma] since I was in third grade, so we're going back there this coming Friday." She began writing songs in 1988 or 1989, shortly afterward moving to Telluride, Colorado, where her writing output increased dramatically.

Most of the music that the Farm Couple performs directly indexes themes that throw into relief notions of the "country" and the "city"—or indirectly, premodernity and modernity—and a particular sense of "us"—the common man—versus "them"—presumably the urban-based owner class. Joli Jensen articulates this duality in *The Nashville Sound: Authenticity, Commercialization, and Country Music* (1998):

> The world is divided between us and them. We are hardworking, honest, far from home, patriotic, vulnerable. They are slick, dishonest, untrustworthy, powerful, cruel. They own the factories, have more education, think they are better than we are. They do not respect other people or what makes this country great. They use big words, hold all the cards and will stab you in the back.
>
> But we are better than they are because we work hard, care for our families, stick together, and keep faith with each other. We made this country. We hold the key to true happiness because we know that happiness is home and family and doing right by each other. We have good friends who go way back with us, and we do the best we can. They can never take those things away from us. (28–29)

While Jensen's characterization takes on a sense of ideological caricature, the main tenets of this perspective are evident in the performative content of the Farm Couple's musical and social exchanges. Yet the dialectics of these exchanges—the resonant images of city and country, modernity and the past, us versus them—intertwine in many ways and are articulated through their engagement with the music business.

As of 1999, the Farm Couple has maintained a Web presence, first through Dust Bowl Records, now apparently defunct, and then on their own at www.the farmcouple.com. The sites have included a brief bio, with information concerning Patrick's family farm, reviews of their music, discographies, and sources for purchasing their CDs. The photograph of Monica and Patrick on their first Web site was reminiscent of Grant Wood's painting *American Gothic* (1930): not in a direct or even intentional way, but rather there was a subliminal and vague similarity.

The Farm Couple sang their first song together, "Little Town," in 1996 at the Walnut Valley Bluegrass Festival in Winfield, Kansas. The song illustrates the duality of city versus country, us versus them in decidedly nostalgic terms:

> Much too long I lived the city life.
> Searched long and hard to find a wife.
> Well maybe I'll meet a gal in a little town.
> But I'm gonna follow an old dirt road.
> I'll find someplace to ease my load,
> park the truck outside a diner in a little town.
>
> Chorus:
> Little town, little town,
> place where I can get around
> Little town little town,
> there's peace of mind for me in a little town.
>
> I'll get a job at an old feed store,
> or on the farm where I can do some chores,
> and everybody know my name in a little town.
> All my friends'll call me country bumpkin,
> the way I'll talk, really something, but
> I'm going to cleanse my soul in a little town.
>
> Chorus
>
> Well I like cornbread and I like beans.
> Like a slice of bacon in my collard greens.
> Well I'm gonna plant a garden in a little town.
> I have a dog and a cat, a pen full of pigs,
> a rooster and a hen and some baby chicks
> We'll be getting our fix in a little town.

The musical accompaniment for "Little Town" is a conventional, up-tempo, country flavored, I–IV–V strophic form that is, in itself, unremarkable. However, the images evoked in the lyrics to the song clearly present the oppositions and fictions of Jensen's us/them opposition. The lyrics in "Little Town," as well as most songs the Farm Couple sings, directly refer to the rural past and present it in nostalgic terms. Yet the final line in "Little Town" illustrates the conflicted nature of their idealization of the past. "We'll be getting our fix in a little town" pits the vernacular of drug use—admittedly the phrase "getting a fix" has worked its way into common usage, but its drug related origins are clear—against the idealized image of rural America.

Their duo guitar accompaniments and vocal inflections and timbres are part of the nostalgic process and part of an unavoidable engagement with modernity. Both musicians strum and fingerpick at times playing typical country and folk harmonic progressions. Patrick punctuates the tunes with solos, mostly single-line melodic flat-picking. His technique is clean and precise and rarely flashy or virtuosic. Both singers have strongly inflected Southern accents, and their vocal performance is practiced and professional.

Perhaps the most striking aspect of the Farm Couple's performance is Monica's voice. Her powerful and emotive vocal technique is remarkable for its timbral quality. A pronounced midrange edge to her voice recalls singers from the old-time music tradition of Appalachia: an upper chest and slightly nasal singing style as opposed to the classical singing from the diaphragm technique. Additionally Monica's singing is punctuated by occasional falsetto events that suggest the old-time style. However, her intonation is precise and she has impressive vocal control: characteristic more of a late-twentieth-century popular aesthetic than the late-nineteenth-, early-twentieth-century "hillbilly" aesthetic. Rather than appearing to be preservationists of some arbitrary traditional genre, the Farm Couple freely idealizes the past, the rural, and the "common man" while negotiating an aesthetic of modernity.

Patrick and Monica call their musical style "red dirt music," and explained that phrase in the following exchange that took place at the Kerrville Folk Festival on 6 June 1999:

PATRICK: We hang around some great singer/songwriters up there in Oklahoma. . . .
   I don't know where it really got started, that title Red Dirt music. . . .
BYSTANDER: Stillwater, wasn't it?
PATRICK: Well yeah, but was it Bob, or who started the title, uh, the name of that?
MONICA: Probably Bob Childers, Tom Skinner, something like that.
PATRICK: Well anyway, we kind of . . .
MONICA: Jimmy LaFave . . . Jimmy probably started it.

PATRICK: Yeah, Jimmy LaFave. . . . It's got some grit to it you know, as far as the songs that come out . . . and they're spiritual. Probably there's a spiritual undertone to . . . a lot of the songs, . . . songs about our Indian heritage . . . and . . . the red dirt of the farmer.

MONICA: The people who came to live in Oklahoma, you know, the land run and before that the Trail of Tears. . . . They had . . . to have an amazing amount of courage and grit—physical stamina to get there and then to survive. . . .

PATRICK: It's an honest music I'd say, . . . a music about roots. . . .

MONICA: Being proud of those roots: like Woody Guthrie.

PATRICK: It's something that I think is really going to take off in these next few years. It's something you can grab ahold of and . . . understand it's just a music from the heart. And I don't think there's very many places where there's such a good gathering of friends that write songs, and they call it red dirt music.

MONICA: And we're all friends for ten to twenty years.

The Farm Couple's comments suggest a number of themes that are common among today's singer/songwriters. In addition to the connections with an idealized rural history, the "Indian heritage," the communal aspects of folk music, and the valorization of forebears,[6] one of the most prevalent themes is the relationship of spirituality to the creative process. For Patrick and Monica that sense of spirituality is implicit in the narratives of their songs and in the performative act. That is, they convey a sense of joy in their performance that doesn't seem contrived or superficial. However, at the same time they are well rehearsed and in some ways very slick—intelligent yet folksy. Like the Bugkiller, the Farm Couple is endowed with an authenticity that winds circuitously between the imaginary and the experiential in both subtle and not so subtle ways.

The common man as a folk paradigm has left its imprint on all of the aforementioned aspects of the popular folk archetype. Fashion, in terms of the outward appearance of performers and performance, as well as stereotypical elements of folk music and lyrics can be attributed in one way or another to the common man idea.[7] The formality of European classical music traditions is antithetical to conventional notions of folk music. Virtuoso performers dressed in tuxedos, playing complicated "art" music from written scores, have little to say to the folk. However, as the folk enter the twenty-first century and folk music increasingly draws reference from widening geographic, aesthetic, and epistemological bases, some of the a priori codes of folkness are straining under the weight of shifting codes of authenticity.[8]

In one form or another, authenticity is a primary determinant for legitimizing performers, performances, music, and song lyrics within the folk community and is either directly or indirectly located within the domain of style. "Style" in this context can indicate particular playing techniques, adherence to various formal musical conventions, or conventions of dress, or it can be a more ambiguous description of particular ways in which people conduct their lives. For today's folk, adherence to conventional styles and indexes of authenticity are often, and at many levels, tied to nostalgic idealism.

Nostalgia for an imagined past has long held a central role in folk music discourses. The sense of longing for the imagined rural homestead, the simplicity of a preindustrial lifestyle, and the freedom to wander the open prairies of America unfettered by the constraints of twentieth-century modernity had particular resonance for folk musicians during earlier periods in the development of American industrialization. Urban migration and the stark realities of life for the low-paid, low-prestige industrial laborer contributed to folk music's appropriation of the rural nostalgia theme. However, the relationship between urban labor migration and the nostalgic imagination was also dialectical. An awareness of a stigmatization of the rural persona and an accompanying desire to distance oneself from the "hillbilly" or "hick" image must have been a primary concern for many migrant industrial workers aspiring to a bourgeois lifestyle. The conflicting predispositions to romanticize the rural past and at once to shed the social and economic constraints of that past resulted in what Archie Green calls a "joint pattern of rejection as well as sentimentalization of rural mores. We flee the eroded land with its rotting cabin; at the same time we cover it in rose vines of memory" ("Hillbilly Music," 223). Songs such as "My Old Kentucky Home" or "Tennessee Mountain Home" approach themes of rural nostalgia from the perspective of displaced "hillbillies" who migrated to Northern urban centers to find work during the rapid industrialization of early twentieth-century America.

Today rural nostalgia presents different perspectives that illustrate a changing world. The following excerpt is from a song entitled "The Man in Me," written by singer/songwriter Jack Williams and released on the Wind River record label in 1999:

> Dodgin' coyotes and free-rangin' cattle
> I got so scared, lost in Seattle
> There's a hole in my hotel wall
> Great big hole in my hotel wall
> New Year's Eve, out of control
> Layin' down rhythm for some bad rock and roll
> Left a good home behind
> My son and a friend of mine

Oh Colorado, you're wild and clear
You're not like me, a prisoner of fear
Don't know what I'm doin' down here
Don't know what I'm doin' down here

Williams's evocation of loss and longing indexes a sense of nostalgia for the "wild and clear" spaces of Colorado within a distinctly contemporary narrative frame. In this piece, leaving the "eroded land with its rotting cabin" no longer resonates with the plight of the industrial labor migrant. Rather it is marked by the implied travails of the traveling musician "layin' down rhythm for some bad rock and roll." For the Appalachian labor migrant, the urban factories of the industrial revolution stood in marked opposition to the country—the rural homestead. For Williams, working as a sideman in the rock and roll band implies a similar opposition: playing music as an economic necessity versus playing the music of his roots—presumably folk music.

While many of the new generation of singer/songwriters have in some ways turned their gaze upon more topical concerns, the "rural" continues to provide a potent source of symbolic reference materials. However, in many cases its referents are manifested in performance practices and stylistic conventions—clothing or the southern accent vocal affect, for example—rather than in literal textual references. In any case, the rural experience, the common man, and their evocation in American folk music, continue to have considerable cachet as primary symbols of authenticity.

Arguably the authenticity fetish has been one of the driving forces behind the popularization of folk music on the twentieth-century American musical landscape. When John Lomax introduced Huddie Ledbetter to white, academic, socially privileged audiences in the 1930s, the appeal of contact with an American "Authentic," or perhaps a "primitive savant," must have been overwhelming for these people, who presumably had relatively little contact with African-Americans. Here, after all, was a black man with practically no formal schooling and a sordid past, including a history of violence and two prison terms, whose singing and 12-string guitar playing embodied archetypal notions of the rural, the primitive, and not coincidentally the exotic.[9]

Yet today the authentic in American folk music is not always as clear-cut as a simple nostalgia for an imagined (or real) rural past. The authenticity of personal excess—a history of hard living, heartbreak, and substance abuse—fits into the equation with the same sort of resonance, and often in conjunction with the imagined rural past. The idea that excessive personal behaviors constitute a level of authenticity, which is clearly and somehow appealingly manifested in the musical performance, is a long-lived tradition in American popular music. In *Country Music, U.S.A.*, Bill Malone calls Charlie Poole[10] "one of the earliest examples in country music of the hard-living, hard-drinking young man who burns his life away, a type which has appeared periodically and which seems endlessly appealing to country music fans" (51). This attraction to what is, in the most conventional view of middle-class American society, usually considered aberrant behavior seems noteworthy on several levels.

The attraction/revulsion dialectic described by scholars within various contexts[11] is apparent in folk (and country) music audiences' acceptance of music whose messages include unmistakable references to drug and alcohol abuse as well as to violence and a general glorification (or sometimes a repudiation) of lawlessness. This particular aspect of the popular music landscape was exemplified by the country rock "outlaw" phenomenon that began in the early 1970s and included such luminaries as Willie Nelson, Jerry Jeff Walker, and others whose work blurred the stylistic distinctions between country music, rock, and folk. The term "outlaw" became a symbolic badge of honor that defined their iconoclastic approaches. In their songs, implicit and explicit references to drug use, primarily marijuana, resonated with audiences for whom getting stoned had become socially acceptable and commonplace.

The folk and popular precedents for these song types are extensive. From "Willie the Weeper" (trad.), to "Cocaine Blues" (ca. 1929[12]), to the more recent "Needle and Spoon" (1970), a popular acceptance of socially marginal behavior has a long history for American audiences and for the folk specifically. However, many older folk songs whose texts deal with drug related issues serve as warnings that these vices will cause certain downfall and ultimately death.

> Now this is the story of Willie the Weeper.
> Willie the Weeper was a chimneysweeper.
> Someday a pill too many he'll take,
> And dreaming he's dead, he'll forget to wake

In recent years the messages have changed. The boundaries of aesthetic/social acceptability are intrinsically connected to a folk demographic: today's folk audiences are overwhelmingly in the forty- to sixty-year-old age bracket.[13] The baby boomers have grown up, and experiences of their youth have been instrumental in determining aesthetic parameters and indexes of authenticity.

In the 1960s and '70s, drug use among American youth became, for the first time, a widespread national phenomenon. Prior to this popularization of drug experimentation, most drug use was, at least in the popular imagination, associated with jazz musicians and Oriental immigrants—and mindful of Edward

Said's notion of Orientalism, here "Oriental" is used in its most othering sense.[14] By the mid- to late 1960s, recreational drug use had achieved a degree of social acceptance. Suddenly it was hip to smoke marijuana and ingest various abundantly available hallucinogens and narcotics, pastimes once reserved for society's marginal elements. Drug use was widely reported by the news media and became the fodder for what could be called its own genre of drug related popular music.

The legacy of this change in attitude regarding drugs is a popular folk aesthetic in which drug use—or, more precisely, the textual evocation of drug use—is one aspect of a new authenticity. If this seems suspiciously similar to the Charlie Poole model mentioned above, it is no accident. While some of the drugs of choice may have changed throughout the intervening years, the same personality traits are being celebrated: the "rebel," the "outlaw," the "tortured artist" have all become literary conventions, conventions that have had long-lasting and sometimes deadly consequences for generations of artists.[15] An excerpt from a *Dallas Observer* article (28 January 1999) written by Rob Patterson about the Texas singer/songwriter Ray Wylie Hubbard, which was posted for a while on Hubbard's Web site, illustrates the dialectic romanticism of the artist as a tortured soul:

> The Hubbard mythology of yore is as problematic as having an anthem for beer-sotted country bucks young and old as one's best known song. Hubbard and his Cowboy Twinkies were legendary for their raw, anarchic and almost punky honky-tonk rave-ups, and his offstage life was lived as wildly as he played his music. It's almost as if, after penning "Redneck Mother," Hubbard was driven to penance by becoming the song's worst nightmare, a substance-fueled wild man and, in the great musical tradition, [having] his hit also serve as his epitaph.

Recently Hubbard contends that he no longer uses drugs. However, his widely publicized history of drug and alcohol abuse continues to index his personal and public authenticity of experience.

On 22 April 2000, Hubbard performed at the Cactus Cafe, a small bar on the University of Texas at Austin campus. Following a competent but unremarkable opening set by singer/songwriter Mark Stuart,[16] the headliner took the stage. Ray Wylie Hubbard has maintained a minor industry presence since his most famous song, "Up against the Wall, Redneck Mother," became an instant hit for Jerry Jeff Walker, who recorded it on his 1973 album ¡Viva Terlingua! Hubbard was dressed in jeans and a blue denim shirt with patches of a matching blue design. He appeared haggard, with the slightly drawn look of someone living on too much junk food and too little sleep for too long. Middle age hasn't been particularly kind to many of the

1960s outlaws. Yet his appearance seemed consistent with the archetypical artist persona he has constructed. Hubbard's stage patter was clever, well rehearsed, and at times very funny.

Like Bugkiller, Ray Wylie presented himself as a kind of ideal hayseed. Where the similarities ended was in the imagery Hubbard used, imagery and direct textual content that unambiguously referred to a history of drug use. The following is an excerpt from "Conversations with the Devil," on Hubbard's 1999 release *Crusades of the Restless Knights.*

> I said oh man, wait a minute there's got to be something wrong
> I ain't a bad guy, just write these little songs
> I always pay my union dues, I don't stay in the passing lane
> and he said what about all that whiskey and cocaine
> I said well, yeah, but that's no reason to throw me in hell
> 'cause I didn't use the cocaine to get high, I just like the way it smells.

In performance the humorous treatment of the subject matter endows the performer with a sense of experiential authenticity. That is, Hubbard's history of drug use provides referential legitimacy to the claims of authenticity implicit in the song. Without this sort of referential exchange between singer and song, the efficacy of a particular performance is questionable. While there are similarities between these drug references and timeworn country music references to alcohol use and abuse, recreational drugs have become a symbolic marker of the baby boomer's "misspent youth." References to past drug use inspire a hazy melancholy, not unlike nostalgia for the rural homestead. However, instead of the family farm, the nostalgia concerns the excesses of youthful indiscretion—either real or imagined.

For the contemporary singer/songwriter, indices of authenticity have become more diverse, more fluid, and often less easily situated within folk's "traditional" thematic contexts. Rather than sentimentalizing places, rural pasts, or romantic love—although these are still fairly common—many singer/songwriters visit and revisit the personal emotional experience as an index of authenticity. This is not a new thing. Love, loss, and longing have been the stuff of songs as long as people have written them. However, one apparent trend for the new folk is a level of introspection that allows for very personal expressions of these traditional themes. For the highly introspective folk, authenticity is indexed through the presumably shared experience of personal drama or, perhaps, trauma.

The realm of authentic experience is constantly referenced by contemporary singer/songwriters in song lyrics and narrative content as well as in the outward manifestations of a folk persona. In lyrics and narratives common thematic threads have begun to emerge as the demographics of folk dictate a certain set of shared experiences. Today's audiences have matured. As middle age has set in for the baby boom generation—folk's common man—the thematic topics of contemporary folk songs have kept pace with that process of maturation. While nostalgia for lost youth may allow for idealizing reconfigurations of youthful indiscretion, the realities of aging for folk audiences and performers have prompted new popular thematic genres within folk repertories, genres through which the authentic experience is translated in performance. One such genre through which singer/songwriters establish bonds of common experience with their audiences concerns resolution of uneasy or broken relationships with parents: the type of reconciliation that is prompted by the immanent passing of older generations.

The songs usually feature emotional imagery nostalgizing individual pasts and suggest that through the expression of loss, either immediate or impending, comes redemption. "My Old Man" by Susan Shore illustrates this emotional trajectory through an implied understanding of the individual frailties that constitute the human condition.

> My old man said we'd go west when the grass got green
> Just to see the biggest sky I'd ever seen
> We took the back roads winding, sang at every turn
> Saw every sunrise, drank coffee so hot that our lips got burned
>
> When we got home and unrolled ourselves from the family sedan
> My grandma said "Baby, you're just like your old man
> You should have been in school with your ABC's
> Instead of playing cowboy and putting holes in your brand new jeans
>
> My old man's not perfect
> He's a prism in the sky
> With all the colors of the rainbow
> In his eyes, in his eyes, in his eyes
>
> My old man makes promises he tries to keep
> Staying up past midnight just to watch me sleep
> He knows who I am and just where I came from
> And those who left us can hardly imagine what their leaving has done
>
> He dreams a life far from the smokestack
> No more shoveling coal until his face turns black
> No more watching bankers in their fancy cars
> Looking right through him as if he were smoke that curls from their cigars

My old man said we'd go west when the grass got green
He makes promises he tries to keep
As he dreams

Performers recall, reconstruct, or invent emotional experiences that they feel will resonate with their audiences. Yet most singer/songwriters do not claim to write expressly for the audience. Rather, writing and performing the song are acts of personal expression. However, a simple statement of emotion is rarely the stuff of a successful song. Clearly the craft of songwriting must be considered in order to effectively convey the emotional message in a noteworthy or memorable fashion. True love, death of a loved one, or affection for one's children must be cleverly phrased and musically appropriate in order to convey the authenticity of experience that determines the efficacy of a song or a given performance. Yet to relegate the bulk of songs written by contemporary singer/songwriters to typical concerns of middle-aged consumers is to do the new folk a gross injustice. Given the breadth of the field, it is difficult to find a topic about which songs have not been written. The efficacy of those songs in performance depends upon the performer's ability to evoke an appropriate emotional response through the convincing reenactment of the authentic.

For a song's narrative, the writer may draw from a diverse well of personal, imaginative, and public texts. Thus the effective presentation of the interpretation of those texts presents a complicated web of signification. When Susan Shore writes and sings about her father "shoveling coal until his face turns black," it is doubtful that she is presenting an accurate picture of a childhood memory of her father. Shore is from New Jersey and is younger than she would need to be to have had a father who shoveled coal into an industrial furnace. Yet the metaphorical image is grounded in a distinctly modern politics of image.

As in Vincent van Gogh's painting *A Pair of Boots* (1887), which Fredric Jameson suggests "requires us to reconstruct some initial situation out of which the finished work emerges" (*Postmodernism*, 7), the stark image of the menial industrial worker in Shore's song implies a similar kind of imaginative construction or reconstruction of content.[17] In each reading the content of the image requires the interpreter to recall or resurrect referential signification. That is, the image has implications beyond its surface meaning. Each interpreter enters into the act of deciphering the subjective content of the piece in a way that makes some sense in terms of worldview. While the interpretive process may present widely divergent assignments of meaning, particularly in the visual arts, unquestionably the process "may be described as hermeneutical, in the sense in which the work in its inert, objectal form is taken as a clue or a symptom for some vaster reality which replaces it as its ultimate truth" (ibid.). Simply put, its meaning is variable depending upon who is doing the interpreting.

The "ultimate truth" derived from the perception of imagery, whether visual, musical, or linguistic, is entrenched in subjectivities each staking its own claim to authenticity. The image of the father shoveling coal may suggest the alienation of the worker and capitalism's innate conflict between the working and owner classes, or it may throw into relief the experiential chasm between the realities of the everyday versus the nostalgic, yet ultimately impotent, world of dreams. In either case, the hermeneutical process relies on codes, which in order for the song to be effective for a mass audience must index common ideas about the world.

The chance that a large percentage of Shore's audience has had personal experiences that mirror those of the character in her song is unlikely and beside the point. The symbolic codes through which meanings are derived have less to do with direct experiential associations than with their applicability to evoke emotional responses. Simply, it makes no difference if her father was actually a menial industrial worker or an accountant from Newark. The arrangement of words pushes emotional buttons for the listener rather than presenting a flat, perhaps irrelevant narrative. The authenticity of that narrative setting is subjugated by the authenticity of its emotional appeal.[18]

In point of fact it is precisely that reaction—the emotional response, whether transitory or not—that is not only welcomed but also encouraged. Folk audiences *want* to feel. They pay the price of admission to *feel* unashamedly. Sentiment and sentimentality provide a welcome respite from a non-folk modernity where sentiment is conventionally associated with weakness.

The poetics of songwriting manipulate the listener through indexing common emotions and the experiential Ordinary that *depend* upon the cultural homogeneity of the audience. However, the efficacy of the song also depends in large part on performative indices of authenticity. Beyond the obvious codes embodied in dress, vocal affectations, and literal references to folk's grand and not so grand narratives, performers may choose to highlight their own authorial and experiential position.

Several months before this writing I attended a concert in Buffalo, New York, in which Darryl Purpose was the featured singer/songwriter. The concert was a typical church hall concert series event. Purpose, who is a moderately well known singer/songwriter and tours nationally, earns his living primarily through music making. An unassuming figure, he is of medium height and stocky build, bearded, and he generally wears a wide-brimmed fedora over thinning hair. After a few numbers, Purpose prefaced one song with an autobiographical sketch in which he remarked that he had once been a professional gambler. As the narrative unfolded, he described such events as being evicted from casinos for counting cards and being chased by the Russian mafia. The story served to set up a song that suggested the danger, intrigue, and mystery of the gambler's lifestyle.

The explicit evocation of the dangerous romance of the outlaw predisposed the song to index Purpose's experiential authenticity—an authenticity belied by the man's unassuming appearance and demeanor. Had Purpose not prefaced the song with his account of personal investment, the efficacy of the narrative would likely have been minimal. Contextualizing the events through the lens of his own experience, Purpose limited the audience's interpretive frame much like Hollywood filmmakers do in creating action/adventure movies. This is not to say that the song was lacking in terms of craftsmanship or delivery. Rather the codes of authenticity foregrounded Purpose, the author, as the primary, if not the only interpreter of the narrative.

For singer/songwriters authenticity is most often claimed by indices of experience: the roadworn, wizened artist or the insightful clever critic of the ordinary. One such performer is Deirdre Flint, whose material seems concerned primarily with funny aspects of life for her largely suburban audience. Flint's guitar accompaniment is technically simplistic, but as with more famous purveyors of "humor folk," such as Christine Lavin, music seems a convenient setting for adding color to the comedic performance. Like Flint's, much of Lavin's repertoire is thematically associated with situations and character types familiar to her audience. Songs with titles such as "I Was in Love with a Difficult Man," "Getting in Touch with My Inner Bitch," and "Biological Time Bomb" provide the audience with familiar codes of the ordinary. In the following excerpt from "Getting in Touch with My Inner Bitch," between the song's verses Lavin intersperses narratives that index typical middle-class experiences.

> Some people have an inner child
> Some people hear an inner voice
> Some people have inner calm
> Good for them!
> But me I've got no choice
> Some people have an inner cop
> Some people hear an inner clown
> But I've got me an Inner Bitch
> And it's hard to keep that Inner Bitch down!
>
> . . . .
>
> Ok, here's another example:
>
> I'm standing in line at the bank because I have to cash a check.

Finally I'm at the head of the line and one of the two working tellers that day decides she needs to take a cigarette break so she looks at all of us standing in line and she smiles as she walks outside and lights herself a Virginia Slim. She's having an Inner Bitch moment. My Inner Bitch salutes her but I'm mad because I'm still in line. Finally the other working teller shouts that magic word "Next!" and I slip my $50 check under the bullet proof Plexiglas barrier she looks at it and asks me for identification "C'mon," I said, "I've had an account here since 1976 just check my name, it's on file." So she goes and checks my signature and she tells me it doesn't match the one that's on file I said, "C'mon! It's only $50, I have to get my dry cleaning" and she says, "Oh? well maybe the dry cleaner will cash your check, but I won't!" And I realize I've been witness to two Inner Bitch moments in the same bank on the same day. What are the odds of that happening? So I get an idea. I say call the telephone number that's on file she does and she hears a recording of my voice telling the caller try my cell phone. "Call my cell phone," I tell her, she does and the cell phone clipped to my exercise shorts doesn't ring because the bank's walls are too thick. Instead my voice mail comes on and the bank teller rolls her eyes and says, "Oh, I'm supposed to be impressed, you have two voice mail accounts on two different telephones. I don't think so!" And she slips that $50 check back under the bullet proof, Plexiglas barrier. She thinks she has won. Her Inner Bitch starts dancing! But I find the bank manager and I have her dial my number, she listens and then she marches me right back to the bank teller and commands her to cash that check! The bank teller's Inner Bitch stops dancing, My Inner Bitch does the mambo. And the bank manager's Inner Bitch cha cha's out to the sidewalk and cuts that Virginia Slim cigarette break short! Ha!

For Christine Lavin, and Deirdre Flint as well, the comedy of everyday life outweighs the specifically musical performance. That is, music provides a setting without being the central focus. Lavin is an adequate guitarist but not virtuosic. Her harmonic vocabulary is conventional to the idiom. Music is clearly secondary, and her audience, which is substantial, doesn't come to her concerts to be awed by musicianship. As for much contemporary folk music, the message is in the lyrics, and in Lavin's case the comedy of her message highlights an easily accessible authenticity of the ordinary.

One of the most apparent and conceptually intriguing enactments of folk authenticities does not concern singer/songwriters per se, but blues revivalists. While some of these performers do write songs emulating various urban and rural blues styles and other styles as well, most appear to play the "torchbearer of tradition" role in folk communities. Along with the increased interest in what D. K. Wilgus called the Anglo-American folk song, contemporary folkies have illustrated a newfound interest in the music of black country-blues artists, most of whom recorded race records from the 1920s through the 1940s.[19] The webs of signification enacted through blues performances by primarily white, well-educated emulators and imitators of black musical expression[20] not only index appropriated codes of authenticity, but also explicitly and implicitly address issues of race and its historical bearing on relative positions of power within the music industry at large and, more recently, within the contemporary folk microindustry.

Shortly before moving from Austin to New York in the summer of 2001, I had lunch with bluesman Roy Bookbinder in a small café in South Austin. A mutual friend arranged our introduction, and I found Bookbinder to be a personable and articulate fellow. He invited me to a concert he was playing that evening, and I happily accepted. That evening Roy met me outside the venue and made certain my name was on the guest list, which as a graduate student living from hand to mouth I found a welcome surprise. When he began his set, person and persona presented an engaging perspective on authenticity, appropriation, and high/low culture. Bookbinder sang in a gravelly baritone, the inflections of which vacillated between his spoken voice and that of an old black man. This emulation of African-American rural speech underscored the musical elements of the performance in striking ways.

Bookbinder has, for more than three decades, been learning and refining a style of guitar playing whose roots lie in the southeastern United States of the early twentieth century. The style employs various techniques including the independent thumb and bottleneck playing.[21] Each of these techniques demands a level of expertise that comes only through extended practice. That is to say, it is not easy to play well. However, the overall effect is, by highbrow technical standards, somewhat loose and sloppy. Strings buzzing from imprecise finger placement are characteristic, and for most of these highly proficient bluesmen a practiced sloppiness is more desirable than clean precision. Through his vocal and instrumental techniques, Bookbinder embodies the black rural bluesmen whose playing and songs he so obviously admires. The indices of authenticity were obvious from a stylistic standpoint as well as from his performative behaviors, choice of guitars, and between-song patter. In a recent conversation with a presenter who admires Bookbinder, the suggestion was made that he has been employing the bluesman persona for so long that it is difficult to say where the person ends and the persona begins. Indeed the level of commitment to the style has blurred the boundaries between experience and the imaginary. For most of his audience, Bookbinder's performance presents a journey into the historical imagination. For an almost exclusively white, middle-class crowd, his performance and persona suggest an authenticity in which race becomes abstract—a vague authenticity that comes without the problematics of actually confronting the conflicted history of black America—an authenticity based upon the performer's personal investment in the aesthetic history of style.

Where Bookbinder and other contemporary country-blues players perform authenticity through the audience's imaginary reconstructions of early twentieth-century black American experience, folk singer/songwriters are more generally concerned with topics through which shared authenticities of experience resonate. These bonds of experience and potential experience enacted in performances may be poetic excursions through which listeners wander in imaginative phantasms or may leave little to the imagination beyond picturing the action of narratives.

At a recent concert by one of folk's rising stars, a woman whose introspective songs primarily concern interpersonal relationships, one song stood out from the rest. It describes, both figuratively and somewhat literally, having intercourse with her partner on the dining room table. Her preamble and the song exposition made it clear that she was describing real events. The audience's reaction varied, but generally it seemed a mix of voyeuristic titillation and embarrassment. Nonetheless the authenticity of experience was effectively manifest.

Sexually charged topics are not a new phenomenon for the folk, but the ways in which they find expression have mirrored a larger social/cultural change in attitudes regarding sex. Radio, television, and movies have been instrumental in these changing attitudes. Violence and overtly sexual images and situations are cornerstones of prime-time television's tenacious grip on popular culture. Through relaxation of conventional, Victorian, Judeo-Christian moral codes, a Western mass media habitus, as it were, has emerged and continues to develop. Singer/songwriters are not immune to a cultural climate in which thematic material can draw from any imaginable source. Recently singer/songwriter Steve Earle came under media fire for writing a song from the perspective of John Walker Lindh, the convicted American Taliban collaborator. In a cultural climate of nationalistic fervor and fear of terroristic menace, Earle's song was interpreted as anti-American, and he was accused of everything short of treason. Earle's subsequent brief interview broadcast on various nationally syndicated television news programs no doubt gave credence to the adage "even bad publicity is good publicity."

As the world changes and the American public is inundated with images once considered too private or emotionally evocative for mass consumption, the new folk changes as well and the lines between public and private expression are redrawn. Since the folk revival of the late 1950s and 1960s, folk music has summarily been discarded and ignored by popular music audiences, "defiled" by pop music influences, reinfused with a vaguely rural nostalgic "Authentic," and lionized as an oasis of aesthetic and emotional expression. Shifting authenticities based on emotional, psychological, chemical, humorous, or topical texts are symptomatic of the changing face of folk music. Ultimately contemporary notions of a new folk aesthetic are defined by the values and perceptions of the people making and consuming folk music. The audience's evocation of emotion and sense of investment in the imagery of song narrative, the "living pictures" of folk song, is pivotal, not only in the perception of authenticities but also in the enactments of an increasingly interconnected folk collective: one which, as it turns out, is driven largely by developing audio and communication technologies.

Normalcy has spoken
And the wistful spell is broken
Time to start my odyssey
Of Internet and pay TV
—David R, "Spark," from *Spark*

3 Wired Folk
Recording Technology and the Internet

Folk music's waning popularity in the late 1960s returned the American folk to its status as a marginalized musical community: a position that was apparently preferred by the die-hard "real" folk who were never quite comfortable in their association with mainstream popular music. The timeworn venues that existed before the "folk revival" continued to present relatively well-established folksingers, while the rest of the live music industry turned to more profitable popular music stars. When singer/songwriters such as James Taylor and Joni Mitchell introduced a more pop-oriented folk music into America's mainstream marketplace, the rift between traditional folk and the upstart popular folk performers widened. The folk landscape in the United States became increasingly fragmented, and the industry of folk followed suit. Folk music seemed destined to be a poor cousin to its polished and more elaborately produced popular rock influenced counterparts. Magazines such as *Sing Out!* and *Dirty Linen* continued to extol the virtues of folk music, but their audience was limited. The Newport and Philadelphia folk festivals continued to present folk music, but the primary focus for music festivals shifted to rock music following the Monterey International Pop Music Festival in June 1967 and the Woodstock Music and Art Fair in August 1969. The business of folk reverted to its prerevival days as a diverse cottage industry based largely upon populist idealism and vague notions of the rural.

Many musicians who made a reasonable living during the early to mid-1960s playing the then ubiquitous folk venues either abandoned the idea of professional music making or followed the industry's lead and switched to various more popular styles of music. During this period the popular music consuming public grew bored with folk. It lacked the excitement and sonic power of rock, and following the folk world's initial sense of betrayal when Bob Dylan—the crown prince of folk—plugged in an electric guitar and played a rock set at the Newport Folk Festival in 1965, American music consumers en masse followed Dylan's lead and put folk music on the back burner of public memory.[1] The postrevival fragmentation of the American folk landscape reflected a lack of centralizing focus: a common practical or ideological foundation through which the factions of the folk music landscape might again coalesce into a cohesive community. Paradoxically, technology was to play a central role in that process.

Recording the Folk

In the late nineteenth and early twentieth centuries folk music's association with technology was situated primarily in preservationist projects. For collectors and folklorists such as John and Alan Lomax, recording technology was a welcome substitute for transcription skills. If a cowboy song could be recorded and played back, there was no immediate need to go about the tedium of transcribing the song into musical notation. When the Lomaxes conducted their now famous music collecting excursions in the 1930s, the wax cylinder and disc recorders with which they preserved hundreds of southern prison songs occupied most of the rather substantial trunk of their automobile.[2] It was also very expensive, as recording equipment in general continued to be at least until the latter half of the century when electronics manufacturers recognized the market potential of consumer tape machines. For the first fifty years or so of the twentieth century, music recording was an occupation for the privileged.

Indeed the history of folk music recording is marked by its inexorable connection to capital, both economic and symbolic. John and Alan Lomax are rightfully celebrated as central figures in the collection and preservation of American folk music. They also made a considerable sum of money publishing that music. However, certainly a central focus for the Lomaxes concerned public recognition of their intellectual and ideological agenda. An article that Alan Lomax wrote for *HiFi/Stereo Review* in 1960 illustrates the paradoxical relationship between folk idealism and technology:

> [T]he recording machine can be a voice for the voiceless, for the millions in the world who have no access to the main channels of communication, and whose cultures are being talked to death by all sorts of well-intentioned people—teachers, missionaries, etc—and who are being shouted into silence by our commercially bought-and-paid for loudspeakers. It took me a long time to realize that the main point of my activity was to redress the balance a bit, to put sound technology at the disposal of the folk, to bring channels of communication to all sorts of artists and areas. ("Saga of a Folksong Hunter," 38)

Lomax's apparent altruism toward the "voiceless" belies his own position of privilege and power within the folk music community and smacks of the paternalistic perspective anthropologists and ethnomusicologists have endeavored to shed over the last several decades. In his essay "The Ethics of the Voice," Steven Connor remarks:

> This privative conception of voice, as something exposed to the ever-present danger of theft, trespass or violation, pervades the politics of voice in feminism, cultural studies, ethnography and postcolonial writing. In this conception, for my voice to issue from another means that my voice can no longer be in my possession. If, by contrast, another forces his voice upon me then it is again impossible for me to speak with my own voice, because the voice of the other must wholly supplant my own. (221)

This notion of the voice as something one possesses, something that can be appropriated by others for sinister or altruistic ends, suggests parallels between ethnography and ventriloquism. Yet to dismiss Alan Lomax as merely a cultural imperialist is to impose an "enlightened" present on a credulous past.[3]

The apparent contradiction with which Lomax at once celebrates the redemptive power of technology while condemning "our commercially bought-and-paid for loudspeakers" illustrates the contested nature of the entire notion of "the folk" within the context of modernity. For Alan Lomax the Janus face of technology subjugates world cultures while offering agency to the powerless.

The apparent optimism with which Lomax views recording technology was reasonably common for mid-twentieth-century scholars. Marshall McLuhan shares that optimism regarding the redemptive potential of technology, and specifically of sound recording, in *Understanding Media: The Extensions of Man* (1964):

> The repertory of the 1920s was revived and given new depth and complexity by this new means. But the tape recorder in combination with l.p. revolutionized the repertory of classical music. Just as tape meant the new study of spoken rather than written languages, so it brought in the entire musical culture of many centuries and countries. Where before there had been a narrow selection from periods and composers, the tape recorder, combined with l.p., gave a full musical spectrum that made the sixteenth century as available as the nineteenth, and Chinese folk song as accessible as the Hungarian. (283)

The love affair that many midcentury scholars had with technology failed to address its dialectical potency. Nearly three decades before McLuhan advanced his optimistic view of technology, Walter Benjamin in his now famous essay "The Work of Art in the Age of Mechanical Reproduction" (1936) addressed the dialectical nature of technology with more guarded optimism. While suggesting that "mechanical reproduction emancipates the work of art from its parasitical dependence on ritual" (224), Benjamin's language occasionally implies a certain nostalgic sense of loss: "changes in the medium of contemporary perception can be comprehended as *decay of the aura*" (222, emphasis added). Yet Benjamin sees the infinite reproducibility of art as empowering the masses, a perspective that was to change radically in the work of Jean Baudrillard, for example, whose notion of "simulacra" paints a decidedly less rosy picture of the "work of art" and the world at large. While the availability of modern sound recording technology may, as Lomax asserts, give "voice to the voiceless," it also potentially alienates the very subjects it aims to empower. In terms of folk musics, for example, the same advancements that allowed for the preservation of cultural traditions have also threatened to consume those traditions, seemingly bombarding the world's folk with the aesthetic products of popular culture.

Peter Manuel in his work on North Indian cassette culture contends, "[T]he spread of mass-mediated music genres—especially film music—has contributed to the decline or even extinction of once-vital folk genres" (*Cassette Culture*, 7–8). Yet the same technologies that have facilitated this "decline or even extinction" are at once celebrated as having a democratizing effect within the context of the international music industry. The dialectics of technology played out in increasingly complex ways as sound recording continued to develop in the last half of the twentieth century.

By the late 1940s and early '50s, magnetic tape became the medium of choice for recording music performances, and the development of professional and consumer tape recorders resolved many of the physical problems of the earlier technology.[4] However, until the early 1970s, professional quality recording gear remained prohibitively expensive. The capital necessary to produce high quality recordings marked clear distinctions between musicians/consumers and the music industry as such. In 1969 a research and development team working for the Japanese company TEAC Audio Systems Corporation began exploring possibilities for a line of semiprofessional recording gear aimed at the performing musician.

In 1972, TEAC marketed the A3340S and A2340S tape recorders. Both machines were four-track recorders equipped with Simul-Sync capability, which enabled the user to record on one or more tracks and then listen to those tracks while recording additional tracks ("TASCAM Company History"). The early TEAC multitrack recorders offered reasonably good sonic quality, which was improved significantly by adding outboard noise reduction systems developed by companies such as Dolby Laboratories and DBX. Thus home multitrack recording became a reality. This event marked the beginning of what was in the years to come, a dramatic shift in modes of musical production.

By the mid-1970s the reasonably inexpensive four- and eight-track machines manufactured by TASCAM and several other companies began to have an impact, albeit minor, on the independent record production market. Home basement recording studios utilizing the new technologies were beginning to become commonplace. For a comparatively small investment, musicians could equip a home studio with sufficient hardware to produce master recordings for commercial LP record manufacture. In comparison to the sonic accuracy achieved by the major recording studios, these home recording projects were often less than stellar, but a skilled amateur engineer with the right equipment and a discerning ear could get quite acceptable results. This was particularly true for folk musicians, many of whom preferred a somewhat raw sound as befitting the authenticity of their musical choices. For three to four thousand dollars—still a considerable sum for a workaday folk musician in the 1970s—a home studio became possible for recording artists who lacked record company affiliations. Technology was again changing the landscape of the music industry, spurring an emerging marketplace for independent recording companies and their products.

As the 1970s ended and the 1980s began, semipro equipment manufacturers continued to introduce reasonably priced recording gear, much of which aimed at improving the quality and ease of home recording. As the semipro recording equipment industry grew, the record industry at large underwent various changes in media standards as well. LP records continued as the primary distribution media for popular and less popular musics. Cassette tapes brought the demise of the four- and eight-track players in the early 1970s, and in 1982 the advent of the compact disc foreshadowed the decline of the LP. For the semipro recording industry, one of the most significant developments occurred in 1987 with the introduction of the consumer digital audiotape (DAT) recorder (Recording Industry Association of America, "History of Recordings").

By the early 1990s, DAT had become the standard mix-down medium for professional and semipro recording studios around the world. Theoretically the DAT format allows for unlimited digital reproduction of recorded sound without the signal loss or degradation that occurs when analog magnetic tape is copied. The merits and pitfalls of DAT are widely debated in the recording community. Arguments against DAT suggest that the medium may not be particularly stable over time. Digital audiotape looks much like magnetic tape, and its containers, which resemble miniature videocassettes, are not particularly robust. Like magnetic tape, digital audiotape is subject to deformation if exposed to extremes of temperature or humidity, and even in the best environmental conditions DAT is likely to deteriorate over time. DAT recorders are also subject to software and hardware inconsistencies that produce various digital errors. Some of these errors are not readily audible and others may produce digital distortion or intermittent cutouts. Regardless of its potential shortcomings, the advantages of DAT—lack of signal degeneration in the copying process and absence of tape hiss—defined it, if only for a moment, as the recording industry standard for producing master tapes.

Digital multitrack recorders followed closely on the heels of the introduction of DAT. Various companies including Alesis, TASCAM, and Sony began marketing to the professional and semipro recording communities. Mirroring rapid technological advancements in the computer industry, recording technology became much less expensive and of much higher quality in terms of sonic reproduction.

By the mid-1990s the ADAT, an eight-channel digital recorder produced by Alesis and introduced in 1991 (Alesis, "About Us"), was ubiquitous in the recording industry.[5] Most professional recording facilities had several of the machines in order to meet the demand for interstudio cooperative projects. The low cost of the machines allowed unprecedented numbers of musicians to produce recordings in their homes or at live performances, which could then be "sweetened," mixed, or mastered at professional facilities with the capability to produce publishable products. It also allowed musicians to record projects in multiple locations, recording bits and pieces in various studios as schedules, budgets, and other considerations came into play. A performer or band could record basic tracks in a studio in New York, for example, and send the ADAT tapes to Los Angeles where a soloist could add a part, after which the tapes could be sent to a studio in London, Paris, or anywhere else that compatible hardware was in use, for additional tracking.

The widespread use of digital tape machines has changed the landscape of the music industry in profound ways: both in how the musical artifact is produced and, as the equipment has become more available to nonprofessional recordists, in decentralized modes of production as well. In a broad sense the development of widely accessible and reasonably good quality recording technologies has allowed for what Peter Manuel has called a "grassroots-based, decentralized, pluralistic, 'democratic-participant' micro-medium in a given region, whose negative and positive ramifications may have broader implications for the spread of such technologies elsewhere" (*Cassette Culture*, 1). While Manuel's study is situated within the context of a specific region, the last part of his statement presages changes that occurred after the publication of his book.

Rapid advancements in recording technology have reached epic proportions in the last decade as hard disk digital recording software and hardware systems have accelerated the availability of multitrack recording capability for increasing numbers of musicians. The integration of computer technology and sound recording has created an opportunity for digitally stored information to be transmitted almost instantaneously anywhere in the world through the Internet.[6] The cumulative effects of these rapid advancements in recording and communication technologies have in some ways leveled the playing field of the record industry. Anyone with a moderately priced computer recording system and a microphone can produce a musical product and market and distribute that product through his or her own Web site. The advent of MP3 technology and file sharing opportunities available through the World Wide Web have made obtaining digital copies of recorded music a simple point and click proposition. The mainstream recording industry, historically slow to respond to trends in popular culture, has been caught with its proverbial pants down and has filed countless law suits against file sharing companies such as Napster, the first highly publicized action. Where the semipro recording equipment industry has provided a means for musicians (folk and otherwise) to record projects less expensively than ever before, the Internet has provided the forum through which musicians can market and distribute their music. It has also been the impetus for the creation of virtual musical communities and, secondarily, the most recent revival and popularization of the contemporary folk singer/songwriter.

Folk and the Internet

In the past decade the business of folk music has in large part grown out of the increasing use of the Internet as a communication medium. Much like the marketing and dissemination of television technologies in the late 1950s and early '60s, during which media pundits, corporations, and politicians recognized and celebrated claims that the vast majority of American households owned a television,[7] the personal computer and the Internet are being generally celebrated as the loci of the information age. By the early 1990s germinal Internet interest groups reflected what appeared to be a steadily growing interest in contemporary and traditional folk music as well as the emerging field of new singer/songwriters. Increasingly, Internet usergroups, newsgroups, and listservs[8] concerning folk music topics were being created as forums for discussing not only the music but also venues, copyright, publishing, songwriting—any and all topics relating to the business and performance of folk music.

Over the next few years the traffic on various lists and groups kept pace with the general increase in Internet use. As the traffic accelerated, songwriters, players, and entertainers began to use the new medium as a vehicle for promoting careers. Internet lists and newsgroups became sites through which an industry buzz could be generated. Granted, the industry of folk was still a somewhat amorphous entity, or collection of entities; however, subscribers to these folk lists and the newsgroups' regular contributors began to have an impact on the lives and careers of what became a new wave of professional traveling folk musicians on a rapidly expanding circuit of folk-related performance venues. On one list or group, a performer might be widely hailed as a gifted performer, writer, or player, and word might spread throughout the various lists as subscribers chime in with their own reiterations of the initial praise. The various groups, of course, have crossover participants. That is, many people participate in more than one of these folk music forums, allowing for information sharing and a wide audience for one's ideas. Rarely will there be explicit disagreement regarding a performer's talent. The community of folk who frequent these Internet newsgroups and listservs is generally averse to negative public commentary regarding individual performers. This is particularly evident in listserv subscription groups and less so in related newsgroups, which have a more transitory readership.

The differences in communicative dynamics between newsgroups and listservs derive, at least in part, from the specific structures of participation. Newsgroups have a less formally defined readership. Anyone with a newsreader can download current messages on a topic and respond with comments, opinions, or observations. If one no longer wants to take part, one can simply choose not to download the group's messages. The listserv requires that the participants subscribe to the group. Messages are generated and received in an e-mail digest form or as individual e-mail messages.

Newsgroups and Usenet

In most of the folk-music-related newsgroups and presumably in non-folk-music groups as well, a stable group of regular contributors emerges. These regulars set the tone of the group's behavior, or "netiquette." As in the world of face-to-face communication, arguments and debates occasionally arise. These altercations may be relatively polite differences of opinion, or they may get heated and deteriorate into personal attacks and insults. For some participants, these more vociferous exchanges apparently provide a great deal of amusement: enter the "troll."

Trolls are people who join a newsgroup discussion for the express purpose of inciting controversy. The troll will usually observe the general tenor of the conversations in a newsgroup in order to determine the most inflammatory tack to take in initiating a thread.[9] In the early days of folk music discussion groups a surefire method of generating heated discussion was to post a message asking, "What is folk music anyway?" The what-is-folk question, while guaranteed to generate debate, is a relatively benign issue for the troll. More provocative fare includes topics ranging from racist diatribes to slurs on various brands of guitars or sound equipment, to colorful comments on sexuality. Oftentimes trolls disguise their identities. Most apparently prefer that their online behavior, considered aberrant in the virtual domain, remain entirely within the context of the virtual.

A social hierarchy of credibility based upon one's history of posting relevant and thoughtful responses generally arises within newsgroups. Such hierarchies and associations that develop in virtual locales encapsulate the larger sociological implications of the Internet as an agent in creating what has been called unbounded communities. The community of folk that has coalesced within this virtual domain is unbounded not only geographically but also with regard to physicality. In this electronic communication, users develop Net personalities that may or may not readily correlate with their daily lives. Relationships are established, friendships develop, and antagonisms surface through the course of discussing music, performers, instruments, personal experiences, and world events. Humor and joking are frequent elements of newsgroup participation and are often used to diffuse hostilities. All of this occurs without the benefit of shared physical presence. Clearly the implications for alienation are staggering.[10]

In the fall of 2000, I attended the TX-1 gathering of the usergroup rec.music .makers.guitar.acoustic, or RMMGA, in Wimberley, Texas, a small community close to Austin. I became involved with the group through a chance meeting with Al Evans, a regular participant of RMMGA, at an informal song circle in Austin, hosted by a mutual friend. The day after the song circle, Al posted a message to the group concerning one of my guitars. He suggested that I read the posting and the subsequent responses, and I was drawn into a discussion regarding acoustic guitars and their perceived value. Over the next several months I occasionally participated in discussions and was invited to attend the first Texas gathering of RMMGA.

I arrived at the rural site of the gathering in the late morning of October 13 to find about a dozen participants congregating around the central building, which consisted of an open room of about twelve hundred square feet with an adjoining kitchen and bathroom. Participants were housed in small, comfortable cottages scattered around the property. Outside the meeting house, where most of the organized activities took place, chairs and tables were set up and small groups were playing music, admiring each other's guitars, and visiting. Al and Cea Evans, who organized the event, and my friends Harold and Kathy Hedberg from Houston who had driven in for the weekend, greeted me. I was introduced to the other participants, most of whose names I recognized from RMMGA. Many of the attendees were from out of state, and some had traveled considerable distances.

As the day progressed the socializing and playing continued, accompanied by a substantial ingestion of beer, wine, and food. A tangible feeling of camaraderie permeated the festivities, and as most of the participants were not professional musicians, the sort of competitive musicianship often evident at festival song circles and other music events was nowhere to be found among this egalitarian crowd. The few professional and semiprofessional musicians and the more adept amateur players were well regarded, but it was clear that all musical contributions were valued. The instruments were the real stars. Most of the attendees brought handmade guitars, many of which had been built specifically for them and carried price tags in the thousands of dollars.

The primary common interest that drew the crowd together was acoustic guitars. The music for those three days of the gathering reflected interests not only in American folk but also in popular and older rock, jazz, and classical music. While a variety of musical styles were represented, the exclusive use of acoustic instruments—albeit sometimes amplified—defined the event. Like the contemporary folk music landscape at large, the gathering illustrated the confluence of stylistic genres that has come to characterize American folk.

On the first night many attendees of the RMMGA TX-1 gathering stayed up until the wee hours socializing and playing music. The festivities continued on Saturday with occasional organized activities including a lutherie demonstration by local guitarmaker Jamie Kinscherff and an elaborate evening meal prepared by some of the wives. That evening an open mic was organized in the main meeting hall. Most of the group participated, and a small public-address system was set up, which served to formalize the performances. All of the performers, regardless of their technical proficiency, received enthusiastic applause, and an awards ceremony honored the organizers and other group members, with humorous door prizes distributed to most attendees. Following the open mic session, some participants retired to their cottages while others continued socializing and playing guitars well into the night.

On Sunday morning Jamie Kinscherff hosted a country breakfast, followed by a tour of his guitarmaking facility on a nearby ranch. Several of the group continued to socialize and play music upon their return to the meeting area, while preparations for departing the site were initiated and farewells and appreciative comments were exchanged as the group disbanded and the event came to a close.

Several aspects of the TX-1 gathering are notable with regard to the more general landscape of folk music and the imagined community of the folk. In terms of demographics, the gathering was a somewhat exaggerated microcosm of the larger picture of the contemporary folk scene. The majority of the primary participants were male, Caucasian, middle-aged, and well educated. The only female attendee who also maintained a presence in the newsgroup was Cea Evans. The preponderance of men at the gathering illustrates an exaggerated, yet decidedly gendered element of the larger folk community. While male participants took some part in food preparation, cleanup, and other stereotypically female activities, these jobs were attended to primarily by group members' wives, the men being excused to play and discuss guitars and socialize among themselves. One of the "guitar widows" confided that prior to arriving at the gathering she had never met any of the participants, had nothing apparent in common with the other wives, and was quite frankly bored to tears.

Women have made considerable headway in terms of gained status within the community of folk musicians, yet there remains an attitude illustrated in comments by one of the old guard Kerrville Folk Festival attendees who, upon hearing Mary Melena playing a technically difficult guitar instrumental, stated, "You play pretty good for a girl." However, that the women of the RMMGA gathering played noticeably secondary roles was less a matter of reinscribing patriarchal notions than a function of the conceptual framework of the event. The participants of RMMGA had gathered to actualize the social bonds shaped within the context of the virtual domain: to see and play the instruments around which their association was shaped and to reinforce those bonds through face-to-face encounter. That most of the group's active participants are male reflects the tenacity of patriarchal values, which are continually reinscribed throughout the spectrum of American life: men are proactive and interested in construction and maintenance of the artifacts of culture, while women are passive bystanders who may enjoy the products of technology but are uninterested in the details of process.

All of this strongly suggests that for those involved with RMMGA, the guitar has assumed the character of fetish. Clearly the instruments are the stars of the show, and for weeks after group gatherings, talk of the guitars in attendance seems to far surpass the mention of individual players. In his essay "On the Fetish-Character in Music and the Regression of Listening" (1938), Theodor Adorno suggests, "The more inexorably the principle of exchange-value destroys use values for human beings, the more deeply does exchange-value disguise itself as the object of enjoyment" (quoted in Arato and Gebhardt, *Essential Frankfurt School Reader*, 279). For RMMGA participants and attendees at the frequent gatherings organized around Internet participation in that group, the guitar provides the impetus for community interaction and exemplifies commodity fetishism in the classic Marxist tradition. However, to assume that RMMGA speaks for the American folk at large would be disingenuous. The group is one of a plethora of Internet interest groups whose primary concerns intersect with folk communities. To argue that the guitar as fetish is ubiquitous on the American folk landscape is to miss the forest for the trees.

TX-1 was one of many similar gatherings that have since continued to occur. Several EC (East Coast) gatherings, as well as UK (United Kingdom), and subsequent TX meetings, and probably others as well, have taken place and have been well attended. Attending gatherings has become an important part of people's lives and can constitute a substantial investment of time, energy, and money. The "real world" experience of the gathering may serve to justify the blocks of time spent in the faceless world of cyberspace.

Participation in newsgroups and listservs can occupy considerable amounts of time spent sitting in front of a computer screen typing opinions and responses to other participants. These discussions can develop into complicated conceptual exchanges in which each participant may write lengthy explanations or recitations, which more than occasionally deteriorate into verbal assaults called "flame wars." Such antagonism is often due to misunderstandings of authorial intent; it is also often due to conflicts of opinion sometimes stemming from the diversity of cultural backgrounds in the forums as well as the lack of physical signals—body language, eye contact, and vocal inflections—with which dialogues are interpreted in face-to-face encounters. One of the most protracted of these exchanges that I have witnessed occurred in RMMGA and brought to the fore the issue of race.

The extended and highly contested thread began with the following posting dated 1 October 2000. The post was from a new contributor allegedly named Tyrone X whose e-mail address was proudnigroid@aol.com.[11] The message subject read: "PROUD NIGGA IS IN DA HOUSE."

SUP

DIS BE TYRONE X. I LUV DEM COUSTIC AXES. I BE FROM DA GHETTO OF COMPTON. I IS DA COUSTIC AXE PLAYA IN COMPTON. I PLAY GANGSTA RAP ON DA COUSTIC GITTA. IS DER ANY OTHA RAPPERS IN DIS HOUSE DAT PLAY DA COUSTIC GITTA?

NIGGA OUT,
TYRONE X

PS RESPOND TO PROWDNIGGA7@YAHOO.COM.

Less than an hour after initial posting, the message was responded to by a regular contributor to the group, Larry Pattis, whose comment set the tone for the contested nature of the thread.

If this posting continues I will personally organize a mass e-mail campaign to get Yahoo's attention in this matter.

I will not sit still for this.

I expect that ALL of you will also NOT sit still.

Let this be a WARNING to whomever thinks that this is either acceptable or funny.

Your behavior will stop.

I will GET you.

I promise.

Larry Pattis.

Pattis's apparently visceral reaction to Tyrone's posting opened the floodgates for a debate implicitly and explicitly informed by racial tensions that continue to resonate within American society at large and in the folk music community specifically.[12] The central issue concerned Tyrone's identity as a black man. Pattis, along with numerous others, was convinced that Tyrone was a Caucasian troll and was aping the "rapeze" popularized by rap and hip-hop artists.

The medium of communication was pivotal in defining the boundaries of the debate as well as the issue at hand. Without the benefit of physical presence, authorial intent was called into question. Tyrone was reviled as everything from a Ku Klux Klan member attempting to incite racial tension to a suburban teenage troublemaker. There were also voices suggesting that Tyrone be accepted as who he claimed to be: a black rapper with an interest in acoustic guitar. Over the weeks in which the Tyrone debate continued, righteous indignation and proclamations of moral rectitude were interspersed with attempts at humor and highly charged emotional rhetoric. Pattis and the contingent of morally incensed RMMGA participants were so enraged by Tyrone's perceived breach of cultural propriety that they successfully lobbied to have at least two of his e-mail accounts revoked.

The discussion and debate indexed some resonant and tenacious attitudes about race and otherness. That Tyrone chose to frame his contributions to the discussion in language foreign and repellant to much of the regular constituency situated him outside the familiar cultural context the group had nurtured over time. For the most part the regular contributors to RMMGA seem to be white, middle-aged, and reasonably well educated in mainstream behavioral propriety. This issue was addressed during the course of the discussion with one participant suggesting that making demographic assumptions without ever coming into direct personal contact with most of the group was presumptuous. While the author's point was well made, little argument ensued regarding the original comment, and the constituencies of the frequent RMMGA gatherings offer at least limited evidence as to the accuracy of the initial generalization.

Tyrone introduced an element of the ethnic Other to the group. However, without the benefit of an authentication born of visual context, many of the group's participants chose to question his obvious claims to otherness, preferring to believe that his comments were an ill-intentioned caricature. In doing so, the notion of otherness, rather than being attributable to ethnicity or race, shifted to Tyrone's perceived transgression of the social order of behavior. Yet this apparent transgression was (given the benefit of the doubt) initiated from an ethnically situated cultural position within which it would not seem at all transgressive, thereby locating the contestation squarely within the context of cultural difference based upon race or ethnicity. Generally those most offended by Tyrone's commentary took particular exception to his use of the word "nigga." While use of the word among younger generations of African-Americans has become widespread, for much of the white American mainstream the word "nigger," or any variation thereof, invokes a public memory of the long national history of racial injustice, bigotry, and division. The antagonism and general controversy that surrounded Tyrone's introduction to RMMGA was indicative of an ambiguous discomfort with the idea of difference, particularly when that idea is based in the realm of ethnicity or race.

Since the 1960s, when media coverage of increasing civil rights activity propelled the civil rights issue into the forefront of mainstream American life, race has been a highly charged and bitterly contested concern. The media, television in particular, were pivotal in making white Americans aware of the social, political, and economic inequities that mark the history of black America. Through mass mediation, ideas about race and race relations came to evoke strong and sometimes dramatic emotional responses.

As the civil rights movement began to occupy increasing blocks of time for the mass media in the 1960s, the issues presented became integral pieces in the social fabric of American life. For the baby boom generation awareness of racial difference became an unavoidable circumstance of public education. School aged, white, middle-class American youth became increasingly aware of the extent to which African-Americans suffered social inequities. In the political sphere, considerable legislation was enacted in attempts to rectify the problems and assure equal rights. Black and white activists made widely publicized attempts to galvanize African-Americans into a voting block. In short, liberal white America became appalled at the past treatment of black America and began making a concerted effort at widespread social change. Yet the images that past generations had inscribed into public memory lingered under the surface of America's new racial awareness. This is not to say that white Americans were disingenuous about black equality; rather it is an observation that images, once seen, cannot be *un*seen. Ideas about racial or ethnic difference and otherness have often been gleaned from social environments in which contact with the other is limited. Conscious efforts to negate the notion of otherness—an otherness reinforced through the experiential, or lack thereof—necessarily operate in a dialectical sphere.

American popular culture of the 1940s and '50s articulated and defined the inevitably conflicted nature of conventional ideas about race. The images baby boomers saw as children and young adults, including television shows depicting characters such as Amos and Andy and Jack Benny's Rochester, did little to dispel the mythologies perpetuated by blackface minstrels since the early nineteenth century. These television images portrayed as humor, informed us at the level of the aesthetic, suggesting what we should and should not find funny. Lazy and incompetent Negroes were widely regarded as funny. By the early 1960s it began to become clear that the American public at large had been deceived. During the course of the decade, the depth of damage done by these and similar characterizations of black behavior became apparent and the entertainment industry eliminated the most obvious derogatory racial stereotyping. Of course, less obvious and no less sinister examples remain and continue to inform television audiences, but that is a topic for another study.

At a fundamental level Americans felt the need for change. What had formerly been the object of hilarity was now considered shameful. For white Americans this change created a potential site for personal/psychological conflict. While the history of the relationship of black and white Americans became clearer and more graphically illutrated throughout the 1960s and the following decades, the memory of families gathered around the television set laughing at the antics of Amos and Andy grew more repellant. This rift in the perception of a nostalgic, emotional past was symptomatic of a larger sense of national shame regarding race and ethnicity. Situated as such in discourses of national pride (or lack thereof) and ideals of home and family, discussions concerning race have tremendous potential for generating highly emotional responses. Such was the case in the RMMGA discussions concerning Tyrone.

From the outset, the emotional content of the responses to Tyrone's initial inquiry and subsequent postings mirrored the apprehension with issues of race many white Americans continue to share. In the course of the continuing dialogue, accusations of racism and paternalism alternated with attempts to locate the controversy in the domain of language and propriety. These attempts to diffuse the racial implications of the discussion rang hollow in the face of Tyrone's culturally specific language.

It is remarkable that the entire controversy, one that generated so many responses and occupied so much time for quite a few people, existed as a function of the medium in which it occurred. This suggests, perhaps, that for the relatively tight-knit community of RMMGA, and possibly for the folk community at large, face-to-face contact between participants serves to guard against racial division. However, the conflicted nature of the issue of race within those communities may also imply that the relationship of visual immediacy to the negation of division is simply another of folk's lingering myths. It remains that without the physical or visual presence of the participants in the dialogue, Usenet is likely to remain a site of frequent confrontation.

The sort of protracted debate illustrated by the Tyrone incident is somewhat less common in the context of the listserv, primarily because of the forum's structure, in which a moderator can censor comments that might be considered offensive.

Listserv Mediation and New Proprieties

Listservs are more formalized and topic-specific discussion forums than newsgroups and usergroups. As mentioned previously, listservs are groups to which the user subscribes. Generally a moderator, most often the person who organized the list, controls the level of discursive decorum among the discussants. When a debate deteriorates into personal attacks, the moderator will often ask the combatants to take their argument off list. In theory the moderator is also responsible for screening content and making determinations about the relevance and general interest of postings. If a message is completely off topic for the group and the moderator subjectively determines that it has little or no general interest, the message will not be posted.

At the time of this writing thousands of moderated Internet lists cover a broad range of topics. The folk music community has been particularly active in creating listservs as local, national, and international forums for discussion of folk-music-related subjects. Perhaps the most broad based and widely referenced lists relating to folk music issues are the FolkBiz and folkmusic listservs created and moderated by Alan Rowoth.[13] Rowoth has been instrumental in defining the role of the Internet for the folk community and in doing so has become a contemporary version of what Benjamin Filene has called a folk music "power broker."

Through his Internet-related activities, Rowoth has taken a hand in organizing numerous "real world" events and has become a high-profile figure on the contemporary folk landscape. As with power brokers of the past, his position within the folk community and his personal stake in that position have come into question among others involved in folk music. Critics have called him a "professional fan," yet even his most cynical critics admit that Rowoth has a deep personal commitment to contemporary folk music. A musician with whom I spoke in July 2000 at the Falcon Ridge Folk Festival stated, "Alan loves the music. . . . I used to think he was involved [in the folk community] from a sort of groupie perspective, a fame by association type, but have changed my mind. All that star business is secondary to his deep feelings for the music.".

As Rowoth's listserv traffic increased throughout the last decade, the forums became important vehicles for disseminating information concerning emerging artists and the new class of American touring folk musicians. Good reviews of performances posted to the lists regularly stimulated additional positive responses and were instrumental in creating an industry buzz. Venue operators became frequent contributors to the lists, and many began monitoring the level of subscriber interest in specific artists as a determining factor in booking decisions. The artists most widely discussed on listservs as well as in news and usergroups became sought-after commodities in the rapidly increasing circuit of house concerts, concert series, and festivals. These venues presented additional opportunities for Internet friends to meet in person and solidify relationships begun online. "Real world" events and get-togethers organized through listserv postings served to galvanize a community of folk performers, presenters, and fans and offered a concrete realization of the virtual community that was becoming an indispensable element in the rapidly developing landscape of the folk microindustry.

Personal Web Sites

The Internet has in a relatively short time become the primary site for folk music promotion. From the most obscure folk musician to older generations of performers, many who have achieved iconic status through longevity, Web presence has effectively become a necessity. Artists' personal Web sites can contain elaborate graphics and may be professionally designed or may be simple informational sites. Most contain pictures of the performer, the artist's bio, scheduled appearances, and contact information. Some have links to other artists' pages, folk-related Web sites, and general music and miscellaneous sites, as well as ways to purchase CDs, tapes, and other products.[14] Since the advent of MP3 technology, samples of the artist's recorded music have become more widely available on individual sites, and visitors can listen online to excerpts or entire songs. Web sites may feature downloadable press kits, and some have posters and other promotional materials that can be downloaded and printed to advertise upcoming appearances by the artist.

Artists' Web sites are frequently referenced sources where presenters gather information to use in promoting concerts, arranging concert schedules, and evaluating lesser-known artists for possible inclusion in future concerts. While the time-honored press kit is still widely used,[15] Web sites have created an environment in which a great deal of information about performers is immediately available and readily accessible. That the Web site has become a standard of the industry in such a short time is remarkable. Acceptance of this new medium by the folk community punctuates the long relationship between technology and folk music as a cultural commodity.

Technology versus Authenticity

Folk's early involvement with technology, specifically with the recording process, was ostensibly related to preservationist projects and was celebrated as providing, in Alan Lomax's earlier quoted phrase, "a voice for the voiceless" (Lomax, "Saga of a Folksong Hunter").[16] That notion was consistent with the emerging folk ideology espoused by early twentieth-century folk power brokers. There was little if any perceived ideological problem with recording folk music for posterity. Yet as the century wore on, technology and authenticity occasionally proved to be incompatible ideological bedfellows.

In 1965 when Bob Dylan plugged in his Fender Stratocaster and performed with a four-piece rock band at the Newport Folk Festival, technology became anathematic for the American folk. Dylan was the golden boy of the 1960s folk revival and his Newport performance was perceived by much of the folk community as an intentional affront to folk music traditions and to the folk revival specifically. Even the mild-mannered and famously tolerant Pete Seeger, upon hearing Dylan's performance, "threatened to cut the power cables with an ax" (Cantwell, *When We Were Good*, 309). Technology was fine as long as it knew its place. When it intruded on stylistic boundaries—the constructed traditions of the folk aesthetic—technology became a tool of the antithetical popular.

The multiple layers of paradox that continue to inculcate the American folk landscape were most publicly aired during the waning days of the 1960s revival. As discussed previously, the "revival" was not a folk revival at all. Rather it was a relatively brief period during which folk music and its popular incarnations became commercially viable stylistic products. It was through technology that these products were mediated, manufactured, and disseminated in their various forms and through which the authenticities imbued in their aesthetic trappings became inscribed in public memory. The high/low, folk/popular distinctions first articulated by Hubert Parry in 1899 were revived by 1960s folkies who loudly reviled pop music and claimed an authenticity born of tradition as justification for their own positions within the popular music industry. Generally the popular, and technology implicitly, was bad, but it was okay that folk music was popular and great that folk musicians were selling records. Folk music was hailed as egalitarian, and its proponents promoted a public image of simple, peaceful social harmony. Yet the outrage and hostility Dylan encountered as a result of his public engagement with the popular suggested that the line of tolerance for the non-folk popular, and perhaps all things technological, was drawn at the level of the aesthetic.

Adorno's notion of the negative dialectic found a new level of interpretive convolution as folk music defined itself by what it was not as well as by what it was—the popular. The technologies that allowed for the 1960s popularization of folk music and notions of modernity in general were alternately ignored in the service of mythological premodern folk ideals and embraced when it served the ideological ends of folk revivalists or of individual self-interests. By the late 1960s it appeared that modernity, technology, and the popular had won the battle for public attention, and folk music returned to its unpopular, prerevival status. The "real folk" continued to revel in their musical otherness and the slick, modern folk stars either adapted to the change in public tastes or faded into relative obscurity.

In the late 1960s and early 1970s, a new folk aesthetic began to emerge on the popular music landscape. Artists such as James Taylor and Joni Mitchell introduced a new folk sound with a decidedly pop musical sensibility. Not unlike the folk music of the 1960s, the sound was characterized by its acoustic guitar and vocal foundation. Yet there were elements to the new folk music that were quite different than their revival counterparts. The modern folk was generally more elaborately produced. String sections, horn sections, and coloristic instrumental accompaniments waxed commonplace, as did electric guitar solos. For harmonic accompaniment, the songs borrowed more from non-folk popular music styles than the folk song styles popularized a decade before. The authenticity of musical simplicity gave way to a broader use of harmonic and timbral resources. Where earlier folk song lyrics addressed events, social issues, and narrative tales, the new folk lyric tended to be more intensely personal. Yet the themes of earlier folk music occasionally resurfaced in the new folk songs, albeit in updated musical and textual surroundings.

These artists unapologetically made free use of available music technologies. Stylistically their songs presented a hybridized folk/pop that found a tremendous audience among 1970s music consumers. While Leadbelly, Woody Guthrie, and others of their generation were iconic figures for the 1960s folk movement, James Taylor, Joni Mitchell, and their ilk achieved iconic status among a younger generation of folk music listeners and players for whom the 1960s held only dim memories. Many contemporary singer/songwriters acknowledge musical debts to these 1970s popular folk music performers who were, not surprisingly, much maligned by the "real" folk for their lack of authenticity. Certainly the folk/pop of the 1970s was instrumental in legitimizing folk's ongoing relationship with technology.

However, as this relationship ceased to appear ideologically incompatible, the new aesthetic did not supplant previous notions of folkness. Rather the newfound tolerance for a folk modern simply added an additional element to the pastiche of the American folk. Acoustic guitars, vocals, and texts reflecting the rural ideals of early-twentieth-century folk songs coexist with electronic effects devices, contemplative poetics (often characterized as navel-gazing), and humorous texts on computer themes—a new folk song genre that emerged as a direct result of the development of the personal computer.[17]

In July of 2001, Janis Ian performed at the Falcon Ridge Folk Festival. Her performance illustrated the hybrid stylistic nature of folk's still often-contested relationship with technology. Ian rose to national prominence at the age of fifteen and has recorded some seventeen albums in her career. She has won several Grammy Awards for her songwriting, had numerous commercial hit records, and is a regular contributor to music industry publications. Her recordings have been stylistically diverse, yet she has, with reasonable consistency, maintained a presence on the folk/acoustic music landscape. She is a regular performer at folk festivals and is a competent, if not virtuosic, guitarist.

When Ian began her set at Falcon Ridge that year, it was immediately clear that what the audience was going to hear was anything but a half hour performance of conventional folk music. She was playing an acoustic guitar, but one in which electronic transducers and a collection of electronic effects produced timbres that rendered the *acousticness* of the instrument nominal and symbolic. Ian's vocal was, as I recall, also at times processed through outboard effects creating a sonic landscape that was more akin to the art-rock of the early 1970s than to any specific folk style. The audience reaction was mixed, perhaps owing more to the high volume and the electronically processed sounds than to a sense that the experience was incompatible with any folk aesthetic. The impression of a hypermodern performance seemed inescapable. However, the music was compelling in its apparent contradictions. While sonically unusual given the context, the songs were harmonically and formally conventional. The songwriting was competent but also somewhat conventional in its sonic context.[18] Yet the conventions of form, structure, and harmony lent the experience a continuity not unlike the sense of uncomfortable kinship embodied by Bugkiller's performance some thirty years prior to Janis Ian's Falcon Ridge appearance. While Ian's use of technology indexed modernity, the musical structure of the songs along with the extramusical element of her historical connection to the folk music industry indexed a peculiar folk authenticity. In combination the overall effect was one of a strikingly postmodern musical text.

Conclusion

The American folk's long relationship with technology is indicative of the contradictions that have come to characterize conventional and academic ideas of folk and folk music. Yet where the development of that relationship at the end of the twentieth and beginning of the twenty-first centuries seems to fly in the face of the historical/ideological foundations of a folk authenticity, in practice it has galvanized communities of common interest and led to the sustained development of a dedicated folk microindustry. However, to unproblematically celebrate the marriage of folk music and technology is to ignore the exclusionary aspects of that association. While the tools of technology—computers, music-related electronic processors, and recording devices—have become relatively affordable, there is still wide disparity in who has ready access to those technologies. America's economically disenfranchised populations—typically African-Americans, Hispanic Americans, and people of color in general—are underrepresented inhabitants of the information age. This disparity is particularly apparent in the demographics of the American folk community. As Peter Manuel observed in the cassette culture of South Asia, technology has in some ways democratized the music industry, yet advancements in technology have thus far failed to provide substantive solutions to basic problems concerning the gross inequities of power that continue to polarize American society at multiple levels.

They brought me up in 1949
My rookie year almost past my prime
One step too slow and batting .205
They said—strictly minor league

I kicked around until the well ran dry
Like a hobo hopping one more ride
Mantle, Mays, Musial they all passed me by
Strictly minor league

But there were days I'd shine
When sweat and nerve and muscle danced in perfect time
So I'd keep on trying
Cause in those moments my dreams would gather right before
    my eyes
—Rich Prezioso, "Good Enough"

The Business
Microindustry and Folk Hierarchy

Like the protagonist in Rich Prezioso's song "Good Enough," the folk microindustry plays minor league to the popular music industry's major. However, the
"small-time" references in "Good Enough" not only implicate the folk business
at large, but also the divisions and hierarchies within this small-time. The minor league is, in this case, a symbol of careers stalled at various levels within the
landscape of today's American folk.

The technological advances in communication and sound recording that occurred in the last ten or fifteen years of the twentieth century raised the stakes for
the increasingly connected folk community. The relative ease with which folkies
were able to communicate with others sharing their interest in folk music created an atmosphere of almost tangible excitement. As traffic in folk newsgroups
and listservs gained momentum and computer hardware and software industries struggled to keep pace with the increasing demand for Internet-related

products, the folk community began to recognize the renewed interest in this music as having potential for actualization in real-world events as well as in its possibilities for revisiting some of the ideological ground covered in the 1960s revival.

Between the late 1960s and the early 1990s, the folk community lacked a collective sense of organization. Some large cities had local folk communities whose social locus was often a music store selling primarily folk instruments and records, a folklore center, and/or a venue in which folk artists performed. These localized communities had loose associations and affiliations but no substantive large-scale unity. This fragmented folk landscape was to change dramatically by the century's end.

At the time of this writing a microindustry that claims its own professional organization, independent record labels, radio programming, artist management and booking agencies, publications, and circuits of venues has developed around the folk music community. Local communities of folk music enthusiasts, performers, and presenters still persist,[1] but now the local is at some level informed by the collective community of American folk. As such, hierarchies exist at every level of the folk music landscape, from the local to the national to the international. The almost class-based divisions within the industry of folk resemble the hierarchies associated with the pop music industry (see Garfield, *Expensive Habits*, and Weissman, *Music Making in America*). I have chosen the term "microindustry" to suggest a general model based largely on the mainstream popular music industry. However, the folk microindustry operates at levels distinct—particularly in terms of economy—from the popular industry dominated by the big six record labels.[2]

> And I could almost feel that rush
> It was close enough to touch
> I believe I gave it all I had
> But that was not good enough
>
> My friends said "Hang it up, turn the page"
> But the hardest thing I'd ever done was walk away
> 'Cause it's all I knew, the only game I'd played
> And I was strictly minor league

The notion of a folk hierarchy, in terms of performer stature within the framework of national and international markets, has implications for a peculiar and paradoxical figure: the folk "star." If there are minor league players there must also be major league players. The idea of the music "star" has roots in the nineteenth-century veneration of the virtuosi, and it became highly developed in the mid-twentieth century with mass marketing of popular performers such as Frank Sinatra in the 1940s and Elvis Presley in the 1950s and '60s (Gillett, *The Sound of the City*).

While stardom and the folk seem mutually exclusive from a conceptual perspective, the social division between performer and audience, along with a historically grounded Euro-American legacy of idealizing the "Artist" has inculcated folk landscapes. Yet folk stars differ from their counterparts in the world of pop, rock, and classical music. Popular rock and pop stars are relatively unapproachable. The police and private security at large concert events, who assure the separation between performer and audience, are testament to that unapproachability. It is unlikely that today's Britney Spears or Michael Jackson fans will ever meet their music idols face to face. The economics of stardom at those levels negate all but the slightest possibility of personal engagement. For contemporary folk singer/songwriters, the distance between performer and audience is literally and figuratively minuscule by comparison.

Folk stars generally perform at venues that are either intimate enough to afford proximity to (and for) the audience[3] or, at larger venues, where they can share public space during intermission and after the concert to sign autographs and visit with fans. Folksingers who adopt the elitist attitude of the star—avoiding the audience and sequestering themselves—are rare. The American folk community is fairly tight-knit and technologically connected. When a performer snubs a fan at a venue whose physical space implies closeness between artist and audience, venting frustration is but a mouse click away.

The idealized folk of the anonymous author, unencumbered egalitarianism, and communalism seem contrary to the idealization of the individual artist as star. Yet the confluence of folk's imaginative past and its enacted present interact to create artist/audience relationships that are inclusive and at least superficially personalized, but unquestionably privilege the artist as special.

In the United States this romantic notion of the artist stems from a mid- to late-nineteenth-century "sacralization of culture" (Levine, *Highbrow/Lowbrow*) in which the conductor was the initial recipient of public adulation. Whether for musician or conductor, the emergence of the music star was a romantic project. That is, in elevating musicians—cultural producers—to the status of star, they become enhanced actors on a stage set apart from the everyday common man and endowed with insights peculiar to the creatively inclined.[4] As such, the star is another construction of modernity, an enduring myth that despite apparent conceptual (and contextual) contradictions is particularly resonant for today's American folk. Stars become stars through their viability in the marketplace.

Economically folk music is a poor cousin of mainstream popular music. The most successful performers, presenters, managers, agents, and even peripheral folk entrepreneurs generally make comfortable incomes, but they rarely approach the levels attained by their pop music counterparts.[5] The highest incomes in the folk world often come partly from crossover relationships between folk and popular music markets. In the folk microindustry as in its popular counterpart, hierarchies of social and economic status have emerged as the industry went through rapid development during the last decade of the twentieth century. One barometer of the changing face of the folk business is the Folk Alliance.

Folk Alliance

The North American Folk Music and Dance Alliance, commonly known simply as the Folk Alliance, is a professional organization that, like many such organizations, charges a yearly membership fee, holds conferences, and engages in activities beneficial to its membership as well as to community outreach programs. Several years ago the following statement could be found on the Folk Alliance Web site:

> In a world of expanding technology, all folk expressions, traditional and contemporary, are fragile and demand the strength that only a united folk arts community can provide.
>
> Founded in 1989, Folk Alliance was created to increase public awareness of the vital artistic and cultural importance of folk music and dance, because we believe that through folk music and dance, living cultural expressions and traditions are shared, heightening understanding of all cultures, and enriching our quality of life. Folk Alliance seeks to create new and better opportunities for all those involved in the performance folk arts, opportunities for growth, to learn, to share the common bonds of appreciation and participation in the Folk Alliance.
>
> Folk Alliance is an energetic body whose members are performers, agents, media, record companies, merchandisers, presenters, and other organizations and individuals actively promoting and fostering culturally diverse traditional and contemporary folk music, dance, storytelling, and related performing arts in North America. Our members encompass the breadth of the folk community: presenters, performers, festivals, agents, folk societies and their volunteers, back-porch players, song circle leaders, record companies, retailers, luthiers, broadcast and print media, folklorists and arts administrators.

Like Alan Lomax's comments regarding technology and the folk, the implied dangers of "expanding technology" to "folk expressions" seemed more than a bit ironic as the introductory statement on the Folk Alliance Web site. It is precisely these sorts of contradictions that illustrate the conflicted nature of a persistent folk idealism on the one hand and multiple engagements with modernity on the other.

The tenacity of an ideology that positions the "enlightened" as guardians of tradition continues to manifest itself in the mission statements of various venues, folk song societies, and related not-for-profit organizations. However, it would be unfair to characterize the nostalgic preservationism so common in American folk circles as insincere. In most cases it appears to be quite the opposite. Organizations such as the Folk Alliance and individuals who espouse the preservation of "folk culture" often do so with the best of intentions, if not the most critical eye. Indeed many of today's folk enthusiasts approach the goal of preserving folk music (in any of its manifestations) with a missionary zeal.

The tendency to sanctify musical traditions also suggests that stylistic codes have aesthetic appeal. When asked why they devote considerable time and effort to preserving folk music, most interviewees said they do it because they love the music. Yet aside from aesthetic considerations, involvement with preservationist projects has implications for individual and collective constructions of identity. Timothy Taylor suggests that the recent "surge of interest in things Celtic . . . has something to do with the increasing consciousness of ethnicity in contemporary American life and the concomitant commodification of ethnicity in music, even white ethnicities: European Americans are loath to be left out" (*Global Pop*, 7). Taylor goes on to cite Bellah et al., who suggest in *Habits of the Heart* (1985) that white middle-class Americans both lack and long for a sense of ethnicity. While Taylor's analysis draws connections between group identity constructions and the increasing interest in folk culture, specifically "things Celtic," it fails to address issues of agency in these constructions. In the folk music community, Celtic music ensembles have become ubiquitous. However, their initial popularity had more to do with the character of the music style than with a constructed identification with its Anglo-Europeanness. These groups generally play lively dance music that is melodically and harmonically familiar sounding to Western ears. For many of its practitioners, the ethnic identification with Celtic music, as with the broader field of American folk music, came as a secondary consequence of the initial aesthetic appeal of the music. These aesthetic concerns are part and parcel of the process of generating meaning, and organizations like the Folk Alliance, as well as individual musicians, are active agents in reconfiguring relationships of signification and meaning. Yet for the American folk, these same aesthetic concerns in the context of a traditionally community-oriented music could also be seen as a result of the hold the middle class is gaining over culture and how class-specific projects disguise themselves as expressions of supposedly universal concerns and values such as freedom, art, beauty, and so forth. This is particularly apparent for American folk music given the relative homogeneity of its current demographic.

The American folk landscape and its accompanying microindustry strikingly illustrate the complex interplay of image, imagination, and shifting subjectivities, which at once indexes an art of the surface and at the same time may represent deeply personal and highly charged realms of meaning.

Folk Alliance Conference 1999

In 1999, the eleventh annual conference of the Folk Alliance was held in Albuquerque, New Mexico, at the Albuquerque Convention Center with the Hyatt Hotel providing the primary lodging and meeting area. The Hyatt is an ultramodern glass and steel structure, which seemed an incongruous setting for a folk music conference. Many of the seventeen hundred attendees, including U. Utah Phillips, a folksinger, storyteller, and noted hobo, took some issue with the idea of hosting the conference in such opulent surroundings. Yet the setting was incongruous only in terms of the conventional notion of folk's association with the common man and seemed fitting surroundings for the contemporary marketplace represented by the Folk Alliance.

The streets surrounding the conference center were crowded with people, many carrying guitars and other instruments, going toward or coming from the space allocated for the exhibit hall. Solo guitarists and instrumentalists in various combinations sat in the shade of surrounding buildings playing music, most of them going unnoticed by passersby in a hurry to attend one of the countless showcases that go on seemingly around the clock during the conference. Before I made it to the exhibit hall I ran into Dick Weissman, who suggested that I join him and his companions for lunch.

Weissman was accompanied by Eric Darling, a slightly built white-haired gentleman in his late sixties and longtime folkie who played banjo with the Weavers after Pete Seeger left that group, and Rik Palieri, a folksinger from Vermont. The lunch conversation consisted primarily of Darling and Weissman's summarily demythologizing some of the popular folk icons with whom they associated in the 1950s through the 1960s folk revival and Palieri's defending some of those icons, particularly Seeger, whom Palieri repeatedly insisted to be totally sincere in his folk ideology. Darling and Weissman didn't dispute Seeger's good intentions but recognized the irony that Seeger's father was a world-renowned musicologist, his mother was one of the most celebrated women composers of the twentieth century, and "Pete became a hillbilly."

After lunch we walked through the exhibit hall, a cavernous space in which perhaps a hundred or more vendors were selling products or promoting artists or services. Record companies, artists' representatives, music publishers and retailers, luthiers, CD manufacturing companies, individuals and groups of artists, folklore societies, and venues were represented, and the hall was teeming with activity. Everyone registered for the conference wore a nametag that included any institutional affiliation, and it became a running joke that people looked more at the tag than at the person wearing it, with at-a-glance evaluations regarding the importance of initiating a conversation. As a graduate student researcher, my own tag was emblazoned TOM GRUNING—UNIVERSITY OF TEXAS AT AUSTIN. Many performers and agents assumed that I booked talent for university-sponsored events. Dozens of artists thrust their CDs into my hands without waiting for an explanation of my motives for attending the conference. Those who waited long enough for an explanation either took back their CDs or assumed an attitude that one more unit given away fell into the category of the cost of doing business.

Outside the exhibit hall attendees met to eat, drink, and converse. Many performers played music anywhere they might be heard by passing presenters, agents, or record executives. The dream of being discovered by a music industry mover and shaker was a recurring theme as I wandered through the area asking people what they hoped to accomplish at the conference. By the third day an almost tangible feeling of desperation accompanied the exhaustion written on the faces of performers for whom this chance at fame and fortune was rapidly coming to an end. Throughout the spaces where the conference was held, musicians gathered and played. Hallways and the hotel lobby were frequently used as performance spaces, often with numerous groups and solo performers simultaneously creating a soundscape in which one performance blended with any number of others in a shifting cacophony. On the evening of 27 February, while sitting in the Hyatt lobby, one performance in particular caught my attention and crystallized the experiential pastiche of the conference.

Sitting on comfortable overstuffed chairs and couches a few feet from my own perch, several musicians began playing songs and instrumental tunes in styles reminiscent of early country music and Kansas City jazz from the 1920s and 30s. Mary Flower, an accomplished dobro player who has long lived in Denver, Colorado, and several guitarists played these tunes with a remarkable stylistic integrity that bespoke a clear reverence for the material. Flower and the others were visually framed against a backdrop of huge glass-fronted shops selling expensive jewelry, Southwestern art, and Native American curios, reinforcing the sense of pastiche that encompassed the visual images, the aural input, and the performance as a social and cultural text.

Did the authentic musical/stylistic reproduction amount to a simulacrum, given the incongruous setting for old-timey music? Or was Flower "doing honor to traditional music" (Weissman, interview, 25 February 1999) and, in doing so, recreating webs of signification that index the past only as another in a chain of signifiers, rather than as some nostalgic quest for an experiential signified? Perhaps these possibilities each share a kernel of accuracy, depending of course on perspective. For the American folk and particularly those involved in the reconstruction or emulation of older musical styles, the reconfigured past has, much like world music, become an exotic Other.

In the mornings and through the late afternoons of the conference, workshops were presented in meeting rooms at the host hotel. These workshops were loosely organized by topics that particular segments of the membership might find interesting. For example, those who work for folk organizations were encouraged to attend workshops that included Board Development; Marketing; How to Grow Your Festival; Song Contests: How to Develop, Present and Submit; Concert Production; The Art of Programming; Non-Traditional Presenters and Venues; and Introducing Spoken Word into Your Festival. Other workshops were offered for those beginning careers as folksingers, for those more advanced in their careers, and for booking agents. Of the forty workshops offered at the conference, only five dealt with non-industry-related aspects of music. The business focus of the conference was inescapable and, for many of the participants, overwhelming.

On the Friday of the conference at 10:30 a.m., a well-attended workshop entitled Music and Politics convened. The panel was moderated by Dave Marsh, a popular music journalist and critic, and included seven performers, record company owners, and political activists of various ideological persuasions. The discussion that ensued touched upon folk music's relationships to social activism. Panelist Dave Elisha, a union organizer and one of the organizers of the second annual Laborfest in Detroit, stated that the music presented at that festival served to "build morale among union members and their families" and "inform the community." The two basic goals in presenting music at the Laborfest were to "reenergize the labor movement and to attract young people to the movement." To serve these ends the United Auto Workers union bought full-page advertisements in the local alternative press and sold T-shirts, key chains, and other items celebrating the union and the event. Elisha's commentary suggests that the role of music as a commodity—in this case, as advertising—divests the musical product of primarily aesthetic function and places it squarely in the service of ideology, a notion explored at length by Serge Denisoff in his many works concerning folk music and politics.

Jim Musselman, another panelist, described his own involvement with the politics of folk music in terms of a personal revelation in which he "heard another side of the world from Woody Guthrie and Pete Seeger." Musselman, an attorney, went to work for consumer advocate Ralph Nader in the mid-1980s, and in the mid-1990s eventually started an independent record label, Appleseed Recordings, devoted to recording music addressing human rights issues. Musselman celebrated the folk music industry as "not being under the control of multi-nationals" and was the first of the panelists to address the issue of "preaching to the choir." Given the historically white, well-educated, and generally socially and economically privileged constituency of the American folk community, Musselman conceded that his was a friendly audience. However, he suggested, "The choir needs to be invigorated so they'll go out into the community and be politically active."

Tish Hinojosa, a performer from San Antonio, Texas, was one of two popular performers on the panel. Hinojosa's contributions to the discussion were minimal, but her presence as a Hispanic woman seemed to legitimize her participatory role. The other performer on the panel was Steve Earle, who began recording independently following a bitter dispute with the major country music label with which he had to that point enjoyed a degree of popular success. Most of Earle's comments concerned issues of ownership, although the abolition of the death penalty is a cause he often advocates, suggesting, "The death penalty is a class issue and not about race." Earle is an advocate for the Kensington Welfare Rights Union, a Philadelphia-based organization dedicated to ending poverty, and Hinojosa's association with the United Farm Workers of America, the National Women's Political Caucus, and the National Association for Bilingual Education are well publicized. However, neither performer was especially articulate in arguing for specific political causes. Yet "to the choir," by virtue of the speakers' status as popular artists—stars—the most innocuous statements seemed endowed with profundity.

Much of the commentary during the workshop reinscribed familiar mythologies of the folk. The common man, the countercultural constituency of the folk community, and the tenacious "giving voice to the voiceless" were all revisited in the spirit of acknowledging the power of music to change society and the world at large. However, regardless of the generally superficial treatment of very complex issues, the panelists were deeply and personally invested in their political beliefs and felt strongly that music must play explicit and implicit roles in political activism.[6]

Workshops at the Folk Alliance serve primarily as forums for sharing information. However, as in the case of the Music and Politics workshop, the meetings can also provide opportunities for voicing complaints and bonding with others who share similar perspectives and opinions. The organization and function of workshops at the Folk Alliance are much like those at any professional conference. Where the Folk Alliance differs from most non-music-related con-ferences is in the presentation of showcases and the constant music making that pervades public space.

For musician/performers who attend the conference, showcases are the prin-cipal vehicles through which industry connections are cultivated. The primary showcases are sponsored by the Folk Alliance organization and take place all three nights of the conference. The Showcase Committee chooses the perform-ers in these events. Each performer or group plays at one evening concert and one afternoon show. For the 1999 conference, eighteen acts were chosen along with four alternates. Some of the performers in the conference-sponsored show-cases are reasonably well known and some are new faces on the folk scene.

Folk Alliance showcases presented by corporate sponsors rival the primary showcases in their high-profile rosters. While rules prohibit showcases being scheduled during primary concerts, the more high-profile shows, many spon-sored by music retailers, tend to occur in the larger meeting rooms at times dur-ing which the maximum number of listeners are likely to attend. At the Albu-querque conference, two well-attended showcases sponsored by Folk Era/Wind River Records and Elixir Strings/W. L. Gore and Associates, Inc., collectively featured dozens of well-known folk artists, each playing sets that lasted from fifteen to thirty minutes. The rapid pace allows for maximum musical variety, and, as in the case of other professional conferences, attendees often go back and forth among different meeting rooms to hear performers they hope might prove interesting.

Members of the Folk Alliance are encouraged to sponsor private showcases. For a fee, anyone registered to attend the entire conference can hold a private showcase in either a sleeping room or in one of the hotel meeting rooms. These sanctioned showcases must adhere to rules set out by the Folk Alliance admin-istration and are listed in the conference schedule that each registrant receives. The meeting rooms are allocated through a lottery system, and the winning sponsors pay an additional room rental fee. For private showcases in meeting rooms, sponsors may set up a sound system, but showcases held in sleeping rooms are generally prohibited from using a public-address system. In addi-tion to the showcases presented or sanctioned by the Folk Alliance, the "guerilla showcase" has become ubiquitous.

Guerilla showcases offer the most numerous opportunities to perform for an audience. These concerts are independently presented almost exclusively in hotel sleeping rooms and may or may not be organized around a central theme. Common themes include groups of singer/songwriters from the same geographical area, but almost any thematic connection can provide a concep-tual backdrop for a showcase. The guerilla showcases are scheduled almost exclusively after the primary conference showcases, and many present performances all night long. Informal song swaps may follow the scheduled performances allowing performers who lack even these loosely formalized opportunities a chance to play for an audience.

The term "guerilla" is laden with its own semantic and conceptual baggage. Like independent guerilla fighters whose covert activities lie beneath the surface of mainstream military actions, the guerilla showcase is, at least in theory, beneath the radar of the conference administration. The paradoxical implications of such a relationship are plain. The Folk Alliance, which prides itself on egalitarianism, takes on the symbolic role of the establishment, with the hosts of independent showcases as underground operators. In point of fact, guerilla showcases are not only tolerated but are encouraged by conference officials, and are loosely governed by strictures including "quiet floor" policies, post-scheduled-showcase restrictions, and so forth.

Guerilla showcases are generally advertised by posting announcements around conference areas. The fliers, which are usually standard letter sized and homemade rather than designed by professional graphic artists, are taped on most available surfaces in the public space. The proliferation of these makeshift posters is an occasional annoyance for the hotel management as well as for businesses in the convention center complex. Some of these advertisements offer inducements including free beer or food for those attending the showcase. Generally the doors of hotel sleeping rooms in which showcases are scheduled are left open so passersby will feel compelled to enter and listen. Hotels designate showcase floors as well as quiet floors on which showcases are prohibited. It is not unusual for several showcases to be going simultaneously on any given floor, giving the listener constantly changing opportunities to be entertained.

In short, the atmosphere was frenzied and relentless. The frantic pace at which almost everyone seemed to be moving continued throughout the four days of the conference. Several cynics remarked on the scores of unknown performers trying desperately and usually unsuccessfully to impress record company executives in order to "get a deal," adding something like, "Even the most successful folk music performers don't make that much money." Yet this oft repeated sentiment ignores some of the most fundamental motivations shared by the army of unknowns struggling for a chance to be heard.

Most of the little-known artists with whom I spoke at the conference and at subsequent concerts, festivals, song circles, and seminars concede that the economic aspect of the profession is only a minor concern. The romanticized ideal of life on the road and public adulation figure prominently in the appeal of the profession. The attention garnered by well-known performers at the Folk Alliance conference reinforces the mythology of the "artist" and highlights the seductive nature of stardom, even within the limited context of the folk music community.

Artists who attend Folk Alliance conferences with dreams of "being discovered" often leave exhausted from several days with minimal sleep and disappointed by a lack of substantive career advancement. Others leave tired but invigorated by the concentrated dose of musical experience the conference affords. For some the event offers primarily social opportunities to visit with friends and meet others involved with folk music. Yet practically everyone in attendance has some financial stake in the folk landscape, and the business orientation of the event underscores folk music's historical relationship to the American cultural marketplace.

The national Folk Alliance conferences present a microcosm of the new folk microindustry, an industry in which performers rely on a varied and intertwined infrastructure of loosely knit associations. While the primary focus for the artist is generally making connections with presenters and venues, the conference also allows for potential interaction with representatives from related music businesses. Record companies, booking agents, artist management firms, publishers, and companies involved with numerous means of promotion, all of which specialize in acoustic or folk musics, present their wares and occupy positions within the hierarchies of priority for contact.

Contact with presenters offers the most immediate potential for advancing the singer/songwriter's livelihood. Record company representatives provide possibilities for enhancing status within the folk community and thereby opening doors to more lucrative and high-profile performance opportunities. Booking agents and artist managers, two of the most misunderstood professions within the folk industry, are also high-profile attendees. Many singer/songwriters who attend the conference linger in the mistaken assumption that their talents and self-produced CDs will be sufficient enticements for gaining representation. The microindustry, like the popular music industry at large, is less interested in selling musical ability than in selling already proven entertainment exchange value. These are aspects of the business of folk that I will address at length shortly. However, first I will briefly discuss the record companies that cater to the folk audience.

Folk Record Companies

Dirty Linen, Ltd., in Baltimore, Maryland—the publisher of the magazine *Dirty Linen: Folk and World Music*—has posted on its Web site a list of more than eleven hundred record companies involved with the types of music covered in the magazine. While the list may seem exaggerated by the inclusion of numer-ous world music entries, it understates the total number of labels releasing con-temporary folk singer/songwriters' material if we are to consider completely independent releases by individual singer/songwriters. Advances in recording technology and the decreasing costs of producing CDs have created a situation whereby record company affiliation is an unnecessary, if usually advantageous, requisite for self-promotion.[7] Anyone with the desire to record and release an album (CD or cassette tape) can, for a relatively modest financial investment, produce salable product.[8] It would likely not be an exaggeration to suggest that the vast majority of short-run audio CDs (less than ten thousand units) pro-duced in the United States in the past five years fit into this category.

However, the symbolic capital that accompanies a recording contract with a recognized label continues to be a factor in defining hierarchical positions in the folk microindustry, as it does within the context of the major label dominated popular music industry. What distinguishes the folk recording industry—what keeps it from appearing merely as purveyor of alienated products disguised as handicraft—is its emphasis on performance as the primary goal of recording rather than as a means to the commodified end. That is, in the popular music market the primary goal of performance is to promote CD sales. For the folk, the CD is generally a means through which performance opportunities can be realized. For a number of performers, the index of live performance is clearly reflected in the production values of the recorded product.

While combinations of musical elements in folk record production are as varied as folk's constituency, there is at least one widely accepted characteris-tic of singer/songwriter recordings: the primacy of the lyric line. Claims to past and present folk authenticities, or contrary anti-folk positions,[9] may be enacted through production choices, but the vocal remains the central feature. Yet be-yond the focus on vocalized text, the authenticities indexed through production values run the gamut of folk's multifarious past and present engagements with modernity. The following examples represent four distinct approaches to that engagement.

Harvey Reid is an enigmatic singer/songwriter and folk song interpreter from Maine. The production values of his CDs reflect a tacit concern with simplicity of production. A note on Reid's compact disc *Steel Drivin' Man* (1991), states: "This album was recorded in 'living stereo' by the artist, direct to digital, using only a pair of Audio-Technica AT-4051 microphones, a Panasonic SV-255 DAT recorder, and a Lexicon digital reverb unit. No overdubs, splices or edits were done, though the temptation was great at times." The songs on *Steel Drivin' Man* are all public domain traditional folk songs and include fourteen songs and five instrumental tunes. The "living stereo" recording mirrors Reid's concern with the nature of the material. The instruments he chose for the recording further demonstrate a conscious index of the folk authentic: slide guitar, standard acoustic guitar, 12-string guitar, autoharp, and banjo all fit neatly into the traditional aesthetic. The choice of material and the live production values situate the recording squarely in the mainstream of folk's engagement with its own past. Yet the final comment in his description of the CD's production provides a clue to the ultimately contested nature of folk's engagements with technology/modernity. The temptation to overdub, splice, or edit—all concessions to the technological—was subjugated in the interest of the authentic: the less mediated exposition of folkness. While Reid's concern with textural simplicity is not uncommon for today's singer/songwriters, it is far from being a benchmark of contemporary folk record production.

Compact discs by artists such as Greg Greenway have infused contemporary folk music with a decidedly pop-eclectic aesthetic, both in terms of stylistic elements and production. In his 1995 release, *Singing for the Landlord*, Greenway's pop sensibilities are marked by the use of a rhythm section, electric organ, synthesizer, and, most strikingly, lush vocal choruses awash in reverb reminiscent of rock and folk-rock groups of the late 1960s and '70s.[10] Generally the CD is engineered much like pop radio records. The sound is somewhat compressed, reverb is used generously, and the instrumentation is for the most part dense and played with technical precision. However, Greenway's CD, like many of the more pop-oriented singer/songwriter projects, includes two songs in which the artist's vocal is accompanied by solo acoustic guitar. The solo acoustic songs along with the ubiquitous acoustic guitar in the rhythm section presumably situate the artist and the project under the purview of the folk.

Alan Whitney, a singer/songwriter from Rochester, New York, has been attempting to carve a living out of the folk landscape for several years. His most recent release, *Juke* (2004), blends country inflected dance tunes, 1950s tinged rock, and pop ballads to create an overall product that is meant to evoke the atmosphere of a honky-tonk roadhouse. *Juke* is an intentional deviation from the introspective folk singer/songwriter model, which reflects the artist's increasing frustration with what he considers the sameness of many of today's folk releases. Much of the production has the sparse character of rock and roll and country music recordings from the 1950s, and the introspective poetics often associated with the contemporary folk is conspicuously absent. While Whitney's critique of sameness is manifest in a production that does honor to various stylistic trends not usually associated with the folk per se, some artists use traditional folk material in decidedly nontraditional settings.

Bethany Yarrow, daughter of Peter Yarrow of Peter, Paul, and Mary fame, is a New York singer/songwriter whose release *Rock Island* (2003), features songs like Leadbelly's "Rock Island Line," the Reverend Gary Davis's "True Vine," and the traditional "Pretty Polly." While the selections reference a fundamental folkness, the musical settings index a sort of techno-rock style that seems antithetical to the folk yet infuses the traditional material with a compelling hybridity. Drums, synthesizers, and modal improvised cello lines accompany Yarrow's acoustic guitar and sultry vocals giving the impression of a rock avant-garde experimentalism.

All of the aforementioned compact disc releases are independently produced, manufactured, and marketed. Many of today's well-established folk record labels began as independent, short-run companies whose founders were performers intent to record and release their own products. While the independently released CDs quite likely outnumber releases by established record companies, the types of material—that is, the variety of stylistic treatments of contemporary folk music—translate across the landscape at large. Many independent folk record companies of whatever size are reasonably open to taking musical chances. While some labels are defined by particular styles, many include a variety of artists and, at least compared to the major labels, diverse offerings. However, like any market-driven capitalist venture, when companies achieve success with particular artists or musics, those become the focus and serve to establish the label's reputation within the community.

Among the labels that specialize in contemporary and traditional folk music, reputations are made in various ways. Longevity and artist rosters play primary roles in determining a label's credibility and stature. Smithsonian Folkways Recordings can be considered the granddaddy of folk music labels, with several thousand recordings in its catalog. Founded by Moses Asch in 1948, the roster of Folkways includes such iconic folk music figures as Big Bill Broonzy, Woody Guthrie, Lightnin' Hopkins, Leadbelly, and Pete Seeger, among many others. The Smithsonian Institution acquired Folkways from the Asch estate in 1987, and the label, like its parent institution, is heavily endowed with the authority of cultural capital. Yet except for some compilations—especially the *Fast Folk Musical Magazine*—the company's catalog of contemporary singer/songwriters is thin, consisiting largely of recordings of traditional musics, world music, and popular folk songs from previous revivals. Both in terms of the musical offerings as well as the cover artwork for its CD releases, the fetish for tradition and authenticity is writ large at Smithsonian Folkways.

Rounder Records has, since its inception in 1970, established a reputation as another premier folk music label, boasting a catalog of over three thousand releases. The Rounder subsidiary Philo Records, the company's label specializing in contemporary singer/songwriters, has a roster of about seventy artists, including some of the best-known artists on the folk circuit. Folk Era Records, while considerably smaller than Rounder, has likewise existed long enough to be considered a significant player in the folk world. Like Rounder, Folk Era's primary roster is comprised largely of more traditional folk artists, and Folk Era also has a subsidiary, Wind River, that features primarily contemporary singer/songwriters. Yet Folk Era and Wind River are, in terms of market share and associated status, at a less exalted level than Rounder.

Other labels that feature contemporary singer/songwriters and occupy a similar secondary station within the folk microindustry hierarchy include Signature Sounds, Red House Records, and Shanachie Entertainment. This is not to say that these labels are by any account second rate. All of these labels are widely recognized in the folk community, affiliation with any of them lends professional credibility, and all of them have under contract some of folk's most popular artists. Several smaller but important companies, whose performers are generally less well known, are Flying Fish Records, Gadfly Records, Green Linnet, and Waterbug. These companies, while not the only labels in a large field of independents, are primarily involved in presenting folk music of various types, and/or specifically contemporary singer/songwriters. Collectively the aforementioned labels represent several levels of the new folk's recording landscape.

The upper levels of the label hierarchy, as might be expected, generally sign artists who have a relatively broad fan base and who either tour extensively or have reached a point in their careers that their audience continues to buy new releases regardless of the frequency of live performances. Alison Krauss, whose 1995 compilation *Now That I've Found You* was Rounder's first platinum record, is an artist whose popularity has for some time transcended the folk microindustry. That she continues to record for Rounder may speak to the nature of the independent recording industry, which generally allows the artist creative freedom to produce projects that may not coincide with the aesthetic direction of the mainstream marketplace. Krauss has received thirteen Grammy Awards and remains a popular favorite with country, folk, and bluegrass audiences. She has been courted by major labels hoping to capitalize on her commercial success. Her continuing relationship with Rounder is apparently a mutually beneficial arrangement in which she retains artistic control, and Rounder distributes and markets her projects to a wide audience. Through its association with well-known contemporary artists such as Krauss and its widely distributed traditional recordings, an artist affiliation with Rounder has come to be, in itself, a mark of status and success within the folk community. Through its association with Rounder, Philo has attracted some of the most recognized names in contemporary folk music, including Christine Lavin, Patty Larkin, Cheryl Wheeler, Vance Gilbert, Bill Morrissey, and Ellis Paul.[11] The nature of the microindustry is such that the artists mentioned above have become tremendously popular with folk audiences yet remain virtually unknown to mainstream popular music audiences.

While Rounder occupies a rarified position within the folk recording industry, a number of smaller labels have grown up around the increased market for contemporary folk music. Signature Sounds, founded in 1995, and Red House Records have responded to the renewed interest in folk by signing growing numbers of actively performing singer/songwriters. Both labels have attracted noted folk artists. Red House, in part by virtue of is longevity, has some well-established performers including Greg Brown, John Gorka, Garnet Rogers, Lucy Kaplansky, and Cliff Eberhardt.

Wind River, the subsidiary of Folk Era Records oriented toward contemporary singer/songwriters, is another recently established label that has attracted moderately popular performers including Jack Williams, Cosy Sheridan, the Australian guitarist Jeff Lang, and the husband and wife duo Small Potatoes. While these artists have established reputations within the folk microindustry, in the hierarchies of popularity for the folk consumer they rank at a level below the top draws. This does not imply that these performers are less effective or less musical than the stars of folk. Rather, the microindustry "food chain,"[12] like the mainstream industry it at once disparages and in some ways imitates, is determined by concert tickets sold and compact discs marketed: the measures of perceived entertainment value to a mass audience.[13] The record company with which an artist is affiliated plays a distinct role in that determination. The more successful the record company, the more likely a CD is to get regular airplay on folk radio shows as well as on programs not exclusively devoted to folk music. The more prominent labels allow for additional distribution possibilities, so the artists' CDs are more likely to be available at larger retail outlets such as Borders and Barnes and Noble. Finally, a label's name recognition plays a significant role in determining its artists' perceived value in the marketplace. Smaller record companies with little or no promotional budgets simply cannot achieve the level of media saturation of the larger, comparatively well-financed record labels.

However, it would be a mistake to reduce a performer's position on the folk landscape to the economics of record companies alone. Things are never so simple. In interviews I have conducted in the past few years, several recording artists have stated that projects for some of the more widely distributed folk music labels have received no company support after the initial release. On the other side of the coin, some smaller labels have invested considerable time, energy, and money into individual artists' careers beyond the release of CDs. Affiliation with the larger folk labels, like affiliation with one of the big six major labels, does not guarantee a successful career on the performance circuit. Rather, establishing a high-profile presence in the folk community is a combination of factors, many of which appear to be common to A-list performers.

Covers, Youth, and Artist Representation

One element of success for many, if not most of the best-known performers on the folk circuit is an authorial association with mainstream country or popular music stars. Writing a song that is recorded by Garth Brooks, Bette Midler, or any other pop superstar serves a potent legitimizing function for the singer/songwriter. Chris Smither, a popular performer on the folk circuit, introduced his song "Slow Surprise" at a 2000 concert series in San Antonio by stating that "this next song paid for my house." Emmylou Harris recorded the song in 1998 for Robert Redford's film *The Horse Whisperer*. The financial rewards of writing for mainstream popular performers aside, the status these projects garner within the community that has embraced the singer/songwriter as the torchbearer of the folk, is considerable. But again, this sort of accomplishment is not in itself a guarantee of fame and fortune as a folk circuit top draw.

Recently I received a press kit from singer/songwriter Steve Gillette. In addition to the promotional photographs, glowing press reviews, and one-page biography, the kit included a page with the heading "Steve Gillette songs have been recorded by these artists." The list included forty-three individuals or groups from the very famous to the somewhat obscure. However, Gillette, while highly respected for his writing and performing, does not demand the fees of folk's top draws, nor does he confine his performances to large and lucrative venues. Clearly Steve Gillette is revered more among his peers than the public at large; other singer/songwriters generally hold him in higher regard than the mass folk audience. The reasons for this are as elusive as any notions regarding public aesthetic sensibilities and must certainly include a multitude of musical and extramusical considerations.

Steve Gillette is a white-haired gentleman with an unassuming demeanor and a quiet manner. His public persona is not exotic or particularly compelling to the growing younger audience for folk music. Where idealistic and decidedly modernist notions of the primacy of the music itself are common themes for folk music enthusiasts, the image—the performance persona—remains a central concern. Most of folk's top draws are in their thirties or forties or have adopted some of the fashionable affectations of a younger audience.[14] The immediacy and cogency of the music and musical text are clearly issues in determining hierarchical status; they are equally clearly not the only issues.

Increasingly, younger performers with more pop-oriented musical sensibilities are becoming dominant forces in the folk microindustry. Where this differs from the mainstream industry's approach is in relative age differences. For the pop industry the youth market constitutes the overwhelming consumer base. For the folk microindustry a considerable percentage of the audience is over forty and even over sixty years old.[15] However, recently there is a growing market for folk music among younger audiences. Where even a few years ago (certainly as recently as the mid-1990s) the median age at most folk performance events was around fifty, folk festivals are reporting increasing percentages of attendees in the twenty- to thirty-year-old ranges.

Another factor in determining levels of hierarchy in the folk microindustry is among the most misunderstood elements in the field of professional performance of any kind: the roles of the booking agent and the personal manager. For the contemporary singer/songwriter the booking agent represents, in some sense, attainment of an advanced level of professionalism. However, within the context of these professions there are also multiple levels of status and function.

For many performers, the time and emotional energy spent dealing with venue operators is the least attractive aspect of the professional musician's working week. In countless interviews, musicians have confided that the business of music leaves no time for the creative aspects of making music. For some performers a spouse or friend with abounding faith in the performer's talent and potential assumes the responsibilities of booking. Such arrangements rarely transcend the level of the hobbyist. With most agents charging between 15 and 20 percent, the artist must make a considerable amount of money to make the agent's time investment worthwhile.

In July 2002 I spoke with Mary Granata, a booking agent who indicated that she regularly receives unsolicited inquiries from relatively unknown musicians seeking representation. Granata lamented the fact that representing artists who do not already have national reputations is, for her, a losing proposition. She asserted that her percentage from unknown artists, no matter how talented they may be, "won't pay my phone bill." In a July 2000 interview with the artist manager Tim Drake, he spoke about the point in an artist's career at which management and a booking agent become viable and desirable for the artist and the representative alike. Drake stated that most reputable booking agents and/or managers are unwilling to consider signing a performer unless he or she is playing approximately 150 dates a year. When artists are consistently booking themselves at that level of frequency, the more high-profile booking agencies should serve as resources for streamlining the booking process by building from the artists' established reputations, attempting to upgrade the quality of engagements. In attempting to be upwardly mobile in the folk "food chain," artists are encouraged to play better and higher-profile gigs rather than small house concerts and obscure coffeehouses that, for many medium-level traveling musicians, constitute filler or bread-and-butter jobs.

The venues through which contemporary folk performers ply their trade frame the boundaries of the microindustry in distinct ways. When folk artists transcend the barrier between folk music and the popular music industry, their presence within the context of the folk landscape and its host venues becomes negligible. Some artists who have achieved a degree of mainstream popularity—Shawn Colvin, Nanci Griffith, and Martin Sexton, among others—illustrate this distinction between the two music markets. All of these "stars" began their careers as folk artists. However, upon achieving a degree of success in the mainstream commercial marketplace, all of them affiliated with representation that specialized in promoting nationally recognized artists to mainstream audiences. Their public images as well as their musical products began to reflect a more accessible popular aesthetic than those of many of their folk contemporaries. Once the line has been crossed from folk to popular there is rarely any return. The economics of folk seldom make sense in terms of career moves for artists who have expanded their audience base to the mainstream.[16]

However, within the context of the microindustry the hierarchy of booking agencies indicates that the economics of folk, while not approaching the level of the popular industry, can nonetheless be relatively profitable. With some of the new folk's more popular artists demanding minimum performance fees of $850 to $5000 per engagement, a busy touring schedule can easily translate into a yearly income of six figures. With touring, income from performing rights, residuals for film projects, or composer royalties for songs recorded by popular artists, today's most successful folk singer/songwriters can make substantial incomes.

For the contemporary folk, there are a few very high-profile booking agencies with which association equates to symbolic capital within the microindustry. In the 1990s, Fleming, Tamulevich and Associates boasted the most impressive roster of folk's top performers. In 2002, Jim Fleming and David Tamulevich parted ways. Following the split, the majority of the agency's artists, including Ani DiFranco, Garnet Rogers, Cheryl Wheeler, Susan Werner, and Lucy Kaplansky among others, affiliated with Fleming and Associates. David Tamulevich founded Tamulevich Artist Management representing Greg Brown, John Gorka, and Ellis Paul, as well as several lesser-known performers. Signing with one of these agencies, particularly Fleming and Associates at this point, is a mark of stature in the folk community and indicates potential for entrée into the higher levels of the folk food chain.

While Fleming and Associates and Tamulevich Artist Management represent many of folk's A-list performers, other agencies represent artists of similar stature within somewhat different contexts of the folk landscape. One perplexing example of the sometimes disparate nature of the microindustry is a sort of geographical isolationism or bounded localism. Many of the artists mentioned above have a degree of national appeal. That is, such artists as Cheryl Wheeler, John Gorka, Greg Brown, and Ani DiFranco regularly appear at venues throughout the United States, with some having an international presence. Yet in certain areas of the country the hierarchies of contemporary singer/songwriters have only incidental relation to the aforementioned luminaries. The Texas folk community offers a particularly striking illustration. Tim Drake suggests, "Texas is like a different world" when it comes to booking or arranging tours for some performers who may have huge followings in other parts of the country.

The Texas folk landscape often seems like Drake's "different world." Texas artists such as Ray Wylie Hubbard, Willis Alan Ramsey, and Robert Earl Keen are revered performers on the Texas music landscape, and they all perform outside Texas. Despite that, within the context of some other geographically situated folk music communities they are comparatively unknown.[17]

In the northeastern United States it is not uncommon for audience members with encyclopedic knowledge of John Gorka or Greg Brown to be completely unfamiliar with stars of the Texas folk/acoustic music world. Likewise Ellis Paul or Vance Gilbert, both very popular on the East Coast, may have a difficult time getting booked at premier Texas venues. These spatially separate music communities share certain ideological, aesthetic, and organizational characteristics yet are constituted of performers, venues, and peripheral industries that may have little or no contact with their peers in other parts of the country.

While organizations such as the Folk Alliance attempt to present and represent a united community of folk, the secondary localism of folk communities in the United States seems at odds with that idealism. The disparity of these local landscapes is even more apparent a rung or two down the ladder from the stars. In a recent Web-based article on the current Northwest folk music scene, including Seattle and Portland, more than a dozen locally popular singer/songwriters, most of whom record for established record labels and tour regularly, were listed. None of the names were familiar to me.[18] Similarly, in 1999 the Thursday evening sundown concert at the Kerrville Folk Festival on 3 June was called Seattle Songwriters and featured Evan Brubaker, Janis Carper, Heidi Muller, and Tracy Spring. For the majority of concert attendees these were all new faces and names.[19]

The localism of folk communities is at times defined in areas as small as cities. However, more expansive regional areas form unwritten boundaries of folk communities, as do circuits of performance venues within those boundaries. The Texas circuit, for example, seems to reach somewhat beyond the borders of that state, with artists from other southern states achieving degrees of popularity in Texas and Texas artists maintaining their local status in neighboring states. The northeastern circuit, with a conceptual/geographic base in Boston, covers New England and the surrounds, from Maine to Washington, D.C. Artists who have become reasonably well known in the Northeast seem to have an easy transition to playing circuits in the Midwest, as the level of popularity translates well from one area to the other. Booking agents are of course aware of these geographic distinctions in markets and book their clients accordingly. Some artists do have large local followings in more than one area. Distinctions in markets are by no means written in stone. Numerous performers have successfully negotiated multiple markets. However, the boundaries of these markets and localized music communities remain, sometimes serving to enhance local performers' reputations, and sometimes limiting a more ubiquitous public presence.

In attempting to cross over the loosely confined boundaries of local folk communities, booking agencies often work closely with management personnel. Like booking agents, personal managers come in different shapes and sizes, from friend-of-the-band managers who often have few industry connections, to big time managers who represent more successful artists. The artist manager's function within the context of the folk microindustry, as well as in the music industry at large, is perhaps the most misunderstood aspect of the music business.

Generally the manager's job is to work in conjunction with the booking agent, the artist's record company, publicist, and road manager (if applicable) to orchestrate and enhance the performer's career.[20] The organization history that Young/Hunter Management once had on its Web site (http://www.younghunter .com) pointed out that a manager's job includes prosaic tasks such as "advancing artists' tour dates," which means "putting together all the little details of a tour like getting directions, booking the hotels, scheduling sound check, etc." In addition the management company might deal with the details of artists' Web sites, mailing lists, and "road press," which encompasses preperformance tour advertising in the locations an artist will be performing.

Without exception, managers with whom I have spoken are regularly besieged by scores of young artists seeking representation. Most of these aspiring entertainers have only a vague idea about what an artist manager does. Some of the misunderstandings about the role of the personal manager result from managers who also take on the responsibility of booking their clients. Kerry Bernard, who at the time of this writing in 2002 works for the Young/Hunter management agency, was, according to the company's Web site, fulfilling this dual role for the "developing artist" Jeffrey Foucault. Still managed by Young/Hunter, Foucault later turned over his booking representation to Mad Mission, a booking agency that works with artists associated with several different management agencies.

For the aspiring professional folk singer/songwriter, representation by management and booking agencies is equivalent to obtaining the proverbial Holy Grail. However, in most cases an artist must have already reached an advanced level of career development to be considered by a highly respected agent or manager. For Tim Drake, among the criteria for considering a potential client is whether the artist has had a hit record or shows marked development in touring history. Musical and performative elements are also taken into consideration. When I interviewed him in 2000, Drake suggested that the artist performing a "great show" is of primary interest. Yet an engaging performance persona, accessible songs, an impressive voice, and advanced instrumental skills do not guarantee that an artist can secure representation. Most of the agents interviewed, both booking and management, reiterated the 150-dates-a-year criteria for determining whether an artist is perhaps ready to employ management and/or a booking agency.[21] The requisite number of dates is in itself also no guarantee of consideration if those dates do not reflect a history of development. That is, if a performer is playing only at bookstore coffeehouses, neighborhood taverns, and the like, major agency consideration is unlikely. If, however, the artist is beginning to perform at major folk festivals, high-profile concert series, and other name venues, the agency may see potential for significant income. As with the corresponding agencies in the popular music industry, substantial public recognition and economic credibility invite acceptance by the management and booking movers and shakers of the folk microindustry.

Folk Music Magazines

Before 1962, *Sing Out!* magazine (whose predecessor was *People's Songs*) was the only folk music publication on the market. From about 1962 to 1972, a publication called *Broadside* was put out by the joint efforts of Seeger, Agnes "Sis" Cunningham, Gordon Friesen, and Gil Turner. This mimeographed publication was designed to put out the songs of the folk music movement (Eliot, 1979), and included the publication of some of Dylan's earliest material (McKeen, 1993). It also included articles about various protest movements, concerts, festivals, record reviews, and more. (Neff, "Media Usage")

Neff's account of the folk music periodicals that marked the genesis of popular folk movements in twentieth-century America suggests that these publications had a limited commercial appeal and consequently a limited economic scope. In a conversation in September 2002 with Sonny Ochs, sister of popular 1960s folksinger Phil Ochs, she commented about the appearance of these publications in contrast to current folk music periodicals. Ochs stated that in the early 1950s when *Sing Out!* was in its infancy, it was decidedly "unglossy." Likewise *Broadside* reflected its folkie ideological conceptual backdrop in its simple, underwhelming appearance. As the new face of folk began to emerge in the late 1980s and 1990s, publications that had informed earlier folk music enthusiasts changed in appearance, and new publications surfaced to fulfill the needs of a changing marketplace. As popular culture seemed to broaden the base of a postmodern politics of image, the landscape of folk publishing bowed to the pressure. Glossy, full-color publications replaced the mimeographed statements of the older folk's ideals, and a new contender began to rise in stature.

By 1993 the long-lived monthly folk magazines *Sing Out!* and *Dirty Linen* faced competition from a new and imposing magazine that targeted segments of their readership. *Performing Songwriter,* the brainchild of Lydia Hutchinson, was introduced at the Kerrville Folk Festival and quickly raised the stakes for folk-music-related periodicals. Published eight times a year, by 2002, according to Hutchinson, *Performing Songwriter*'s circulation reached approximately fifty thousand. The magazine's appearance is glossy, professional, printed on heavy paper, and Hutchinson has assembled an illustrious team of regular and occasional contributors including such notables as Paul Zollo and Janis Ian.[22]

The magazine's content is both specialized and general, part fanzine and part instructional. It deals with topics and songwriters of interest to folk music enthusiasts and mainstream popular music enthusiasts. It is directed toward songwriters beginning their careers and to professionals as well. The material is presented in an image-driven format that appeals to active participants in the music industries but doesn't exclude the casual reader. Altogether *Performing Songwriter* is a well conceived and executed commercial project.

The magazine targets potential consumers by listing interests both broad and more specialized. The studio equipment "gear listings," for example, might appeal to anyone interested in recording technology. The "salute to the masters of the American songbook" might tempt a traditional music enthusiast or, depending on who is being saluted, a fan of Broadway musicals. The magazine has adeptly tapped into a large cross section of markets. That is, it does not give the impression of a jumble of only marginally related articles and columns. As a whole, it usually appears as a reasonably cohesive package.

In a 1999 interview with Lydia Hutchinson, the publisher/editor was clear about her magazine's focus on songwriters and songwriting rather than on specific styles of music. While folk singer/songwriters figure regularly and prominently in the magazine, so do rock and pop stars, country music songwriters, and Broadway musical composers. Hutchinson contended that the high-profile pop songwriters featured in *Performing Songwriter* attract a large readership that might otherwise never hear of the folk singer/songwriters. According to Hutchinson, including performers such as Sting and Alanis Morissette does the folk world good by increasing the exposure of folk music across a larger segment of the music consumer marketplace.

In appearance, content, and development, *Performing Songwriter* both mirrors the folk microindustry and seeks to transcend that industry in pursuit of a larger piece of the pie. These two characteristics are not mutually exclusive. The folk world's oft-expressed antipathy for the mainstream pop music landscape notwithstanding, much of the contemporary folk singer/songwriter population would unashamedly admit a desire to expand its audience beyond the limitations of folk music consumers. The pop music audience is both the faceless, undiscerning mass and the brass ring as well. Thus the pages of *Performing Songwriter* reveal images of introspective poet-songwriters alongside sneering pop stars, pouting divas, and full-page advertisements for Martin guitars, Yamaha electronic keyboards, Shure microphones, countless independent record companies, and miscellaneous musical accessories.

The glossy color images of *Performing Songwriter* illustrate the new face of folk: a face that is heavily informed by a recent popular music history yet that iconizes figures whose work predates their own musical roots; a face that looks on the present as a time of opportunity and fetishizes the past as an idealized authentic; a face whose strength signifies the independence of the common man yet unquestioningly embraces the tenets of late capitalism; a Janus face.

Sing Out! and *Dirty Linen*, while adopting a somewhat glossy and produced look, tend less toward the mainstream than *Performing Songwriter*. *Sing Out!*'s mission statement says the magazine intends "to preserve and support the cultural diversity and heritage of all traditional and contemporary folk musics, and to encourage making folk music a part of our everyday lives. We are a tax-exempt, not-for-profit, educational organization" (http://www.singout.org, *Sing Out!*). *Sing Out!* maintains a degree of folk traditionalism and is more style specific than its eclectic competitor. Each issue includes transcriptions of songs, along with the lyrics, melodic line, and guitar chord charts. True to its mid-twentieth-century roots, the magazine's appearance continues to be a bit Spartan and, perhaps, proletarian. That is, except for the cover and some ads there is little color. The majority of the pages of the magazine are black and white. This starkly contrasts with *Performing Songwriter*, whose pages teem with color. *Sing Out!* is also smaller than its counterparts. Sonny Ochs recalled that in the 1950s, the magazine was quite small compared to most periodicals.[23]

Dirty Linen, like *Sing Out!*, is less opulent looking than *Performing Songwriter*. What is most remarkable about it, and the primary difference between one magazine and the other, is its subtitle, *Folk and World Music*. While *Dirty Linen's* content concerns both contemporary and traditional American folk music and musicians, it has also become an important source of information about music and recording artists who fit the category of world music. West African drummers, Peruvian altiplano ensembles, and Tibetan monks share the pages of *Dirty Linen*, implying the it's-all-folk-music cliché. *Dirty Linen's* association between American folk music and world music underscores some of the folk's darker moments, moments that will be addressed at length in chapter 7.

Of the three primary general readership folk music periodicals, *Sing Out!* is the only one that also publishes books. Its catalog includes instructional texts, songbooks, and historical accounts of iconic folk music figures. This publishing concern preceded a recent trend toward do-it-yourself publishing, which has grown more popular with continual improvements in computer technology and desktop publishing software.

Mirroring those improvements, video technology has become more readily available than ever before, bringing with it a tremendous market for music-related instructional videotapes. It has become relatively commonplace for performers to sell these videotaped guitar, banjo, mandolin, or fiddle lessons alongside their CDs at shows. Many of these instructional aids focus on teaching the purchaser one or two songs in the particular style that the teacher is known for playing. Some of these video offerings include tablature so that the student may follow written instructions for playing a note-by-note transcription of the instructor's performance. The most popular of the folk video instructional materials appear to be those dealing with blues-related styles. During the 2002 Kerrville Folk Festival, Steve James, an entertainer known for his accurate representations of older blues styles, remarked that sales for his recent video on playing blues mandolin had been brisk. James markets his video lessons through Internet outlets as well as at his performances. Other folk artists such as Roy Bookbinder, Keb' Mo', Rory Block, and Bob Brozman market their blues guitar video lessons through a company called Homespun Video.

Homespun Video, headed by a longtime fixture on the folk scene, Happy Traum, has been in existence for nearly forty years and markets a wide variety of videos ranging from beginning guitar and bouzouki instruction to piano and ukulele lessons. Many of their products teach folk or folk-related styles, but Homespun's catalog has become extensive and includes children's music, jazz, rock, and even world/international music. The nature of the company, as well as others involved in similar pursuits, and its range of offerings reflects the expanding diversity of today's folk landscape and its increasing interconnections with and dependencies on technology.

Workshops and Weekends

As the folk community grew in the last decade of the twentieth century, opportunities for learning to play folk instruments in a range of styles increased accordingly. Many of the larger and more prestigious folk festivals host performance workshops, as do groups of interested folkies throughout the country. Seminars and workshops may occur over a period of hours or days. For several years the Kerrville Folk Festival has offered a three-day seminar in which participants study blues guitar styles with several well-known acoustic blues performers. For a few hours on each of three days, small groups of students study with each instructor. The small groups switch from one instructor to another after the individual lessons are completed. Such workshops have become a staple of folk festivals and cover songwriting, presenting a house concert series, and more general topics such as succeeding in the music business. These workshops offer amateur and budding professional performers and presenters opportunities to interact with microindustry insiders in an informal setting. The participants get to know the instructors, reinforcing the general sense of accessibility to folk music and the performer. The workshop, as an entity unto itself, has become ubiquitous on the folk landscape.

Weekend instrumental, vocal, and songwriting "camps" are popular vehicles for reinscribing the communal aspects of folk ideology. Participants in these events spend several days together during which their mutual interest in music is the locus for group interaction. Weekend and multiple-day workshops have become regularly occurring events that provide returning participants opportunities to renew friendships initiated at previous meetings and to support online relationships with face-to-face interaction. The sense of being part of a community and the idealism of that community are strong motivational forces in the maintenance and longevity of these retreats. As the world becomes increasingly complicated, intertwined, and dangerous, the folk retreat is a welcome respite from the pressures of highly technologized and rapidly changing social and political landscapes. As do the folk in general, folk music retreats index simpler times when the individual subject was the locus of communal interaction and identification. That they do so at an often exclusionary economic level speaks to the underlying social hierarchies that define the arena of folk.

The communal embrace of these musical associations comes at a price. One prominent songwriting camp, NashCamp in Middle Tennessee west of Nashville, offers weekend and weeklong camps. In 2005, tuition, meals, and lodging for the three-day fall Banjo Retreat cost $550; the summertime Songwriting Week costs $795. For an aspiring writer who hopes to break into the industry at one level or another, the price may be money well spent, providing opportunities to refine playing and writing skills as well as to network with industry professionals and other aspiring writers and performers. While NashCamp illustrates a businesslike approach to music and songwriting, it is only one of an expansive array of songwriting and folk music workshops, seminars, retreats, and full-fledged folk music schools. The prices of admission are as varied as the offerings, and they range from modest to opulent, depending upon accommodations, length of study, and the prominence of the faculty. Many are organized by not-for-profit arts groups and hold to Jim Fleming's apt description of today's folk performers as "making a living, not a killing" (quoted in Neff, "Media Usage").

Peripheral to the folk microindustry, musical instrument manufacturers and related companies have seen substantial growth in the last decade. The market for handcrafted guitars, banjos, dulcimers, and other folk instruments has mirrored the increasing interest in folk music. Some of the better-known lutherie businesses have grown to the extent that formerly one-man operations have become medium to large manufacturing concerns. One of the most successful of these, Taylor Guitars in El Cajon, California, from inauspicious beginnings in the mid-1970s has grown into a 143,000-square-foot complex with 335 employees (Taylor Guitars, "From the Beginning . . ."). Longtime companies such as C. F. Martin and Co., Gibson, and Guild have also capitalized on the resurgence of interest in acoustic music. These companies, Martin in particular, feature advertising in which "regular folks" as well as prizewinning musicians wax nostalgic about "always wanting a Martin guitar" and eventually getting one. These accounts suggest that by purchasing one of their guitars, the consumer becomes part of a revered tradition. Once again the past becomes a measure of capital exchange.

Folk Radio

As increased interest in folk music has created relatively lucrative markets for the impresarios of folk, radio has responded accordingly. Where size and market potential for this music limits its widespread dissemination, many university radio stations and small commercial stations have allotted time in their broadcast schedules for folk programming. For the legions of performers playing for a living in local, regional, national, and international contexts, airplay is an important means of drumming up interest on local turf as well as paving the way into new regional markets.

At the time of this writing well over three hundred radio stations in the United States feature folk music programming.[24] Many of these are university-based stations with low-powered transmitters. In the past, this would limit their potential audience, yet given the folk community's widespread reliance on the Internet, a growing trend for folk radio lies in audio streaming. The Internet allows radio programs to extend far beyond the range of conventional transmitters and can be an effective tool for exposing new artists to a wide listener base.

Program titles often index folk's grand narratives: the common man, the egalitarian nature of the folk community, and traditionalism. Programs with such names as *Homemade Music, Common Threads, Back Porch Music, Acoustic Harvest*, and *Us Folk*, reinscribe these narratives in attempts to draw listeners. Many, if not most, of these shows feature interviews with musicians, interspersing live in-studio performances with prerecorded selections from the artist's repretoire. They also afford an opportunity for the program host to converse with performers in an informal, unrehearsed interview setting. These broadcast or Webcast visits may be quite effective in drawing larger audiences for the performer's concerts within the local listening area. Yet depending upon the context, sometimes the radio show *is* the concert.

Recently I attended Bound for Glory *at WVBR on the campus of Cornell University. I accompanied a friend who was the featured performer that night. Phil Shapiro, the show's host, has been presenting the series for some thirty-eight years as of this writing, making it America's longest-running live folk broadcast. The concert was held in an upstairs meeting room or lounge that seated thirty-five or forty audience members. Upon arriving, my friend was briefed on what he could and could not get away with saying on the radio. The evening progressed much like any concert series event save for the timing of sets, which were scheduled to conform to station identifications and other regularly occurring broadcast conventions. The audience was warm and appreciative, and desserts, coffee, tea, and so forth were served.*

Bound for Glory is somewhat unusual in its dual roles as a performance venue as well as a radio broadcast. Many radio interview/performance opportunities take place in tiny control rooms barely large enough for the disc jockey and a guest. Frequently the hosts of these local/regional folk radio shows are themselves performers. Wanda Fischer, who hosts the *Hudson River Sampler* on WAMC in Albany, New York, is a folksinger who sells her CD, *Singing Along with the Radio*, on her Web site and presumably at public appearances. Matt

Watroba is the host of *Folks Like Us*, an Ypsilanti, Michigan, based radio show that Watroba presented for some eighteen years on WDET-FM before moving the show to WEMU-FM. Matt is a guitarist and folksinger who records and performs frequently. Phil Shapiro of *Bound for Glory* is also a performer. These are not isolated cases. Rather, many of folk's cultural intermediaries play multiple roles within the microindustry. The distinctions between performer, presenter, and audience become increasingly blurred and cycles of reciprocity become starkly evident when intermediaries produce cultural goods while mediating the cultural production of others.

Conclusion

> So I watch these kids playing Single A
> It's batter up against the hand of fate
> We're all praying good will somehow turn to great
> And not be strictly minor league
>
> But there are days we shine
> When sweat and nerve and muscle dance in perfect time
> So we keep on trying
> But in one moment our dreams might shatter
> Right before our eyes
>
> And you can almost feel that rush
> It's close enough to touch
> I believe we gave it all that we had
> I believe I gave it all that I had
> I believe we're giving all we can
> Will it ever be enough?

The contemporary folk microindustry can be defined in terms of the multiple layers of hierarchical relationships that exist, either stated or unspoken, at every level of the musical landscape. From the artistic food chain, to record companies and artist representation, to the presenters whose efforts are rewarded by positions of power within the microindustry, the folk operate as a small-scale version of the popular music industry at large. Yet the oft-repeated claims of community and folk identity tell a different story, one that is immersed in notions of egalitarianism. The apparent contradictions between folk's egalitarianism and its engagements with market and late capitalism underscore the general ambiguity of the contemporary folk arena. All the elements of the microindustry converge in the performance spaces. Where the pop music industry has traditionally used artists' tours as vehicles to promote record sales, the folk are more performance-oriented, and recordings function as secondary artifacts through which the live performance can be recalled in memory. Since the late 1980s the proliferation of folk music venues has reflected the overall development of the microindustry and the increasing multitude of semiprofessional and professional performers. As the next chapter will show, the hierarchical relationships that have emerged at each level of the microindustry are most apparent in the areas of public performance.

Oh, the interstates and backroads might be paved with gold

But my heart keeps pulling me back home

The show last night in Abilene wasn't much to write home about

But it was pretty good pay

—Annie Benjamin, "The Road," from *Life's Blessings*

5 Folkspace

House Concerts, Coffeehouses, and the Concert Series

The rapidly evolving folk microindustry of the 1990s and the increasing public demand for venues featuring singer/songwriters, proved to be a boon to American folk music communities at large. The market for and interest in traditional folk musics in the United States also appeared to undergo a marked resurgence during this period. However, given the burgeoning population of professional and semiprofessional singer/songwriters vying for performance opportunities, old-time folk music was, in the marketplace, a poor cousin. During the course of the decade, venerated halls where stars of the 1960s plied their trade achieved iconic status for the new folk. Venues that survived the lean years of the 1970s and '80s, when disco reigned supreme, became signifiers of folk music's past: place as symbolic bearer of tradition.

For performers, playing at places like Club Passim in Cambridge, Massachusetts, or Gerde's Folk City in New York was, and continues to be, a mark of success. Singer/songwriters' promotional material is rife with references to past performances at well-known venues. Oftentimes presenters inundated with promotional material take these references with a grain of salt. All too often players claim to have shared the stage with folk luminaries when in fact they may have played at an open-mic[1] where some folk legend once played. Clearly identification with, and valorization of, place occupies a central position in the hierarchies of the folk microindustry.[2] The venerated halls of folk's past glories serve to reinscribe the more general notions of "tradition" that continually surface within the context of music and performance. However, as folk music changes, so do the sites in which that music is presented.

As increasing numbers of singer/songwriters entered the professional and semiprofessional realms during the 1990s, new venues opened to accommodate the growing interest in folk music. However, it may be as easily stated that during the 1990s, new venues opened their doors to accommodate the growing interest in folk music, and thus increasing numbers of singer/songwriters entered the professional realm. That is, one circumstance cannot be determined as a causal agent for the other. Rather the field became more crowded with performers and venues simultaneously. House concerts, "church basement" concert series, the traditional coffeehouse, the bookstore chain coffeehouse, and folk festivals offered a growing field of opportunity for aspiring and established folk musicians.

The House Concert: Bringing the Folk Back Home

The house concert has a number of historical precedents, including European parlor concerts and various music events within many folk traditions. Comparable to today's house concerts were "rent parties," which took place in urban areas since the 1920s and continued at least throughout the 1940s and '50s. Generally the host of a rent party would supply food and beverages. The partygoers would eat, drink, and listen to (or play) music and contribute money toward the host's rent payment (Weissman, pers. comm.). The most significant differences between such rent parties and today's house concert series lie in the structural and economic organization of the events.

The contemporary house concert is structurally similar to larger concert events or parlor concerts involving distinct divisions between performer and audience. Generally chairs are arranged in rows facing a front central area where the performer plays and sings. While group participation in the performance is occasionally encouraged in the form of sing-alongs, there is a clear distinction between artist and audience. The ways in which the audience is expected to respond and interact with the performers are well defined.

Social protocols surrounding house concerts have much in common with behavioral expectations at most symphonic or operatic events, expectations that formed as class-based protocols of politeness in early nineteenth-century Europe.[3] Like concert music audiences, the house concert audience is expected to sit quietly and attentively, respond when directed to do so, and refrain from behavior that might be distracting.[4] According to all of the presenters interviewed, serious breaches of behavioral stricture are rare. The notion of folk music as a participatory "people's music" or a music accompanying everyday life has in large part been supplanted by a division between the active and passive roles of performer and audience. In some respects politeness takes on an even more central role at a house concert than at a public venue. It remains easier to dismiss spilled coffee or dropped food in a performance space that has a maintenance staff to deal with such matters. Spilling coffee on someone's living room couch is a different matter. The performance place itself is personalized. The space is also relatively small, making any breach of acceptable behavior all too apparent.

It seems unlikely that the rent parties of the early twentieth century were as carefully delineated in strict performer/audience relationships as are modern house concerts. Admittedly this unlikelihood resides perhaps primarily within my own retrospective imagination. Once again the past—a past that for this author never existed—is imbued with a sense of power. The mythology of authenticity finds its most potent allies in the fallibility of memory and the fictions of imagination. While the structural differences between the house concert and its immediate predecessor may be matters of conjecture, the economic organization of the two is more clearly differentiated.

Many of today's house concert series are presented by people who have little or no interest in deriving personal financial gain from the concerts. This is not to say that the concerts are free from economic constraints. Generally attendees pay a "suggested donation" before the performance begins, usually between seven and fifteen dollars.[5] In most cases the performer receives all of the proceeds as well as the opportunity to sell "product."[6] Occasionally the presenter will take a small percentage of the door to cover expenses (coffee, tea, and desserts that are available for the audience), but that seems to be an exception to the rule. For the most part presenters are financially secure apart from their involvement with music and are therefore in a position to provide refreshments without concern for reimbursement.

As the term "house concert" suggests, these events are usually held in people's homes. In order for the series to attract better-known professional singer/songwriters, the house must be large enough to accommodate a relatively large audience. The successful and high-profile house concert series must comfortably seat enough people to pay a performer's minimum fee requirements. The smaller the presentation space, the smaller the audience and the income generated by the performance. Thus a living room that will seat only twenty to thirty people is less likely to attract performers who have achieved significant national attention than a room that will seat a larger audience. Depending upon several factors, including proximity to neighboring houses, weather conditions, and topographical concerns, presenters may host outdoor concerts in their backyards, thereby minimizing or eliminating the space constraints of their living rooms.

The availability of houses large enough to host such audiences suggests that changes have occurred in the folk's economic landscape since the 1960s revival popularized folk music among America's youth. Today's folk audiences are generally older and have more disposable income than 1960s audiences did. Today's new generation of middle-aged folk power brokers—the occasional presenter in this case—generally has independent economic resources and is, at least theoretically, unconcerned with profiting from the experience. Yet the house concert presenter profits in other ways, not coincidentally in social status or symbolic capital. Presenting a nationally known artist in the comfort of one's living room imbues the presenter with substantial cultural capital. Proximity to stardom can be a seductive enticement to work at generating significant numbers of paying customers. The proximity to folk's stars is important not only for presenters, but for the audience as well.

The house concert draws performer and audience into a relatively close relationship. Sitting a few feet from the artist, without an elevated stage or elaborate lighting, audience members can make direct eye contact with the performer, request particular songs, and learn guitar parts for their favorite songs directly from the source. During intermissions, audience members may engage the performer in conversation, buy a CD, and have the performer personalize it with an autograph. The house concert humanizes the performance experience and speaks to one of the primary attractions of the folk: the sense of community. At times it can appear to be a very small community. The audience for a house concert often includes other house concert presenters, hosts of folk music radio shows, and folk aficionados who regularly attend concerts, festivals, and "competing" house concerts in a specific region.

"Folk music: you can hear and understand the lyrics, and you want to," say Glen and LaJeanna Pilant, who for about seven years hosted Hill Country House Concerts in Bulverde, Texas, a bedroom community outside San Antonio. Prior to moving to Bulverde in 1998, the Pilants hosted a concert series in San Antonio called Urban Campfires, a continuing series presently hosted by San Antonio residents Steve and Jayne Wood.

Arriving at Glen and LaJeanna's large new home in the hill country northwest of San Antonio, I parked in the driveway at the rear of the house and found my way to the front door. Glen and LaJeanna met me there and offered to help carry my guitars and equipment. The living room, which adjoined dining and kitchen areas, was large enough to accommodate a considerable crowd. It was about 4 p.m. and the Pilants were preparing the house for the evening's concert at which I was to play an opening set before the main act.

I helped Glen rearrange the living room furniture to make room for rows of folding chairs. We set up quite a few chairs, and I asked Glen if he was expecting this many people to show up. He replied that some fifty people had called for reservations and that they often had a significant number who didn't bother to call ahead. A minimal but nice sounding public-address system was set up at the front of the room. The feature act for the evening was Dave Carter and Tracy Grammer,[7] an increasingly popular act on the national folk circuit, who arrived for a sound check about an hour before the show began.

Approximately half an hour prior to the scheduled time of the show, the audience began to arrive. As do most house concert series, Hill Country House Concerts has its regular crowd: people who attend the concert regardless of who is playing and some for whom the series simply affords an opportunity to socialize in pleasant, nonthreatening surroundings. There were also a considerable number of people who were fans of Dave and Tracy. At least one other presenter was in attendance. Rod Kennedy, founder and longtime producer of the Kerrville Folk Festival, arrived and claimed a spot on the comfortable couch, which had been moved to one side of the room. Dave and Tracy seemed honored that Kennedy came to hear them perform. The industry buzz surrounding the duo's growing popularity and their recent association with Fleming, Tamulevich—the premier management/booking agency for the new folk—notwithstanding, they had yet to play at the Kerrville main stage.

Following my set, which lasted about thirty minutes, there was a brief intermission during which the audience visited, admired the house and backyard, and drank coffee, tea, or water provided by the hosts. Some brought coolers of beer; others brought wine. Carter and Grammer played their first set and were enthusiastically received. During the intermission a potluck dinner was served, and the performers and audience were invited to partake.

The culinary aspects of the house concert environment vary. Some hosts provide light snacks and dessert, while others suggest that the audience bring covered-dish items, and a full-scale dinner is shared. This association of food and folk music is an important aspect of the American folk's construction of an aesthetic community. However, the addition of food to the house concert has its own set of potential problems. Glen and LaJeanna have lamented the food aspect of their series, complaining that guests have spilled food and drinks on furniture and carpeting, leading to considerable cleaning expense added to the general cost of presenting the series.

Dave and Tracy played their second set and an encore after which some of the audience left immediately. Others stayed to speak to the performers, buy CDs and have them autographed, or visit with friends. For some there was a discernable sense of unwillingness to let the evening end. Generally, house concerts are not late night events. By 11 p.m. the audience had left. Glen and LaJeanna had much earlier asked if I wanted to spend the night at their house rather than driving back to Austin, and I accepted. Carter and Grammer were also invited to stay, but they declined explaining that they had matters to attend to. They had to be in Seattle within a day or two for a meeting with Joan Baez to discuss some sort of collaborative project.[8]

It is common, if not expected, for the presenter's home to be large enough that guest rooms are available for touring musicians. This practice is often appreciated by traveling performers but sometimes has negative aspects. Touring musicians may play several dates per week. Often these jobs are separated by considerable distance. It is not unusual for a performer to play a night in Bulverde, Texas, for example, and have a job in Tulsa, Oklahoma, or Clovis, New Mexico, the next night. However, presenters may want to have what amounts to a private party following the audience's departure. The performer is the guest of honor, and through either affection for the host or a sense of professional obligation, musicians regularly participate in these celebrations.

Late nights, little sleep, and the potential for overconsumption of alcohol or recreational drugs are common features of life on the road. Of course this is true for traveling musicians of any genre or description. However, as the folk microindustry expands its base of venues and touring artists, many performers have become aware of the pitfalls of excess on the road and monitor their partying closely, allowing for adequate amounts of sleep and nutrition. The hard living hedonistic artist is a notion that persists for some: a modernist image with destructive and often fatal consequences. However, folk performers tend more and more to be concerned with maintaining their health while on tour.[9] The house concert provides the opportunity to perform in a setting where smoking is usually banned, no alcohol is sold, and food is usually plentiful and well prepared. If the performer wants to stay awake all night drinking, visiting, and partying, the opportunity is never far away. However, most house concert hosts are aware of the pressures on touring musicians and are sensitive to the individual performer's choices regarding social activities following the show.

The house concert has become a familiar and ubiquitous venue for the folk and reinscribes codes of communal value, both in terms of aesthetics in a broad sense and also as an aesthetic of community. The home as a place of cultural production is symbolic of a longing for more immediate and personalized involvement with that production. In an age when mass media permeates the postindustrial world; where television has become America's favorite pastime, a pastime that requires no personal interaction; where Internet communications have created disembodied communities of technophiles; the house concert allows for a redemption of the social body. Much like settlers on the frontiers of America's preindustrial past who would gather occasionally to share stories, gossip, and local news, the house concert provides an idealized respite from isolation on the frontiers of the depersonalized information age.

Max Weber, the early German sociologist, suggests in his essay "Science as a Vocation" that rational thought creates disenchantment with the world, a permanent state of dissatisfaction, and that the alternative to this disenchantment is to sacrifice rational intelligence and return to the premodern, to "the arms of the old churches" (175). Symbolically the house concert represents such a return—a reenchantment with the aesthetics of community. The music presented in these settings can signify a similar reenchantment with the premodern. Acoustic instruments that can be heard by everybody within earshot, a certain musical simplicity, and accessible, thoughtful, understandable lyrics are the most commonly quoted reasons for interest in contemporary folk music.

The "Church Basement" Concert Series

The church basement concert series is much like the house concert except usually on a larger scale. Oftentimes the concert series is presented in a church meeting hall or some other public use building that can be rented at a relatively small fee. Church halls are common sites for folk music concerts, usually offering not only inexpensive rental charges, but also rooms acoustically suited for theatrical and musical presentations. However, the so-called church basement series has evolved to include venues not associated with churches per se. The Urban Campfires concert series, for example, takes place in a community building at Brackenridge Park, a large popular urban recreational area close to downtown San Antonio. In fact many presenters are beginning to shy away from using church facilities, suggesting that an implied association with a specific religious group may alienate potential patrons and decrease the audience for the series. This appears to be less the case in rural areas, where churches are often primary locations for social interaction. The "concert series" has come to be associated with the idea of public space and provides a venue for the presenter whose home may not be suitable to accommodate a house concert audience or whose series has simply outgrown the living room. One of the most appealing aspects of sponsoring a series is that the presenters can go home after the concert and separate themselves from the business of folk both emotionally and spatially.

For the presenter, the concert series may also secure a relatively high-profile presence within local folk communities. Opportunities for becoming involved in presenting festivals or other collaborative productions increase the presenter's network of contacts within the folk and business community. Along with the more widely dispersed public presence, comes a corresponding increase in symbolic capital. The presenter, through his presence at the crossroads of the folk world has become one of the stars of the show: fame by association.[10] For some, the increased social profile that comes with promoting a concert series may afford the opportunity to promote individual local artists whose talents are yet unrecognized by general audiences. Playing as the opener for one of the acknowledged stars of the new folk is a sought after way of gaining exposure to a wide audience and can be instrumental in creating an industry buzz. Yet there is an ideological incongruity between the folk ideal of the local and the prestige of association with decidedly nonlocal stars. A concert series can effectively outgrow local and lesser-known touring performers through presenting acts with considerable drawing power. Such was the case for the now defunct (since February 2003) 12 Corners Coffeehouse series in Rochester, New York.

In the early days of the series, presenter Glenn Drinkwater's booking decisions were based almost entirely on aesthetic determinations of quality. Many relatively unknown local and touring artists benefited from this quality-oriented booking practice. Drinkwater contends that the obscurity of many of these artists contributed to economic losses incurred in the first three years of the series. By 1996 he was ready to try his hand at presenting a top-tier artist in the folk world. The first of these performers was Cheryl Wheeler, who had attended the same high school as Drinkwater and Cilla Shaw, the 12 Corners copresenter, and with whom they had maintained contact. Largely because of their personal connection, Wheeler agreed to play for a reduced guarantee. I was booked as the opening act. The evening of the concert arrived and to Glenn and Cilla's delight, a capacity crowd filled the Presbyterian church hall. Financially the concert was a resounding success, and Cheryl Wheeler made considerably more than her guaranteed minimum. I received a substantial fee as the opening act, and the series covered their expenses.

This first big-time 12 Corners Coffeehouse concert with Cheryl Wheeler marked a turning point of sorts for the series and reflected a larger trend among the more successful concert series operators: a tightening of the ranks, a more distinct separation of folk artists into the hierarchies described in the previous chapter. In presenters' language, folk artists were classified in terms of "tiers," which represented the specific artist's level of prominence in the folk "food chain." Undoubtedly these qualifiers were not new to presenters, but they more clearly defined the hierarchical nature of the folk world in terms of drawing power. The artists were not the only elements of the folk that were subjected to a tiered system of classification; venues were also assigned qualifiers. However, the most common designations for any folk concert series are either an A-list venue or a B-list venue.[11] As in the case of the popular music industry, the folk music marketplace became a site for the arbitration of aesthetic value.

At the 2000 Falcon Ridge Folk Festival in Hillsdale, New York, several conversations between A-list presenters revolved around the dynamics and logistics of presenting top-tier artists, and all appeared to be concerned primarily with the economic realities of booking these well-known acts. "Love of the music" entered into practically all of these discussions but seemed more an obligatory tip of the hat than a meaningful consideration. The "draw" was the main concern for these entrepreneurs. They also turned to the practical and much discussed notion of a group of regional A-list presenters creating a loosely knit network with agents for important folk artists and block-routing tours. The idea behind this sort of network is not new. Lawrence Levine documents a remarkably similar union that occurred in the late nineteenth century: "[T]heaters in an area attempted to increase the efficiency of the booking process by banding together in theatrical circuits. In 1896 a half dozen important theater owners and booking agents from New York, Philadelphia, and Boston forged these local circuits into a centralized national booking system, which ultimately functioned as a national theatrical monopoly" (*Highbrow/Lowbrow*, 78).

Where the theatrical monopoly Levine mentions was apparently successful at drawing factions of the industry to function cooperatively, shaping a similar effort in the contemporary folk arena has been less fruitful. Communication between presenters is often sporadic, and the time involved in organizing a centralized booking/routing entity appears to be prohibitive. One of the fundamental differences between earlier and more recent efforts to organize regional circuits lies in the nature of the presenters.

In the nineteenth century, the theater owners and agents who "forged these local circuits into a centralized national booking system" were presumably professional promoters, presenters, or entrepreneurs. In contrast, many of the current folk music concert series presenters do not expect to make a living promoting music. For these part-time power brokers, involvement in the folk music world—and the personal advantages of that position of power—appears to be the primary motivation. The presenter is a fairly high-profile actor in the folk arena. Aspiring artists and established stars treat presenters with a degree of deference. For novice singer/songwriters, the presenter is someone who can jumpstart their careers. However, for the most part, few concert series presenters are interested in fulfilling that function. Although some do it, presenting unknown artists, no matter how exceptional their musical abilities, doesn't fill seats. As in politics and advertising in general, name recognition is what sells. Even if presenters are part-time entrepreneurs, most attempt to operate their concert series with a degree of professionalism, a professionalism that is usually measured in economic terms. Yet the acquisition of economic capital is a secondary consideration, a corollary to cultural capital acquired through fulfilling the role of what Pierre Bourdieu has called "cultural intermediaries."[12]

That the contemporary folk have effectively canonized specific performers, repertoires, stylistic characteristics, and even performance spaces, allows the presenter, Filene's "power broker" or Bourdieu's "cultural intermediary," to "divulg[e] legitimate culture" (Bourdieu, *Distinction*, 326)—made legitimate by highlighting its difference from the "nonlegitimate" and indirectly through its exchange value—and to drive the process of that canonization to some extent, regardless of any possible deficiency in terms of "intrinsic value." Bourdieu suggests, "The petit-bourgeois spectators know that they have no need to be alarmed: they can recognize the 'guarantees of quality' offered by their moderately revolutionary taste-makers, who surround themselves with all the institutional signs of cultural authority" (326). For the folk, however, the institutional signs that mark that authority are primarily the same associations that define the presenter's standing in the community: that is, the artists being presented—along with their position in the folk food chain—and the success of performances in terms of audience size and economic viability. Yet their cultural capital may also be built upon public perceptions of taste.

Concert series presenters build audiences through an ongoing process of developing public trust in the presenter's sense of taste. Within the context of the contemporary folk community, presenters may, perhaps deservedly, take on the role of arbiters of the public taste. I guardedly say "deservedly," because the arbitration of a public aesthetic—one determined by the intermediaries—is only part of a much more complicated picture. If the presenter's elevated status within the community of folk, and whatever "special quality" afforded that position, allowed for a universally accepted aesthetic standard, the folk audience would indeed be made up of hapless pawns, devoid of agency. Yet perhaps because of the relative homogeneity of the folk community in terms of race, age, and educational capital, the presenter's sense of taste is not necessarily the final word in determinations of musical quality. Among both amateur and professional performers, there is a great deal of debate regarding presenters' choices, and discussions denigrating this performer or that—the "I just don't get it!" commentary—are common fodder for the rank-and-file folkie. But the rank-and-file performer rarely plays the successful concert series except perhaps as an opening act.

For the well-established performer, the concert series can yield a relatively substantial amount of money for an evening's work.[13] These series afford opportunities to play for more sizable audiences than at house concerts, and, as at house concerts, folk audiences are almost invariably receptive and appreciative. In the case of the professional touring folk act for whom performing pays the bills, the concert series plays an important role in generating revenues as well as contributing to a higher public profile that eventually translates into industry buzz.

In the past decade house concerts and independent concert series have become the most popular venues in the United States for presenting singer/songwriters. However, they are not the only markets in which the new folk have found a growing audience. Large bookstore chains have found that integrating a coffeehouse and presenting singer/songwriters, whose CDs are available for sale, may be a profitable enterprise. Additionally, neighborhood and independent coffeehouses—popular venues in the 1960s, many of which closed following the demise of folk's commercial heyday—appear to be enjoying a revival as well.

Traditional and Corporate Bookstore Coffeehouses

By the 1970s the traditional coffeehouse as a venue for contemporary folk music had become somewhat anachronistic. After the "folk scare" of the 1960s, the coffeehouse—the classic bohemian artist hangout, owing as much or more to the 1950s beat generation as to the 1960s folkies—ceased to embody the same level of cultural cachet that it did during folk's brief commercial heyday. Folk music was the stuff of the common man. It had quiet dignity and spoke simply or poetically to the concerns of a generation in the process of recreating heroic rural pasts. Those histories became increasingly irrelevant to a generation caught up in the social turmoil of its own time—a time in which the electric sounds of rock bands began to speak more decisively than the dulcet strumming of acoustic guitars.[14] The coffeehouse was passé. Like many folk musicians, coffeehouses felt the declining commercial interest in folk music and many began changing their image to fit the prevailing popularity of rock and roll. Many others simply closed their doors, as the baby boom generation seemed to turn its back on folk music.

As in the late 1950s and early 1960s, groups of die-hard folkies continued to play the music they had come to call their own. However, after the "death" of the folk revival, making a living as a folk musician became significantly more difficult than it had been in the previous few years. The decline of folk music's mainstream popularity wrote a similar epitaph for the coffeehouse. Yet there were die-hard coffeehouses as well, the proprietors of which were more concerned with beat idealism than the politics of image that threatened to consume them.

In the late 1980s and early 1990s the coffeehouse began to reemerge as a viable commercial enterprise. However, the competition in terms of music presentation and the nature of the coffeehouse as a business whose primary income is derived from beverage and food sales, relegated many of these venues to booking local, inexpensive performers. There are, of course, exceptions to the rule. Some of the better-known coffeehouses are organized around the concert series model. That is, on evenings that well-known artists are to perform, the venue will charge customers a competitive admission fee. Thus the coffeehouse can realize a profit from food and beverage sales, and the artist will receive most if not all of the door as well as CD sales. In some cases the coffeehouse management will guarantee the artist a set amount and simply take that fee from the total receipts for the evening.

Another contemporary coffeehouse venue that offers the workaday singer/songwriter opportunities to play for an audience, sell some CDs, and make a few weekday dollars, comes in the guise of the corporate chain bookstore. The Borders Group, which includes Borders and Waldenbooks, as of 2005 operates more than twelve hundred stores around the world, mostly in the United States but also in England and other countries. This corporate giant has been responsible for adding yet another interpretation of "coffeehouse" to the folk lexicon. In many of the Borders bookstores, an area has been designated in which designer coffees and desserts are served, and customers can sit at tables or on comfortable chairs and couches and enjoy snacks while perusing potential book and magazine purchases. Much like the coffeehouse of old, the corporate coffeehouse offers a break from the fast paced world beyond its borders, and many stores feature contemporary folk singer/songwriter performances. Generally the performers are local artists or traveling musicians who have not achieved a regional or national reputation. The corporate coffeehouse is most often perceived as an "exposure gig" where economic gain is often less a consideration than is the opportunity to expand the performer's audience base.

Performers at corporate coffeehouses are situated squarely in the center of unabashed capitalism, the proverbial belly of the beast. The presentation of folk music surrounded by a supermarket bookstore highlights folk's engagement of capitalism with very little pretense of egalitarian authenticity like that promulgated by many not-for-profit coffeehouses. Once again the nature of the common man has changed. The flannel and corduroy that used to signify the rural working-class aesthetic of simplicity has become the leisure attire of the bourgeoisie for whom the surroundings of the corporate coffeehouse are more natural than the remote fields and valleys of a fictional folk past.

"Coffeehouses," Booking, and Employments of Power

What may be the coffeehouse's central contribution to the contemporary acoustic music landscape is its lexical association with folk music. Various venues have adopted the term "coffeehouse" even when they have been anything but coffeehouses. 12 Corners Coffeehouse is one of many examples. In its last few seasons, Glenn Drinkwater changed the name of his series because it was no longer presented in the 12 Corners area of Rochester, and it was never a coffeehouse per se. Thus every aspect of the name was inaccurate. Today the term appears to be used most often to convey the idea of an informal listening venue at which the audience will not be subjected to overly loud music, cigarette smoke, and inebriated patrons. Oddly, the archetypal coffeehouse of old—the beatnik, poetry and bongos, countercultural, late-night hangout—was, at least in my admittedly flawed recollection, pervaded by a constant haze of cigarette smoke. Today's concert series "coffeehouses" are, to my knowledge, smoke-free and offer the folk audience an alternative to the club scene. In many if not most large urban areas, the traditional coffeehouse has reappeared as a folk-music-oriented venue. However, the new version often relates to its namesake only in title and vague associations of historical context. The use of the word "coffeehouse" as a synonym for "concert venue" has become part of the contemporary folk habitus.

The responsibility for booking each venue in folkspace may fall on individuals or groups—committees who meet periodically and vote on who they want to perform. Individuals responsible for booking, or perhaps representatives of booking committees, often attend the national or regional Folk Alliance conferences looking for talent to fill season rosters. They may also attend concerts at other venues in the area. Their positions as bookers within the folk community make them targets for the attention of performers.

The social baggage that comes with the responsibility for making booking decisions, and the hierarchy of the folk in a general sense, was once characterized to me in conversation as like a "high school popularity contest." While networking is important in any business, it can be conducted with dignity or can stoop to sycophancy. Venue operators—presenters—have become folk's most plentiful power brokers. As such, the power relations at the most fundamental level of the microindustry—the level of the public performative—depend upon the subjective whims of this group of aesthetes, some of whom are themselves folk musicians and many of whom don't know much about music but know what they like. The presenter or booker as power broker wields a potent weapon in the pursuit of advantageous position in the hierarchy of the folk. As a result, personal relationships and the degree of hustle an artist employs may be as important, or even more important, than strictly musical considerations. When invested subjectivities are so intimately involved in decisions that ultimately affect the performer's level of public exposure, the extramusical may assume a disproportionately meaningful role in those decision-making processes.

Paul Barker, a house concert presenter near Austin, addressed his own preferences in an e-mail exchange with me in May 2001. Barker asserted emphatically that performers should look and act "in a professional manner" while on stage. He stated, "My profiles are scored toward what I am looking for—performance *and* songwriting. Some of the songwriting competitions (Napa, etc.) instruct the judges to listen only for the words—I can't do that for my house concert series—audience reaction, humor, etc. are integral to the mix of what my audiences want—not someone in cut-offs staring at their feet and singing the most beautiful lyrics I could imagine." When Barker auditions performers he uses a printed form on which he grades such criteria as guitar style, use of imagery and rhyme, vocal range, use of humor, audience rapport, overall appearance, and a six-tiered cumulative rating.

Barker is not alone in his use of a standardized form for assessing performers. In July 2001, Dave Cambest, who is involved with the South Florida Folk Festival, stated that he also uses a form to evaluate singer/songwriters, and his criteria are similar to those on Paul Barker's scorecard. Both presenters use evaluation forms to organize their evaluative processes and to help them remember individual artists in what sometimes seems a vast ocean of sameness. The sameness that may be the impetus for form evaluations of contemporary singer/songwriters is most evident and most immediate in the other important venue for today's folk—the festival.

The folk festival has become the site where actors at all levels of involvement within the folk microindustry converge. Both spectacle and a deeply revered expression of community, folk festivals combine the best and worst elements of folk idealism in the same extended space for several days and nights: the warmth of communalism and the chill of elitism, the unifying character of folk music and its exclusionary organization, egalitarianism and individual power—all fill needs within the social body of the festival.

Walking through the grass at a summer fest

Intending to see the grandstand best

I'm stopped by the sound of a fiddle

through the trees.

—Lisa Bigwood, "Woodland Band," from *Woodland*

6 The Folk Festival
Spectacle, Community, and Race

The past fifteen years have seen the number of folk music festivals in the United States and around the world increase dramatically. At the time of this writing, nearly 450 folk-music-related festivals occur each year in the continental United States and upwards of seventy-five in Canada.[1] These include bluegrass festivals, storytelling festivals in which music regularly plays a role, dance and music festivals, as well as a number of specialized instrumental festivals—dulcimer and banjo festivals being prevalent. Celtic music festivals, Irish music festivals, and events featuring diverse musical offerings, such as the Festival International de Louisiane in Lafayette, Louisiana, have become yearly attractions for thousands of people interested in music-related activities and those simply drawn by the nature of the festival as spectacle. Of five hundred plus annual folk festivals approximately two thirds regularly feature contemporary singer/songwriters. Folk festivals may be one-day affairs, weekend events, or may occur over multiple days and nights.

The festival as a venue type is one of the primary vehicles through which performers enlarge their base of listeners, thereby increasing individual standing within regional and national folk communities. Yet the festival provides more than an opportunity for the fortunate few who perform as part of the scheduled lineup. Many festivals offer weekend, amateur, and semiprofessional players places to meet and play with each other and with professionals in the context of the campground. For some, the opportunity to spend extended periods of time in which music is the central daytime and evening activity is the primary attraction to the festival. For others, the campground music sessions are an opportunity to network with other musicians, venue operators, folk radio show hosts, and a variety of microindustry power brokers who may conceivably be able to advance aspiring performers' careers. For a researcher, the festival presents a microcosm of regional folk landscapes and the folk community at large. In *Reflections on the Folklife Festival* (1992), Bauman et al. suggest that the event "is a complex, dynamic, and highly problematic undertaking, in which a number of factors (themselves highly subject to revision in the course of the festival) intersect: personal agendas for participating, hierarchies of relating among disparate categories of individuals, and the need to draw upon, to adapt, and to reframe customary activities" (57–58).

Like the folklife festival, the folk music festival presents a rich, multilayered, and often contradictory cultural framework. The suggestion that elements thereof are "highly subject to revision in the course of the festival" is considerably more pertinent when regarding festival culture over a period of several years. Each folk music festival has its own following, its own overall social dynamic, and its own sense of social hierarchy, which have all developed through multiple presentations of the festival. In some ways these elements seem relatively fixed and stable, yet they are dynamic processes that change, sometimes incrementally, and at other times quite dramatically.

The Philadelphia Folk Festival is the oldest annually presented folk festival in the country. In August 2004 the Philadelphia Folksong Society—the sponsor for the festival—hosted its forty-third annual event. The festival is a three-day affair that boasts an impressive array of popular and not so popular artists performing on several stages throughout the festival site. Approximately five thousand people stay in the campgrounds, allowing extensive postconcert opportunities for the professional and nonprofessional musician to participate in campfire jam sessions and song swaps.

Certainly, the longevity of the Philadelphia Folk Festival contributes to a general sense of its stature among events of its type. Like the venerated coffeehouses and other performance venues that have survived folk's lean days following the 1960s revival, its history has endowed the Philadelphia festival, as well as its long-time presenters, with unequivocal symbolic capital. The only other festival in the United States that approaches the iconic stature of Philadelphia is the Newport Folk Festival.

While the Philadelphia event is the longest-running annual folk festival in the country, the Newport Folk Festival appeared a few years earlier in 1959. However, in 1971 it ceased operation and did not resume until 1986. Newport is another three-day event but lacks on-site camping. In 1988 the Newport festival became affiliated with Ben and Jerry's, a successful ice cream company, which perhaps foreshadowed the increasingly intertwined relationship between folk music and late capitalism that became so prevalent in the last decade of the twentieth century.

Both the Philadelphia and Newport festivals are important historically and iconically for the American folk (both also feature very high-profile folk and popular entertainers), but their three-day durations are, from an ethnographic perspective, less than ideal. In terms of fieldwork, festivals of longer duration have the potential to yield somewhat more in-depth insight into these annually constructed folk communities.

To my knowledge, the Kerrville Folk Festival, which has taken place each summer for more than thirty years, is the lengthiest annual folk festival in the United States, running for eighteen days from late May to mid-June. While I was living in Austin from 1996 to 2001, the Kerrville Folk Festival, an important venue for contemporary singer/songwriters, provided multiple opportunities for conducting festival "fieldwork."[2] The festival has been held annually since 1972, and singer/songwriters consider it one of the premier American festivals. The annual New Folk songwriting competition attracts hundreds of entries each year, and many winners of the contest have gone on to achieve elevated stature within the folk microindustry and the popular music industry.

My first Kerrville Folk Festival experience was in May 1998. The site for the festival is a forty-acre parcel of south Texas land called the Quiet Valley Ranch, located approximately nine miles from Kerrville. During the opening day or two, as well as prior to some more high-profile weekend concerts, a continuous stream of cars, trucks, and motor homes lines the dusty dirt road that leads to the festival entrance. During late May in south Texas, most years the weather is hot, leading some to question the wisdom of spending days in a tent exposed to the elements. Yet each year thousands camp at the ranch, much of which has minimal or no natural shade. Smiling and cheerful volunteers at a small shack that serves as the ticket pickup area issue festival attendees wristbands and happily exclaim, "Welcome home!" to everyone entering the main gates.

Two large hand-painted signs at the entrance read WELCOME HOME and IT COULD ALWAYS BE LIKE THIS! An additional group of volunteers checks wristbands on people coming and going from the campgrounds and excitedly welcomes home all incoming festivalgoers.

In the midafternoon of the opening day of the festival, I entered the main gate and began driving through the ranch, which was already crowded with tents, camper trailers, motor homes, and thousands of people. Not knowing where I was going exacerbated a growing feeling of unease. As I drove down the winding dirt roads through armies of campers packed tightly together I wondered if any space remained on the ranch in which I might set up my tent. After driving aimlessly for twenty minutes or so I came across an area large enough for my vehicle and tent. The spot was located in the "lower meadow," a large open area of dust, rocks, and scrub grass with no shade save for that of tarps mounted on tent poles, which people set up in attempts to block the relentless sun.

Bordering the meadow was a heavily treed area. Under the protection of the tree cover, the temperature was easily fifteen degrees cooler than in the meadow. However, walking through the wooded area was difficult because of the high density of tents and camper-trailers. Oddly, very few people were around. Guitars were perched on picnic tables and instrument stands; all manner of personal belongings lay in plain view; tents were open and unattended. Despite the relative absence of people, the sound of guitars playing and voices singing seemed at once distant and constant.

I met some acquaintances from Austin who asked if I would like to accompany them to Chapel Hill, a heavily treed hill with a clearing at the top where a daily afternoon song swap took place. On top of the hill was an extended trellis approximately fifty feet long with two or three rows of benches underneath. The benches and surrounding area were crowded with people, many of whom had guitars and were listening to a performer standing in the sun singing a song. The audience applauded enthusiastically when the young man finished and the next performer took his place.

Each day of the festival, the Chapel Hill song sharing sessions are hosted by a moderately well-known singer/songwriter who begins the session with one or more songs after which names of potential performers are drawn from a hat. These sessions, which begin at three in the afternoon and go until five, are always well attended by songwriters eager to share their songs with an extensive audience. For some, the dream of being discovered by a microindustry mover and shaker is the primary impetus for this and other public displays. For others, the songs are the stars of the show and their authors are secondary. As is the case with many of the more egalitarian performance venues at the festival, performers run the gamut from the novice to the seasoned professional.

Concerts held at the main theater on weekends of the festival began at six o'clock. The theater is at the opposite side of the ranch from the lower meadow and the dirt roads that lead there are the primary passageways for the mass of humanity attending the event. There are hundreds of camps, many with hanging placards denoting the camp's name: Camp Calm, Camp Duct Tape, Camp Stupid, and the like. That first evening while walking to the theater I was again struck by the constant din of strumming guitars and singing. The blending of these voices provided a constantly mutating soundscape as I walked down the campground's main road. The theater is a moderately crowded outdoor affair with a large covered stage, a "formal" seating area, and several rows of booths in the rear of the site at which food, drinks, CDs, T-shirts, and various handicrafts are offered for sale.

During the course of that first day on the ranch, a musical sameness was beginning to become apparent. Most of the players on the main stage were competent musicians and/or performers, but few seemed noteworthy except for one husband-and-wife duo called the Kennedys. Their performance typified folk music's increasingly codependent relationship with the popular. For the most part the Kennedys played energetic pop tunes, their performance replete with animated rock star–like poses. In the context of the festival, their stage antics seemed antithetical to common notions of folk performance and might have been more at home in a lounge in Las Vegas. This wasn't authentic folk music in any conventional sense. Yet despite the unmistakably pop sensibilities of their set it was clear that Pete Kennedy was a competent and perhaps accomplished guitarist, and the audience enthusiastically cheered the performance. Whether their music was real folk or acoustic pop was meaningless. In *The Study of Folk Music in the Modern World* (1988), Philip Bohlman suggests, "Stratification is no longer a meaningful designation of folk music as a genre. Separation of musical genres into strata of folk, popular, religious, and art or, alternatively, into class structures results from aesthetic and political exclusiveness and avoids the empirical consideration of musical change. It is still possible to separate elements of folk and popular music, but we most often encounter them in a state of confluence" (139).

In terms of the Kennedys' performance, the confluence of styles was immediate and pervasive. The audience was apparently less concerned with authenticity, and indeed musical or stylistic convention, than simply celebrating community. For the rest of the evening, and for weeks following, there were occasional islands of musical virtuosity in an ocean of the ordinary. It took returning to Kerrville the following year and staying for the duration of the festival to fully understand that the main stage performances are for many attendees the least important element of the festival experience.

After the concerts that first night, the campground came alive with music. Where earlier in the day music was a constant background hum, after midnight it became a cacophony. I picked up my guitar at camp and began walking through the campground stopping and listening to songs at "campfires" along the way.[3] As I stood listening, people invited me to sit down and play a song or two. Offers of food and beer were plentiful, and the atmosphere was strikingly congenial: the excitement of the beginning of the festival was practically tangible. From the rudimentary to the sophisticated, from the folk strum[4] to elaborately embellished fingerstyle playing, from solo guitar to bagpipes to didgeridoo, the campgrounds were clearly the locus of the Kerrville experience. What seemed most apparent was the general celebration of music making. At some of the more heavily trafficked campfires, novice players might share their songs with performers who had played the main stage earlier in the evening. Some of the unknown players in the campground put many of the main stage performers to shame. It seemed that everyone had something to say, and the community was infatuated with its own musical egalitarianism. Like the infatuation of a love affair, when life is beautiful and passion masks imperfections that time and familiarity make evident, the festival seemed the embodiment of folk idealism.

The next three days passed much as the first. Each evening, concerts at the theater featured singer/songwriters and bands of different stripes. After the scheduled shows the campground became the site for the enactment of communal music making. Each night I wandered the camps playing music until sunrise, at which time I retired to my tent for a few hours of rest before the heat of the day made the inside of the tent unbearable. When I drove away from the festival on Sunday evening, tired and dirty, I was determined to return the following year and conduct additional fieldwork.

The Kerrville experience had, over the course of those few days, presented a complex web of representational associations and relationships between the folk and the popular, the past and the present, history and modernity. Richard Bauman et al. suggest, "The ideological foundation of contemporary American folklife festivals is a species of liberal pluralism, which promulgates a symbolically constructed image of the popular roots of American national culture by traditionalizing, valorizing, and legitimizing selected aspects of vernacular culture drawn from the diverse ethnic, regional, and occupational groups seen to make up American society" (*Reflections on the Folklife Festival*, 1).

Like the folklife festival, folk idealism at the Kerrville Folk Festival—the valorization of the "traditional"—plays a central, if often implicit, role in the general ideological milieu of the spectacle. Yet the relationships between that idealism/traditionalism and popular culture appear much more complicated than the occupational representations of vernacular culture at the folklife festival.

Indeed the "selected aspects of vernacular culture" that are traditionalized, valorized, and legitimized have less to do with clearly defined crafts in which artifacts are produced than with vague notions of musical authenticity: efficacy in the creation of meaning and expressive evocations of experiential "truths." While these aspects of musical production are often perceived as subjective, the levels of mass public acceptance for stylistic conventions promulgate self-perpetuating boundaries of style: "less is more," simplicity over complexity, and, more explicitly, the folk over the popular.

However, these relationships, though frequently stated or tacitly referred to, are deceptive. As discussed in chapter 1, "traditional" has become a very fluid term for the contemporary American folk. Where at once the old-time country tinged songs of artists such as *Jason Eklund*, whose Woody Guthrie influenced songwriting and vocal affectation belie his Midwestern upbringing, stand as testaments to the simple straightforwardness of folk tradition, popular traditions have emerged from the adolescence of the baby boom generation. Songs that graced top forty airwaves in the 1960s and '70s have become part of a new traditional folk repertoire for today's aging folk audience/participants. As a primary source for musical inspiration, the Beatles stand out as a pivotal juncture in the relationship of folk and the popular. This became evident at the 1999 Kerrville Folk Festival.

In *The Politics and Poetics of Transgression* (1986), Peter Stallybrass and Allon White suggest, "[T]he observer at the fair [or folk festival, in this case] is also a potential participant and so the relation between observer and observed is never fixed" (42). Their point was in evidence during my initiation into the cultural life of that festival in 1999. My work has since that time continued to be a matter of public interest and considerable speculation among festivalgoers. Many Kerrville relationships were initiated by curiosity about just how I would portray the actors on this cultural stage.

Wendy Wentworth, the host of a monthly song circle in Austin and a longtime Kerrville Festival attendee, suggested that I plan on coming to "land rush" to claim a camping spot in the shade near her usual camping area. "Land rush" occurs on the weekend prior to the opening of the festival. Veteran Kerrville attendees and others in the know gather in the large grassy parking area of the festival site. Vehicles line up in rows along the length of the field in the order of arrival. Many set up tents and make themselves comfortable for the weekend. The event serves as a preview of the festival. On Sunday at noon the gates open, and the rows of vehicles make their way into the campground to secure prime camping spots. Having selected a spot, many participants leave the ranch to return on the opening day of the festival. Others remain, thus extending their stay an extra four days.

For numbers of these "Kerrverts,"[5] the festival marks one of the most anticipated times of the year, if not *the* most anticipated. Several people with whom I spoke even quit their jobs in order to have the time to stay for the duration of the event. For others, vacation time accrued in their jobs is used at once during the eighteen days. One Kerrvert told me that after the festival he spends the rest of his year anticipating the next festival. The social bonds created over several years, and in many cases several decades, of attendance may or may not extend into lives beyond the festival. Each year weddings and memorial services take place, their anniversaries to be celebrated at subsequent festivals. The personal attachments formed by sharing experiential milestones cement long-term, if only once yearly, familial relations. These festival "family" relationships are in large part location dependent. That is, the camp with which one associates becomes the locus of social life in the culture of the campground.

When the gates opened on Sunday at noon, I proceeded to the area Wendy had suggested. Her extended Kerr-family camps in the vicinity of a large (now unfortunately dead) tree affectionately called the "energy tree." I found a shady spot on the periphery between two pop-up campers and erected my tent and long folding table on which my camp kitchen would reside.[6] Having established camp I returned to Austin to prepare for the opening of the festival the following Thursday. Most of the singer/songwriters I knew in Austin were busily preparing for the festival's opening; some had chosen to stay at the ranch after land rush.

As I arrived around eleven on the opening morning, the festival site had taken on much the same appearance as the previous year. The crowds had swelled the population of the tent community to several thousand. I was glad I had already set up my camp. I unloaded provisions and guitar and began making the camp as comfortable as possible. My neighbors were guardedly friendly. I introduced myself to people in the area, some of whom seemed completely apathetic. It soon became clear that despite the proximity, there were distinct divisions in the social groups sharing the area. I was a newcomer and as yet was not associated with a particular group or camp.

That evening I attended the concerts at the main theater. One of the first performers to make a memorable impression was *Don Edwards*. Edwards was dressed in a cowboy outfit with large brimmed hat and boots and performed material that was intended to recall the romance of the Old West. His brand of cowboy songs included classics from the Lomax collection as well as several songs featuring yodeling. The audience was particularly enchanted by the yodeling songs. Edwards's repertoire also included some Tin Pan Alley hits of the 1930s, which, rather than seeming incongruous, added to the nostalgic grace of the performance.[7] Clearly their origins in the 1930s allowed sufficient time for them to have become "traditional." The obvious nostalgia and its re-creation of a past that never existed for a huge majority of the audience, was enthusiastically received. Edwards sang in a smooth baritone voice, and his guitar accompaniment, which was not virtuosic but practiced and elegant, charmed the audience. The white-haired gentleman's performance reflected a competence nurtured by many years singing these songs for which his affection was obvious. Nostalgia for simpler times and premodern idealism permeated the performance and accentuated that element of contemporary folk romanticism: a fitting opening for the festival, during which cultural constructions made free use of fictive and recollected histories within the pastiche of the spectacle.

Following Don Edwards, a trio took the stage. Rod Kennedy, the enigmatic producer of the festival, introduced the featured singer/songwriter as having "knocked him out" at the Albuquerque Folk Alliance Conference earlier that year. The contrast between Edwards's and *Marianne Osiel*'s sets foregrounded contemporary folk music's disjuncture with the past. Osiel's guitar skills were adequate but, like Edwards's, not virtuosic. An electric bass and "ethnic" drum accompaniment[8] laid down a pop rock groove over which Osiel played a repetitious progression revolving around a clear tonal center. Her vocal quality was competent if unremarkable. Melodically the song meandered around the tonic but seemed to lack conventional musical development. Where Edwards's popular old-timey cowboy songs had a predictable Western sense of melodic development with clear harmonic implications and distinct organizational features, the structures of Osiel's melodies seemed to eschew the notion of melodic primacy. Rather, the overall groove appeared to play the central role. Likewise the lyrics of most of her songs seemed secondary to the setting, which appeared to be employed in the service of mood over message.

Providing additional stylistic contrast, the Austin Lounge Lizards followed Osiel. The Lounge Lizards are a quintet from Austin who write and perform satirical material. Increasingly the folk music landscape is a site for self-directed as well as social and political humor. Some prominent figures in contemporary folk have attained their relatively lofty status through repertoires steeped in comedy. *Christine Lavin*, for example, combines conventionally simple folk music performance with comedy to further reconfigure performative hierarchies. For Lavin humor is central and music is subordinate, a background setting. Melody and harmony plainly serve a self-conscious wittiness. In contrast the Austin Lounge Lizards are accomplished musicians whose country-western and bluegrass influences stand on equal ground with their comedic lyrics. The songs are intelligent and topical and the settings provide not only musical interest but stylistic consistency as well, which articulates the satirical elements of the lyric.

As I walked back to my campsite that night I passed several groups of campers who appeared to have stayed at their camps rather than attending the concerts in the theater. I recall wondering why people would bother coming to the festival without attending the concerts. Isn't music the point of it all? As I became more thoroughly ensconced in festival culture over the next few weeks, the answer to that question became clear. For many attendees the social aspects of festival life outweigh the formal presentations of music. The festival affords opportunities for extended relaxation during which eating, drinking, and visiting frame selective occasions for listening. As the festival wore on, I found myself adopting this selective mode, traversing the road to the main theater only when a highly recommended artist was scheduled to play. In fact, over the next several years of attending the Kerrville festival, my visits to the theater became less frequent. The most memorable musical experiences occurred in the campgrounds.

On Friday, May 28, I awoke to the sound of loud voices and even louder laughter coming from outside my tent. Several people were sitting in lawn chairs in front of my most immediate neighbor's tent. The group was happily visiting, and occasionally one or more of the revelers would pick up a guitar and entertain the others with a song. A few members of the group acknowledged my presence with a nod or an unenthusiastic "good morning." The campgrounds were beginning to awaken, and the constant din of music pervaded the morning. Many of the players were not professionals, but their enthusiasm for making music was unmistakable and infectious. My first impulse was to attempt to make an ambient recording rather than disturb the spontaneity of the exchange, but the ethics of the situation dictated active involvement. I exited the tent, sat down in a vacant chair next to the singers, and between songs asked if they would object to my recording the proceedings. On the contrary, all seemed flattered by my interest. Apparently word had spread that I was an ethnomusicologist doing research on folk music.[9] What seemed to ingratiate me was my interest in not only the current and upcoming stars of folk, but also the nonprofessionals for whom music plays important roles in coping with everyday life.

While taping songs and conducting unstructured interviews, the general mood of spontaneous expression that had marked the earlier musical exchanges changed. Songs became performances. Other players and listeners joined the once small group, and the discursive field of the morning's project began to extend well beyond the immediate area. At one point an observer said, "Setting up a microphone and recorder around here attracts singer/songwriters like flies to shit." The taping session lasted through most of that afternoon. Camp regulars spread the word and brought artists by to speak with me and have their songs recorded. Some of the crowd seemed to view the interview process in terms of its potential for advancing careers as singer/songwriters, as if the document resulting from the project might spotlight them as individual performers. Others saw it as an opportunity to make public their personal reflections on music and its redemptive power. As an academic conducting research on folk music, I was a curiosity: one who was welcomed into a community, but a curiosity nonetheless. However, as a musician and singer/songwriter the relationship between researcher and subject began to blur. In the folk community at large, I remain an Other, while at the same time a valued member. During the course of that initiation into the social life of the festival, my position as researcher at times became a source of symbolic capital—personal as well as for the camp—and I was frequently invited to elaborate dinners at neighboring camps.[10] Yet a certain reticence regarding the relationship between the studier and the studied and a reverence for the ordinary continues to be evident at times and mirrors an all too common knee-jerk anti-intellectualism.

The paradoxical elements of a folk community, which is for the most part at once educationally privileged but retains the fiction of the common man, continue to inculcate folk discourses. One popular performer who has a bachelor's degree in music commented sarcastically, "Look how much good that's done me." In a brief conversation I had with Pete Seeger, one of folk's patron saints, he proudly stated that he was the one in his family who dropped out of college. However, my own position as an academic and much of the stigma that may have been attached had I been merely an impartial observer were offset by my position as a musician and performer. The commitment to spend nearly three weeks camping in the south Texas summer further ingratiated me to the local community.

After several days of recording, the novelty of the situation diminished to the point that interviews became more candid and less self-consciously performative. During that first week of the festival, a number of common patterns became apparent. The professional players with whom I spoke were, by and large, more heavily influenced by popular music than by the iconic figures from folk's recent or extended past. An overwhelming majority of performers both professional and amateur suggested that listening to Beatles records constituted their earliest musical memories. For those under the age of forty, the records often were part of an older sibling's collection. Of the hundreds of singer/songwriters I interviewed in the course of my research, no more than a handful recalled their earliest exposure to music to be family sing-alongs or other nontechnologically mediated musical practices. The only notable exception was Tao Rodriguez-Seeger who fondly recounted his childhood throughout which music played an important and frequent role. Given Seeger's well-known family investment in music and folk music specifically, his example is not surprising. Yet generally the road to folk music was paved by early exposure to the Beatles and the long line of rock groups that followed.

While most accounts of the popular music landscape in the 1960s position Bob Dylan's songwriting as fundamental to mid-1960s Beatles musical production (for instance, Hibbard and Kaleialoha, *The Role of Rock*, 1983; Kastin, *I Hear America Singing*, 2002; Stuessy and Lipscomb, *Rock and Roll*, 1999), the vast majority of the folkies with whom I spoke began their musical journeys listening to the Beatles and subsequently discovering Dylan's work. That their early musical experiences were almost exclusively mediated by recording industry production speaks to the primacy of that industry in shaping mass aesthetic sensibilities.

For the folk, as for most of the Western world, recordings have become the de facto standard of musical experience. If, as Walter Benjamin famously suggests in his essay "The Work of Art in the Age of Mechanical Reproduction," that loss of "aura" marks a degradation of music's immediacy, it also seems to have had the corresponding effect of elevating the act of music making to an almost sanctified position. The festival is a vehicle through which all manner of participants can immerse themselves in the physical act of making music daily for an extended period. The opportunity to play and sing at any time of the day or night, to find an appreciative audience, or to play simply for one's own enjoyment, is for many a primary motivation for festival attendance. While main stage artists and countless other performers sell and trade their CDs during the festival, actually playing those CDs in anything but a personal player with headphones is forbidden by ranch policy. Any sort of "canned" music is discouraged so as not to interfere with the almost constant music making in the campground. This celebration of music making is, for many Kerrverts, a yearly ritual through which their musical predilections are enacted in concentrated form: when the lack of musical outlets in daily lives can find extended resolution. However, the celebration has a dialectical nature.

By the seventh day of the festival, most of the people there for the duration had been, for a week, staying up until all hours of the morning playing music, listening to music, or unable to sleep due to the persistent noise. Temperatures in the high eighties and low nineties by eight in the morning were enough to drive most campers out of tents and trailers. The lack of sleep, intemperate weather conditions, and nonstop activity began to show.

The night before, after making the rounds of the campfires, I lay on my inflatable mattress and wondered if I could stand another two weeks of relentless strumming, the repetitious, tonal, and thoroughly predictable musics whose cacophonous thunder resonated from the walls of my tent and precluded anything but the most disturbed sleep (at that point I had yet to discover the heady joy of foam earplugs). The egalitarian ideal of folk music as the vehicle for profound expressions of meaning was wearing thin as lack of sleep and a mounting sense of musical sameness permeated my consciousness.

By four or five in the morning musical activity in the campground usually subsides to the point that sleep is possible. However, this is not always the case. If a camper wants to continue playing and singing during the more quiet times of the early morning, it is, except under extreme circumstances, considered acceptable behavior. Rarely is musical sound unacceptable unless it interferes with other musicians and listeners.

The nearly constant sensory input during the first week of the festival, along with lack of sleep, ubiquitous alcohol consumption, and exposure to the elements, dulls the celebratory nature of the event. Festivalgoers who stay for the duration generally begin to pace themselves after the initial celebration, which might last one or two days or for a week or longer. The general mood among participants tends to be subdued after the initial excitement. During midweek, when weekend crowds have left the ranch, the pace is more relaxed and campground activity begins comparatively early. After the opening week of the festival, the main theater is closed Mondays through Thursdays. Each evening, "Sundown Concerts" are held at the Threadgill Theater, a smaller venue than the main theater. The concerts begin at seven p.m. and are generally over by nine. Subsequently, the campfire activities begin some three hours earlier than on the weekends. By the end of the first week, Kerrvirgins have generally become enlightened to what is common knowledge among longtime Kerrverts: the campfire hierarchy.

Campfire Pecking Order

Several established camps at the Kerrville festival, as well as at other festivals, reflect the sort of hierarchies discussed previously in terms of the folk food chain. While in other areas of contemporary folk landscapes the hierarchies may be more implicit, campfire social/musical divisions are often very explicit. Camp Cuisine, so named because of its well-equipped camp kitchen in which elaborate meals are regularly prepared, attracts many of the main stage performers and is noticeably selective regarding contributions to the song circles that take place each evening.

Arriving at Camp Cuisine one night I observed a substantial crowd of listeners around the main song circle area underneath a large orange tarpaulin suspended six or seven feet off the ground by poles and ropes. Some of the better-known main stage performers were seated on folding chairs in a circle, exchanging songs and pleasant conversation. The audience was appreciative of each performer's songs, and the distinction between audience and performers was immediately apparent. It was obvious that this was not a song circle in which casual players were welcome

*to join uninvited. The general attitude of egalitarian participation common at most
song circles was noticeably absent, bringing folk music's socially stratified nature to
the fore.*

The evening circle at Camp Cuisine was one of two by-invitation circles reviled by some for their exclusionary practices yet clearly a source of symbolic
capital within the campground community. Camp Nashville hosts the other
long-established song circle in which unknown, guitar-wielding passersby are
summarily ignored in favor of more high-profile folk personalities.

The reasons for the exclusionary practices at both camps are apparent. By
excluding the unknown players, hosts can maintain a subjective level of musical quality. That the quality may be in large part determined by extramusical
considerations is plain to see. Main stage performers, winners of the New Folk
Competition, and established writers or players are frequently the only performers in these circles. Some of these relatively high-profile artists are accomplished musicians, singers, and writers each demanding recognition by virtue
of professional achievement. Others gain entry through long-standing personal
relationships with the camp's hosts. However, regardless of criteria for inclusion in the high-status song circles at Kerrville, these two camps continue to
elicit strong conflicting reactions among festival participants. Many of the less-
known performers at the festival revile the elitism of the high-profile circles yet
regard inclusion in those same circles as a badge of honor. The attraction/revul-
sion dialectic in evidence speaks to a more generalized and conflicted notion of
folk's discourse of egalitarianism versus its multilayered discourses of power.

In some sense the exclusionary nature of the two aforementioned campfires
may serve practical purposes beyond the subjective determinations of musical
quality. One of the well-established song circles at Kerrville, Camp Stupid,[11]
occasionally provides ammunition for exclusionary arguments. Camp Stupid
is headquartered in a large red and white striped tent under which a considerable number of song circle participants have been known to gather. The camp
offers an inviting egalitarian atmosphere in which seasoned professionals and
absolute beginners may feel equally at home. *Ken Gaines*, a Houston-based
singer/songwriter, is the resident host of Camp Stupid and is a warm and congenial fellow who is also a proficient musician, writer, and singer.

On the weekends particularly, the Camp Stupid song circles may host as many
as thirty singer/songwriters at any given time. It is not unusual to find accomplished musicians, some of whom may be main stage performers, sitting in the
circle next to novices whose playing, singing, and writing skills are minimal.
The less practiced performers have an opportunity to play for an audience that
rewards even incompetent performances with polite applause and words of encouragement. However, Camp Stupid's inclusiveness can have negative conse-

quences in terms of that elusive notion of quality. Oftentimes more advanced musicians are discouraged by the large numbers of song circle participants and move to smaller circles in which the wait time may be considerably less. There have been evenings at Camp Stupid when performers have waited up to an hour and a half to play one song. Depending on one's aesthetic sensibilities and level of musical tolerance, the wait can seem interminable.

While each of the many campfires at the Kerrville Folk Festival has its own personality—personalities that vary according to time of day, weather conditions, and specific participants—making music is the common bond that draws people from all over the country (and the world) year after year. The dynamics of power in hierarchical relationships notwithstanding, Kerrverts see themselves as a community with all the inner rivalries, personal foibles, and individual agendas that characterize human interaction. Through the enactment of this occasional community, participants embody the recalled or reconstructed collective consciousness of imagined pasts and idealized value systems. Angry confrontations are rare, violence is practically nonexistent, and theft is generally limited to helping oneself to an occasional beer from someone else's cooler or a cigarette from a package carelessly left on a camp table. The standard of ethics at Kerrville, as at most of the festivals I have attended, is a curious blend of elements of folk idealism and 1960s "Love Generation" communalism. These ethics of behavior are apparent at many, if not all, American folk festivals, but the dynamics of each may vary greatly. In July 2000 my five-year-old son and I attended the Woody Guthrie Folk Festival in Okemah, Oklahoma, Guthrie's hometown. A relatively recent annual festival, it was considerably smaller in scope than the Kerrville event. The campfire scene was underdeveloped and lacked the sort of organization that characterizes its older Texas cousin, but the festival proved to be a striking example of the folk community's penchant for mythologizing its icons.

As was expected, the event celebrated the life and music of its namesake and featured such folk luminaries as Woody's son, Arlo Guthrie, and Pete Seeger. Most in the long list of performers included at least a token Woody Guthrie song in their sets, and much ado was made of the man's musical and ideological legacy. Within the first day or two, it was clear that memories of Guthrie had far outstripped the man. In the minds of countless festival attendees, Woody Guthrie had achieved sainthood. Festival promoters as well as various local businesses and performers had vested interests in this canonization process.

For festival promoters and local businesses, the event had the potential to highlight Okemah's favorite son and thereby stimulate tourism for the otherwise unremarkable small town. This is not to say that the promoters' motives are entirely mercenary. The politics of tribute are as multifaceted as the politics of folk or any other ideological project. However, the economic benefits of creating heroes can be a substantial motivation. The taverns in which festival-related music events took place following the main stage performances were often crowded to capacity during the five-day event, no doubt a rarity in a town the size of Okemah.

At all activities related to the festival, Guthrie's name was spoken reverently and often. Outside the confines of the festival grounds, townspeople seemed relatively unconcerned. One older man, a grocery store clerk, suggested that he "didn't know what all the fuss was about." He asserted that the elder Guthrie was a good for nothing who was always going off and leaving his family to fend for themselves.[12] This antithetical perspective was somehow a refreshing change from the rampant glorification that was inescapable in the festival and campground areas.

Though economics plays a major role in the tribute festival, it is perhaps the least interesting aspect of the event. The mythologization of Woody Guthrie, conceptually problematic but intriguing, was particularly evident in public accounts by performers whose association with the legendary figure provided a potent source of cultural capital. Pete Seeger took any number of opportunities to recount anecdotes concerning his adventures with Guthrie, reconfigured/recollected in nostalgic detail for eager consumption by the festival audience. The process of establishing Guthrie as an American folk music icon, which began during the man's life, escalated after his death in 1967. Woody Guthrie museums, biographies, documentaries, and even conferences have further mythologized the man in the popular imagination. The generally unconditional celebration of Woody Guthrie as a larger than life figure has become a ubiquitous preoccupation of American folk music journalists and historians, including Ronald Cohen, whose romantic "Woody the Red?", among similar works, serves to reinscribe conventional folk mythology and feed the already corpulent beast of modernist iconic construction. In Pete Seeger's book *The Incompleat Folksinger*, the author's accounts of Guthrie do little to dispel the romanticized recreation of the man or to focus the blurred images of historical recollection: specifically the 1940s and '50s when American folk music's now legendary forebears, either by design or by accident, established the bases for what were to become enduring narratives of the folk. Guthrie has become a cultural commodity through which folk ideals of tradition, the common man, and more general notions of authenticity can be referenced without the possibility of critical reprisal.[13]

The festival presented direct opportunities for folkies to feel some connection to the historical backdrop of today's folk landscape, a backdrop that retains a level of cultural cachet but the nature of which becomes more imaginative as fewer and fewer participants in folk's formative years survive into the twenty-first century. Where the Woody Guthrie Folk Festival represents explicit connections to a historical period in the development of the folk, a number of festivals are less concerned with past indexes of folkness than with its present manifestations.

Falcon Ridge, Seducing the Youth Market

Each year since 1988 the Falcon Ridge Folk Festival has been held at the Long Hill Farm bordering the town of Hillsdale, New York. The festival organizers, Anne Saunders and Howard Randall, through their years of presenting, have developed a well-organized, well-attended three-day annual event. The performers presented at Falcon Ridge are primarily contemporary singer/songwriters. Like the Kerrville festival, Falcon Ridge features a showcase competition for emerging artists, which takes place on the first full day of the festival.

The campfire scene at Falcon Ridge is considerably less developed and plays a less central role than at the Kerrville festival. There are a few large and established song circles, including the "Big Orange Tarp" presided over by Alan Rowoth. At times Rowoth's song circle resembles Kerrville's Camp Cuisine in its exclusionary nature, though not so dramatically hierarchical. However, the most remarkable aspect of the Falcon Ridge festival is the increasing population of listeners who diverge from standard folk audience demographics.

In 1996, Maryl Neff compiled demographic data on the folk that confirms my own informal observations over the past decade. Neff's findings indicate that 91 percent of the respondents were white; 80 percent were between the ages of 35 and 77; 79.6 percent had college educations (with almost half of those holding advanced degrees); and 52.9 percent had incomes of $45,000 or more.

While Falcon Ridge and most folk festivals continue reflecting the aforementioned statistics in most respects, one aspect that appears to be changing is the age group involved. Falcon Ridge seems to be making a concerted effort to attract a younger audience by featuring popular crossover acts such as *Ani DiFranco*. In 2002, DiFranco was booked to play the final set of the festival on Sunday evening. Throughout the weekend a younger than usual crowd comprised roughly a third of the audience. Most in their twenties, the Ani crowd presented an intriguing pastiche: retro hippie, retro punk, heavily pierced and tattooed—popular badges of fashion commitment. Many of these young fans challenged conventional gender roles and sexual modalities through appearance and public behavior: men wearing colorful, flowing Indian-print dresses with off-the-shoulder necklines showing pierced nipples, and openly affectionate gay couples—mostly female—many of whom appeared to be challenging the values of the older and presumably conventionally heterosexual folkies.[14]

Ani's audience aside, each year I see greater numbers of younger attendees at folk festivals. The increasing youth audience may at times reflect booking decisions that serve to attract that audience and may also represent the children of folk's standard audience. Many middle-aged baby boomers have adolescent or young adult children who accompanied their parents to festivals over some length of time. The festival as a community spectacle has, for many of this younger generation from folk families, become a traditional event. Many teenagers and young adults with whom I have spoken at festivals are more interested in the festival as carnival than as a specifically musical event. However, this too is changing. Perhaps through habit or repeated exposure, some of the younger generation are developing interests in folk/acoustic music. The continuing popularization, modernization, and reconfiguration of folk aesthetics will, no doubt, present a rich field of study as reminders of folk's past grow more distant and its future emerges.

Festival Folk and Memories of Minstrelsy

The notion of a changing demographic and the landscape of the folk festival as a gathering of diverse interests stand in stark contrast to one of contemporary folk music's enigmas: the dramatic underrepresentation of people of color. Within the performing community the number of African-Americans and other American minority participants is minimal.[15] *Vance Gilbert*, one of the few successful African-American singer/songwriters on the national circuit, is fond of telling the overwhelmingly white sea of faces at concerts and festivals, "I'm the only chocolate chip in the cookie." Gilbert is a competent guitarist with a powerful, resonant baritone voice, whose stage presence and engaging performance style have made him a favorite among folk audiences.

Besides Gilbert, only a handful of nonwhite artists are regular participants in festival events and folk concerts in general. *Ruthie Foster*, a Texas-based black singer/songwriter has become a regular festival performer in the past few years, as have *Tom Prasada-Rao* and *Guy Davis*, whose concert schedule seems more active than his festival dates. *Kim and Reggie Harris* are relatively popular folk circuit performers whose performances and material often recollect the political nature of folk's revival history.

That American folk music's history is steeped in African-American musical contributions is plain to see. Leadbelly, the Reverend Gary Davis, Mississippi

John Hurt, and scores of other black singer/songwriters provided the white icons of today's singer/songwriter traditions with inspiration and influence. This is not to say that Anglo-American artists and traditions have not also exerted important influence. Rather it is to acknowledge the pivotal role that black artists played in the development of American folk music and the singer/songwriter phenomenon specifically. That African-Americans are so underrepresented in the contemporary folk world seems incongruous given their central role in folk's history. Clearly the politics of race and power were at stake in the associations between black artists and folk's early power brokers. Benjamin Filene suggests this in *Romancing the Folk,* as do Charles Wolfe and Kip Lornell in *The Life and Legend of Leadbelly.* Both accounts document the relationship between John and Alan Lomax and Leadbelly and situate it in terms of relative positions of power and privilege. The inequitable relations of power reflected in the Lomax/Leadbelly relationship represent what were considered liberal attitudes toward race in the given historical context, attitudes that would not be considered particularly liberal with regard to current notions of power and race.[16] Yet in each account, Leadbelly's associations with white folksingers in the 1940s proved to be highly influential to the white performers' development. However, regardless of the historical debt owed to African-American folk forebears, today's singer/songwriter landscape is decidedly pale.

Some have suggested that covert racial prejudice plays an implicit role in this imbalance. While the folk community vocally supports racial equity and diversity, there is little doubt that notions of the racial Other linger, in many cases almost subliminally, manifestations of which are apparent in the Tyrone controversy discussed in chapter 3. Performances at folk festivals—as primarily white enterprises—accentuate these persistent reminders of difference.

On Sunday, 29 July 2001, I awoke at the Falcon Ridge Folk Festival to a bright, cloudless day. As the first organized musical event of the day, the Gospel Wake-Up Call began on the main stage at the bottom of the large hill upon which I was camped. For this regular feature of the festival several performers who have played the main stage during the course of the weekend gather on Sunday morning to sing gospel songs. The manner in which these performers chose to sing recalled the sorts of performances one might hear at any number of black Southern Baptist churches. That is, the singers imitated black religious singing in obvious ways: improvisatory solo exclamations interspersed with call-and-response sections in which the singers emulated the vocal characteristics of black gospel singers.

Yet all the performers were white and the mimetic performance, while apparently enjoyed thoroughly by all involved, left a sense of unease. Given the overwhelmingly white audience and the virtual absence of black faces in any of the festival's contexts, the performance took on an undertone of caricature, one that Eric Lott might call, "an affair of copies and originals, theft and love" (*Love and Theft*, 40).

The associations of blackface minstrelsy were difficult to ignore in light of the mimetic presentation that constituted the Gospel Wake-Up Call. Unlike white blues preservationists whose acts are often like musical/historical snapshots of performances that may have occurred some fifty to seventy years ago, the singer/songwriters who made up the Gospel Wake-Up Call seemingly had no historical stake in the re-creation of the gospel concert. Black gospel groups usually sing in the context of religious services,[17] and the setting of the festival as a decidedly secular event exacerbated a sense of parody. The show seemed a superficial enactment of an imagined cultural context that completely lacked experiential, historical/epistemological, or religious grounding. Eric Lott states, "The minstrel show was, on the one hand, a socially approved context of institutional control; and, on the other, it continually acknowledged and absorbed black culture even while defending white America against it" (ibid.). In the context of the folk festival, at which the vast majority of the audience and all of the performers on stage were white, Lott's comments are particularly apropos. Mimesis as defense against the Other aside for the moment, we must turn our attention to the acknowledgement and absorption of black culture. The Gospel Wake-Up Call, simply by virtue of its presentation on the festival stage that Sunday morning, constitutes a general acknowledgement of black Americans' contributions to the folk music landscape. Yet that none of the participants in this performance were black raises an important question. Was the performance doing honor to the musical style—and implicitly to black America—or did it constitute another episode in what can be seen as the historical process of co-opting black expressive culture: a process that perhaps began when T. D. Rice first "jumped Jim Crow" in the early nineteenth century?[18] The Gospel Wake-Up Call was indeed a wake-up call for a folk community whose appropriations sometimes reference an "American Popular" in which the sinister side of mimesis played the central role.

However, references to the minstrel show in the performance of the white, apparently middle-class gospel singers at the festival were, for most of the audience, surreptitious codes concealed in an external celebration of sameness. Michael Taussig, in *Mimesis and Alterity: A Particular History of the Senses* (1993), suggests that "mimesis registers both sameness and difference, of being like, and of being Other. Creating stability from this instability is no small task, yet all identity formation is engaged in this habitually bracing activity in which the issue is not so much staying the same, but maintaining sameness through alterity" (129). Following Taussig, Barbara Fuchs proposes in *Mimesis and Empire*

(2001) that this dance of difference and sameness—the concept of mimesis—is "the fun-house mirror, the reflection that dazzles, the impersonator, the sneaky copy, the double agent—mimesis, that is, as a deliberate performance of sameness that necessarily threatens, or at least modifies, the original" (5). The modification of the "original" that occurred during the Wake-Up Call was one in which the performers and the audience were at once complicit and presumably unaware. It seems unlikely, given the folk's overt celebration of diversity, that the performers' mimetic adoption of black vocal inflections and performance style represented self-consciously sinister motives. Still the legacy of inequity embedded in the black American experience readily allows readings in which history renders intent meaningless.

The temptation is great to subsume the appropriative process at the Wake-Up Call under what Dave Laing has called the cultural imperialism thesis ("The Music Industry and the 'Cultural Imperialism' Thesis"). However, to do so implies an oversimplification and, as Laing rightfully suggests, negates the notion of agency. Christopher Waterman, in his essay on Bo Chatmon and the song "Corrine, Corinna," says, "The analysis of such forms, and of the circumstances of their production and reception, can help us to understand musicians and audiences not as instances of idealized types, but as human beings working under particular historical conditions to produce, texture, and defend certain modes of social existence" ("Race Music," 168). Perhaps the particular historical conditions and ideological positions under which the Falcon Ridge performers were operating served to moderate the implicit racial inferences in the performance. However, Waterman's essay deals with the appropriation of a specific song recorded and reinvented by various artists. This situates his argument in a somewhat different light. In the appropriation of a particular style of music and performance, the reconfiguration and re-presentation of a historically racialized expressive form must either do honor to that form (if indeed that position is tenable at all) or become caricature. The distinctions between the two are not always readily apparent. Yet the extent to which musics associated with African-Americans, particularly gospel and blues, have become part of a popular and perhaps raceless musical habitus—and as such are so thoroughly ingrained as to be inextricable from all popular musical production—is obvious and has been thoroughly explored in recent years (see Charlton, *Rock Music Styles*; Evans, "Blues and Modern Sound"; Garofalo, *Rockin' the Boat*; Stuessy and Lipscomb, *Rock and Roll*; Szatmary, *Rockin' in Time*).

While African and African-American musical contributions are not in dispute, what is in dispute are the ways in which performative enactments such as the Gospel Wake-Up Call index a musical semiotics of race. Like the "musical semiotics of gender" that Susan McClary suggests was a conscious construction of seventeenth-century opera composers—"a set of conventions for constructing 'masculinity' or 'femininity' in music" (*Feminine Endings*, 7)—the concept of a popular music semiotics of race presents problems. While certain elements in much contemporary popular music can be directly or indirectly attributed to African and African-American contributions—so-called blue notes, syncopated rhythms, and even the ubiquitous rock and roll backbeat, for example—their use has become so widespread that claims to specific cultural or racial or ethnic ownership seem disingenuous. McClary contends that the codes through which the musical semiotics of gender are manifest change through time. The same would apply to any musical semiotics of race. As codes initially perceived as indexing race become deeply embedded in a generalized popular musical habitus, they lose their racial/symbolic signification (or that signification changes). Unquestionably certain performance practices, vocal inflections and affectations, and types of music continue to index race: some obviously and others not so obviously. Whether racial/musical codes can constitute a distinct semiotic system exceeds the scope of this project. However, in the case of the Wake-Up Call, the stylistic coding through which gospel music was re-presented to the festival audience seemed perilously close to the surface.

Through this apparently unself-conscious negotiation of racial positions, the Falcon Ridge gospel show reflected a contemporary folk landscape in which conventional "liberal" ideas about race that may be regularly reinscribed in folk discourses—the association of folk with the civil rights movement in the 1960s, for example—continue to serve more as idealized precepts than applicable constituents of life experience. White folkies of the world can march for racial equality but will never really know what it's like to be black. That situation is unlikely to be dramatically altered as long as the folk landscape continues to be primarily the domain of the white middle-class. That generally it is so presents the question of why people of color are noticeably underrepresented.

Recently Glenn Drinkwater asked gospel musician Chuck Campbell, a virtuoso steel guitarist and member of the Campbell Brothers band, a similar question. Drinkwater wondered why so few African-Americans seem interested in the solo blues guitar and vocal styles popular in the 1920s and '30s, precisely the music that has captivated so many younger white blues preservationists. Campbell replied that those styles are considered "old man music." The rest of his explanation implied that most African-Americans consider the old-fashioned music of the solo bluesmen to be a relic of the past, a past not to be celebrated but consigned to its historical context.[19] Similarly the contemporary folk landscape apparently has little to offer African-Americans. Its reconstructions of the past are of a white past, one that simply does not speak to most black Americans.

The history of Anglo-American engagement with black folk musicians may further explain the apparent lack of interest most blacks have shown for contemporary folk music. Beginning with the Lomaxes in the 1930s, finding "authentic" folk music performers, particularly black folksingers, and introducing them into the white mainstream public eye became a trend that continued to gather steam, perhaps culminating during folk's commercial heyday in the early 1960s. Scholars and such venerable institutions as the Library of Congress combed the hinterlands of the country, looking for authentic vernacular examples of American folk culture. Black performers such as Leadbelly, Mississippi John Hurt, Elizabeth Cotton, Mance Lipscomb, and Big Joe Williams reaped the obvious benefits of these expeditions, but there was a price to pay. In the ideological project to construct a national folk heritage, these men and women were put on display (and exoticized, as Filene points out) for primarily white audiences by exclusively white power brokers waving the flag of cultural pluralism. The artists themselves remained subordinate to the cause and to the ideologues whose positions of privilege allowed for their magnanimity.[20]

While the American folk's formative past suggests a restrained (and constrained) discourse of difference, its reflective present speaks to the concerns of its audience through musical, textual, and thematic conventions that may, as Eric Lott suggests, defend that audience against the possible encroachment of difference. That defense may in part explain why the festival presenters chose not simply to hire a black gospel group for the Wake-Up Call.[21]

Conclusion

The folk festival presents a vivid microcosmic arena in which the grand and not so grand narratives of the folk all come into play within geographically and temporally bounded contexts. The conflicted and intersecting spheres of egalitarian idealism and hierarchical social strata, inclusion and exclusion, tradition and the popular, aesthetics and commodity, converge in an imaginative spectacle of the Ordinary. Above all, for many attendees the events mark focal points in their lives: times when, emancipated from the constraints of the everyday, they celebrate community through the common bond of music.

A conversation I recall hearing late one evening at the Falcon Ridge Folk Festival concerned the notion of the folk and the role of the festival. The temperature that night, despite the late July date, was quite chilly. Two men stood around a large metal barrel in which a wood fire burned. One fellow, whom I have seen at the festival each time I have attended, explained the attraction the event held for him. He asserted that the friendships made at the festival were like a family relationship: "You might not see these people all year until the next festival, but then it's like you have never been apart."

Clearly folk and family ties provide the rose-colored lens of the imagination. In recent years festivals have attempted to extend the communal ideals of the folk to the global stage by regularly featuring non-Western performers. This trend toward considering world music part of a global folk music community, as well as folk's general association with non-Western musics, has a long and contested history. However, as the following chapter will show, its present manifestations further blur already ambiguous notions of high and low, popular and folk, and present complicated webs of signification in which representational uncertainty is the only certainty.

In the jungle, the quiet jungle

The lion sleeps tonight

—"Wimoweh," lyrics by Hugo Peretti and Luigi Creatore

7 Music for Export
"World Music," Folk, and the Global Imagination

Folk's engagement with global musical exchange has been well documented at least since the 1950s when Pete Seeger and the Weavers released a number of songs from various non-Western parts of the world. The Weavers' commercial success with songs like Solomon Linda's "Mbube" (released as "Wimoweh" in 1952), "Tzena, Tzena, Tzena," and "Guantanamera" implied not only that these appropriations were a type of benign international exchange, but also that their performance by popular Western artists was a form of cultural altruism. Popularizing these songs in the West was considered a good thing for all involved. The Weavers' position as liberal intellectual folksingers was enhanced by the inclusion of multinational repertoires, and the cultures from which the songs originated were spotlighted in the Western world arena. However, the relations of power that marked these exchanges/appropriations are disturbing at many levels.

The popular press, and often academic literature as well, tend to locate the primary issues surrounding cultural/musical appropriations in economic contexts: how much money is generated and who gets it. One of the better documented examples of this sort of economic analysis made its way into the public sphere in a *Rolling Stone* article entitled "In the Jungle" (25 May 2000). The author, Rian Malan, documents the appropriation of Solomon Linda's[1] "Mbube" by Pete Seeger and the Weavers, its subsequent popularity, and multiple rereleases by the Tokens, Glen Campbell, Brian Eno, R.E.M., and others. Malan contends that Linda's share in the popular success of "Mbube/Wimoweh/The Lion Sleeps Tonight" amounted to some twelve thousand dollars, out of approximately fifteen million the song has generated in composer royalties since 1952.

Beyond the economic implications of "Mbube/Wimoweh," the musical development of the song in its different versions illustrates a highly charged symbolic field in which the violence done to Linda's original piece further reinscribes contested and inequitable power relations between the West and Africa. That is, the issue shifts from conventional notions of cultural imperialism to a more convoluted and complicated process in which "plundering and counterfeiting of black culture" denies the racial authenticities claimed by their "token act of equal exchange to the original" (Erlmann, *Music Modernity, and the Global Imagination*, 264).

"Mbube/Wimoweh/The Lion Sleeps Tonight" is but one example of folk's engagement with non-Western cultural appropriation. Its relationship with Africa—the "dark continent"—marks it as a particularly palpable case of folk's continuing attraction to the musical Other. However, the fascination with the Other permeates folk's history in less obvious ways.

Since the early twentieth century, folk's cultural intermediaries have played upon racial/cultural otherness and the historical imagination to authenticate and sometimes exoticize folk music. Indeed the entire history of folk music in the past century is rife with examples of cultural and historical appropriations through which folk authenticities have been claimed or laid siege to. The most apparent of these is, of course, the early to mid-twentieth-century white intellectual preoccupation with the folk music of black America. This fascination with the Other, while most recently defined by its non-Westernness, is at the very core of the American folk's construction of a musical heritage, a heritage in which imagined pasts—the historical Other—fashioned a mythology that conflated sameness and difference. The taming of the West, the building of transnational railroads, cattle drives—the stuff of collections such as the 1938 Lomax compilation *Cowboy Songs and Other Frontier Ballads*—are all part of the cultural coding of historical and rural ideals that first determined folkness for a decidedly bourgeois American audience. The experiential contexts were the stuff of romantic fiction for most of that audience even during those first few decades of the century. By the beginning of the twenty-first century, the relics of these grand folk narratives—particularly the association with a frontier past—mark the process of historical othering in which the American folk is steeped. Where history (and the racial Other) provided much of the formative material for early constructions of national musical identity, world music has become the contemporary folk's exotic bedfellow.

The American folk have, albeit sometimes reluctantly, embraced world music as a kindred soul. Just plain folks are still just plain folks even if they don't wear flannel shirts or sing in English. In the past decade, quite a few singer/songwriters from non-Western cultures have established themselves within the contexts of folk circuits in the United States. Folk Alliance showcases frequently include international musicians interspersed with more conventional American folksingers, and many of these travelers increasingly tour the coffeehouses, folk festivals, and concert series of this country. In and of itself, this phenomenon appears to be, at least in part, a result of technological advancements in communications and transportation.

Since the demise of the Soviet Union and the subsequent multiplication of interconnections between world cultures, travel has become more accessible to more people than ever before. The relative ease with which singer/songwriters negotiate the global landscape has increased American awareness of the world in some remarkable ways, yet it also presents thorny issues in terms of shifting contexts and perspectives of the international folk. The "exotic" is, and has long been, a salable commodity for the American folk audience. When music's exotic non-Westernness is integral to an artist's stock and trade, that very same non-Westernness presents a complex investment in a politics of image.

On 17 March 2002, a South African group, Sharon Katz and the Peace Train, played a concert for a church-based concert series in Schoharie, New York. The concert took place on a Sunday afternoon and was attended by approximately fifty people. The group consisted of the front person, Sharon Katz, on lead vocals and acoustic and electric guitars; Kozee, the backup vocalist; Lynn Riley on alto saxophone; Sylvester Bryant on electronic keyboards; Darren Keith on drums (trap set); and Junius Pop Wilson on electric six-string bass. The group's presence was striking on various levels. That a South African group playing plugged-in electric instruments and a drum set was performing for what is ordinarily a folk music series illustrated the new folk's widening view of its own stylistic boundaries. That the group consisted of three white performers and three black performers was unusual in that, as mentioned previously, the American folk landscape is not exactly brimming with dark faces.

The group's symmetrical multiethnic makeup seemed symbolic of the message Katz reiterated at length between songs: that they were representatives of the new South Africa, which is happily healing the wounds of colonialism.[2] The notion of folk music's uplifting or redemptive qualities is a recurring theme, not only in terms of folk's globalized nature, but also for the more pedestrian, everyday folk. Katz's performance painted an optimistic picture of what is a complicated and contested situation. The music was lively, generally cheerful, and mixed a folkie sensibility of uplifting songs with a pop/jazz musical setting. Clearly the optimism was appreciated by a Sunday afternoon upstate New York audience whose primary goal was to be entertained. Between-song patter about inequities of power and continuing ruptures in South African society would likely have guaranteed no return engagements for the Peace Train. It would also be counterproductive to the group's conflated message of exoticism and inclusion.

Most of the group wore colorful outfits that emphasized their Africanness. The bright, cheerful designs of fabrics worn by Katz and other members of the band underscored the generally light, unproblematic, and cheery musical message. Yet those same designs and the clear attempt to Africanize/exoticize their performance image present some of the same problems that ethnomusicologists have been grappling with at least since the 1986 release of Paul Simon's album *Graceland*.

For Paul Simon, Ladysmith Black Mambazo lent his project an exoticism welcomed by American and international popular music audiences. Joseph Shabalala's group dressed in colorful African patterns and the performative exchange between the group and Simon painted a powerful picture of egalitarian inclusion coupled with the appeal of the exotic—the cultural and musical Other. Jocelyne Guilbault has suggested that the label "world music" "ends up being implicitly associated with musics from Africa and the African diaspora" ("Beyond the 'World Music' Label," 2). Simon cemented this idea into popular consciousness. Sharon Katz and the Peace Train reinforced it with the celebration of their own exotic Africanness. Indeed it is Katz's Africanness that is a primary locus for the group's marketing.

A picture on Katz's Web site depicts the artist dressed in a colorful African print dress, strumming her guitar amidst a group of smiling black dancers. The image of Katz surrounded by black faces and bodies suggests a number of conflicted discourses of postcolonialism. Again we are confronted by the exotic other on the one hand with a clear message of inclusion on the other hand. The celebratory nature of the depicted experience mirrors Katz's overall social/political stance as evidenced by her musical and textual discourses.

Yet there are a number of subtexts to the image. Katz as the central figure, playing the music to which the others dance, echoes this dialectics of exoticism and the familiar. She is the lone white face, which stands out as either the exotic—if taken in the context of the larger group in the picture—or as the island of normalcy surrounded by the Other. The dancers with their arms lifted, as if in praise, frame the centrally located Katz. Certainly, without intentionally doing so, Katz reinscribes the colonial notion that posits blacks as wards of the benevolent white architects of society: that oppressed blacks need whites to lead them out of their miserable station in life.

The image also indexes notions of the black body as a site for enactment of physicality: the dancers' bodies in motion surrounding the relatively inert figure of Katz with her guitar. The cross-racial attraction/revulsion dialectic implied by the image of Katz surrounded by dancing dark bodies revisits themes of the minstrel stage.

The image is reminiscent of an early 1990s film set in World War II–era South Africa entitled *The Power of One* (1992). It comes to mind not only because of similar implications of colonial ideals, but because the climactic moments of the film involve a choral performance in which imprisoned South Africans of several tribes are united by music and lyrics written by the two central characters—P.K., played by Stephen Dorff, and Professor von Vollensteen, played by Armin Mueller-Stahl. Professor von Vollensteen, a German music professor, was imprisoned for failing to register as a German at the outset of the war. P.K., a precocious British youngster displaced by his parents' deaths and marginalized by his classmates in the Dutch Afrikaans school to which he was sent, found in the German professor a mentor and guardian.

The film's characters and the development of the story are predictable, if superficially pleasant. The film's primary agenda is to highlight the inequities of power in mid-twentieth-century South Africa. The white prison guards, the Dutch Nazi students in the boarding school, the Afrikaner politicos, are all patently evil. The central black character, Geel Piet, played by Morgan Freeman, is predictably wise and thoughtful, as are the two primary white characters.

Perhaps the most striking moment in the film occurs when P.K. is leading the prison chorus. The image of Stephen Dorff, the very young, blond, and very white protagonist, bouncing up and down while conducting the massive black chorus, illustrates one of popular culture's least appealing qualities: an almost absolute lack of critical distance. The scene depicts what is intended to be an empowering moment for black South Africans, a moment in which music and raised voices make a bold statement of resistance. However, the leader and focal character is the benevolent, white British character. It is a similar insensitivity to the residual cultural remnants of colonialism that marked the Peace Train performance.

For *The Power of One*, as for Sharon Katz and the Peace Train, the obvious intent is to enlighten the audience as to South Africa's troubled past and comment on its potential for racial equity and equality. Clearly, Katz is committed to a project of healing the wounds of her troubled homeland, and she has been an active proponent/practitioner of music therapy in the service of that end. However, for Katz, as for John G. Avildsen, the director of *The Power of One*, and as for Pete Seeger, whose appropriation of "Mbube" marked the American folk's most publicized initial foray into the music of the world, good intentions are sometimes belied by unfortunate legacies.

Mr. Jones: Pfarrkirchen Is a Long Way from Lukenbach

"At the same time that world music is homogenizing and human diversity is shrinking, clearly the mark of the new, the exciting, the revitalized, the 'long distance call' is still the mark of otherness . . ." (Feld, "Notes on World Beat," 36).

In May of 2000, while attending the Kerrville Folk Festival, I met *Mr. Jones*. My friend Harold Hedberg introduced me to Jones and his traveling companion, a pleasant young woman in her twenties. Mr. Jones, whose real name is Jürgen Bichlmeier, is a singer/songwriter from Pfarrkirchen, Germany. A German singer/songwriter might not seem particularly noteworthy. However, Mr. Jones presents a complicated example of mimesis and the imagined Other. In appearance Jones is hardly unusual: the well-worn blue jeans, T-shirt, and cowboy boots do not set him apart from anyone at any American folk festival. He has a medium build, medium length brown hair, and a light growth of facial hair. Bichlmeier's command of spoken English was, at the time, as halting as my own command of German, which made conversation between us difficult.

After our initial brief meeting, Harold explained that Jürgen was a singer/songwriter who performed under the name Mr. Jones, emulating the sort of Texas singer/songwriter style characterized by Eric Taylor, Townes Van Zandt, and others. Again in itself the mimetic character of this sort of appropriation seemed relatively common, reminiscent of young white country blues emulators, Japanese Salsa ensembles, or any student "ethno" ensemble playing non-Western music "with an American accent." As I was to observe later that night, Jones's performative mimesis takes the imaginative interrelations of space and cultural identity to a different level.

Sometime in the wee hours of the next morning, I was sitting in a song circle at Camp Stupid when Ken Gaines introduced Mr. Jones to the group. With merely a nod, Jones began playing what seemed like a conventional strummed guitar introduction. He proceeded to sing a convincingly Texas-style folk song, his south Texas drawl adding a familiar country inflected twang to the piece. When he was finished, the other singer/songwriters in attendance gave him a polite round of applause. For all but Gaines and myself, Jürgen might just as well have been another fairly competent singer/songwriter from any of a thousand small Texas towns. But Pfarrkirchen is a long way from Lukenbach.

There are a number of differences and similarities between this performative transformation from Jürgen Bichlmeier to Mr. Jones and the musical/stylistic simulations by contemporary bluesmen, ethno ensembles, and various intercultural mimes. Like the modern country bluesmen, Jones imitates a specific acoustic style of playing and singing. However, the country blues style is grounded temporally and historically in the first half of the twentieth century.[3] The Texas folk style that Bichlmeier emulates, while deriving stylistic characteristics from country and folk styles of the past, has no such clearly framed historical boundaries. Rather, it is an amalgam of popular styles that have developed primarily over the past half-century.

Some contemporary white bluesmen adopt the vocal character of their early black forebears, with idiomatic accents, inflections, and growling affectations. Yet for all the imitation, the semantic frame presents no significant boundary. However, for Bichlmeier, whose conversational English was minimal, the simulation presented a situation similar to the student singing phonetically in an ethno ensemble. The imitation of idiomatic Texan semantics is an act of not only speaking in a foreign language but also simulating the characteristic regional accent. Yet Jones writes the lyrics as well, composing music and text within the stylistic restrictions of very localized traditions.

In personal correspondence that I received from Bichlmeier, dated 8 November 2002, he writes about the process of translation that occurs when he composes English lyrics.

Of course the reason for singing in English first of all was because all my heroes sang in English. But I didn't continue this and start writing in English because it might sell better or at least have a larger market. Whenever I sit down with my guitar tryin' to find words for a song they come to me in English. Not all fluently, and it's not that I sit down and the words flow and there is the song. It needs hard work, but I guess that is the same for American writers too. You don't just sing it and it's perfect. You rethink it, try to be as intense as you can be, try to be as good as you can with every single line. So rework is done to the lines that flow out in the first place, even though [they] are great at the time they first come along. But I never sit down and think about it in German and then translate. Probably because I've heard so many English songs this just sounds so much better to my musical ear. I cannot make things rhyme in German and feel comfortable with it. I only know one or two German writers that I think can really do it, but I just can't write like they do.

From my first to my third record I think that my writing has become a lot better. People in England during the most recent tour told me that they love my lyrics. And that's a good sign, isn't it? In 2000 in Kerrville there was this guy from West Texas who asked me where in his neighborhood I came from after he heard me sing. And after a short conversation he was able to tell I'm not an American. I think it's different if you work it out, write it down and sing it, or if you talk to somebody. After two more years in the States I must say that . . . my English is a lot better, there's less of an accent and there's less feelin' "uncomfortable" as you put it—with conversation. So when I talk in English now it's not that I translate in my head. I just speak and only if I run out of words—I mean if there's something I want to say and don't know the word—then there's a stop in my talk and that might make me suspicious of not being a native speaker.

Since our first contact, Bichlmeier's English skills have improved dramatically. It remains to be seen how the effects of an increasing fluency color his writing process. To date his songs present a fascinating interplay of cultural similarities and differences made manifest in idiomatic language.

Like Jack Williams, who chose to reference the "wild and free" spaces of Colorado, Mr. Jones does so with his song "Colorado." The song begins with an extended guitar and harmonica introduction that establishes a mood of melancholic nostalgia. As Jones sings the opening lines of the lyric, the tangled web of signification is apparent only to listeners with a grasp of the Jones/Bichlmeier context of the performance.

> *Colorado*
> Grew up in Corpus Christi
> There I spent my life
> I met young Nancy
> She became my wife
> We raised three children
> One just turned forty-five
>
> Chorus:
> One day I'll ride the cold wind up to Colorado
> Yes I'll ride the cold wind up to Colorado
>
> Lost my job
> In nineteen sixty eight
> My kids were starving
> And I was afraid
> Got me another job
> That just barely paid

Chorus

Five years later
Yes I saw some snow
I longed for more of that
But I could not go
Up to the hills
Where oaks and pine trees grow

Chorus

The eighties went too fast
Now I'm all alone
The dusty winds
They hit me to the bone
My beating heart
Must now have turned to stone

Chorus

Now I'm old
And I'm waiting for to die
Please teach my ashes
How they're gonna fly
Then a wind will come
And carry me up high
And I'll ride the cold wind up to Colorado
Yes I'll ride the cold wind up to Colorado
Yes I'll ride the cold wind up to Colorado

That the lyric claims Corpus Christi as home establishes an immediate link to the Texas landscape from which Bichlmeier draws inspiration. He indexes the authenticity of experience through referencing the protagonist's relative age; one of his three children "just turned forty-five." The tribulations of losing his job and the message of loss and longing references a general sense of regret and an apparently unfulfilled notion of redemption in the imaginary Colorado.

Yet idiomatic inconsistencies in the lyrics hint at the subtle process of cultural appropriation that underlies the song's composition. The first small inconsistency occurs in the third verse. Referencing the attraction of the Colorado landscape, Jones sings, "But I could not go / Up to the hills / Where oaks and pine trees grow." That oak trees are not a feature of Colorado mountain topography may be chalked up to artistic license. However, as a clue to the underlying mimetic process, it suggests a free use of generally appropriate signifiers, whose specific referents are somewhat skewed. In the fourth verse a similar inconsistency provides additional semantic markers. Jones sings, "The dusty winds / They hit me to the bone." The phrase "hit me to the bone" implies the German *schlagen* or *treffen*, both more nuanced and multifunctional than the English "hit." In English "hit me to the bone" seems vague and misplaced, a conflation of phrases such as "hit me hard" and "cut me to the bone" that a songwriter might use only if hard-pressed for a rhyme.

Still Jones's colloquial accent and stylistic character are convincing enough that for the casual listener, the semantic markers of translation perhaps seem more like weak lines in an otherwise conventionally competent piece than subterranean symbols of the linguistic Other. Jones is not simply aping Texas singer/songwriters for academic or economic reasons. Rather Jürgen Bichlmeier is heavily invested in the personal construction of self that is Mr. Jones. They seem destined to coalesce, drawing newly configured boundaries between public and personal identities. Jones expresses personal and public meanings through the semiotic content of language. That is, the lyrics of his songs must in themselves carry semantic weight recognizable to their listeners. However, in terms of global cultural representations and misrepresentations, the webs of signification attached to language are not always so easily defined.

Performing the Imaginary Other

Rich Prezioso and Jacquie Manning, a Chicago-based husband and wife duo who perform as Small Potatoes and are quite popular in the national folk circuit, recorded a song, "Mad Mouth," that presents a peculiar sort of "depthlessness," to use Fredric Jameson's term. They sing the song entirely in vocables, simulating canntaireachd, or mouth music, originally a vocal technique for learning bagpipe tunes. The song was inspired by a trip to the United Kingdom.

Canntaireachd takes a great deal of time to learn, and Small Potatoes, whose repertoire is quite diverse, traversing stylistic ground from Western swing to jazz to folk to Mexican ballads and more, did not pretend to have studied the technique to mastery. Rather, they constructed their own linguistic field resembling the technique that so appealed to their aesthetic sensibilities, creating a chain of overtly random signifiers that references mouth music—which in itself represents a simulation of bagpipes—but in a superficial play of signification. Yet the tune in performance is very appealing to their audiences, who for the most part couldn't care less about the authenticity of the musical materials. Manning and Prezioso's musicianship and engaging stage personae frame what is an aesthetically compelling piece of music and performance. The Celtic references effectively convey mood and meaning that is exotic while simultaneously indexing a familiar imagined Anglo-European heritage,[4] all within the framework of the popular music foundation of the contemporary folk's public memory. Small Potatoes chooses material that the couple finds musically interesting. The play of intercultural images in some of their material is highlighted by skilled musicianship and, at the same time, relegated to an "art of the surface" in terms of semantic signifiers. This vague interplay of musical/aesthetic meaning and language as sounds reinforcing the musical material presents a decidedly accessible, nonthreatening exoticism, a cornerstone of contemporary folk's discourses of difference. For contemporary singer/songwriters, the trade in difference often belies the relatively homogeneous cultural backgrounds of their constituency.

Tom Prasada-Rao is a popular fixture on the contemporary folk landscape and one of the few folksingers of color on the national circuit. He was born in Ethiopia of Indian parents and was educated in the United States, England, and India. Each time I have heard Prasada-Rao at folk festivals or concerts, his ethnicity is used to introduce him to audiences. The commodity of difference serves the artist by inscribing visual codes—Prasada-Rao's performance attire indexes either his own cultural background or some less specific non-Western exotic Other—that set him apart from the common-man conventions of folk fashion. Beyond visual expressions of otherness, Prasada-Rao appears to play on popular assumptions regarding the spiritual exoticism of the East. Many of his songs tend toward uplifting feel-good themes that reference a somewhat vague nondenominational spirituality. This is not to say that he is insincere in expressing a spiritual connection with music. This idea has taken on a life of its own throughout the histories of Western and non-Western musics. Rather, his subtle and overt references to Indian mysticism serve to reinscribe popular cultural imaginative constructions.

Yet the general stylistic character of Prasada-Rao's music is conventionally Western and tonal. Consonant harmonic developments using traditional Western voice leadings, mellifluous melodic material, and a smooth American-sounding voice provide contrast to Prasada-Rao's visual otherness. The relationship between sameness and otherness that defines Prasada-Rao's public persona is but one of many examples of how today's folk negotiate a balance of the exotic and the familiar. The exotic Other is never presented as musically, personally, or ethnically threatening: the familiar is almost exclusively presented in terms of a musical dependence upon clear, predictable, consonant tonal characteristics.

Contemporary singer/songwriters have become cultural and musical tourists who rarely give more than perfunctory notice to boundaries of style, genre, space, language, or culture. The ease with which they negotiate geographic space mirrors an increasingly free exchange of global popular music resources.

The problematics of these exchanges vary depending upon the relative positions of the actors. For example, when Jürgen Bichlmeier, a white European singer/songwriter, appropriates a Texas songwriting and performing style, the exchange seems relatively benign. Likewise when Jeff Lang, an Australian slide guitar virtuoso, played Mississippi Fred McDowell's "61 Highway" at the 2002 Falcon Ridge Folk Festival in Hillsdale, New York, the appropriation of blues stayed within familiar and comfortable boundaries. Lang is white, personable, and speaks English, albeit with enough Australian accent to warrant a degree of exotic capital. When Third World performers assimilate Western popular musics into their performances, they are either denounced as sellouts to the cultural imperialism of the West or celebrated as world beat ambassadors of new diversities.[5] When Western artists appropriate musical materials from the Third World, the exchanges are often perceived in a less sympathetic light. Criticisms of such exchanges are ordinarily framed in terms of economics or symbolic violence. In cases involving folk musicians and their Third World appropriations, the artists most often appear either devious or naive or some combination of the two. In terms of increasingly globalized cultural interconnections, a generalized folk naïveté seems to prevail, which locates appropriative strategies squarely in the realm of aesthetic subjectivities.

While the global interconnections that inform contemporary folk aesthetics and identities may resonate with the call of the exotic or the lure of reinvented selves, the more central appeal lies in unproblematic aesthetic choices. That is, contemporary singer/songwriters, like their folkie forebears, make appropriative choices that may eschew critical thinking in favor of a generalized feel-good folk authenticity. When Jürgen Bichlmeier fell in love with the music of Texas singer/songwriters, it was the sounds, the messages, and the overall aesthetic that inspired him to model his own cultural output in that image. When Pete Seeger "discovered" the recording of Solomon Linda's "Mbube" and took it for his own use or when Paul Simon "discovered" Ladysmith Black Mambazo and introduced isicathamiya to Western popular music consumers, they did so because the sounds they heard were intriguing and aesthetically appealing.

That ethnomusicologists and critical theorists perceive such appropriations as arrogance or as sinister reinscriptions of colonial power relations likely comes as a surprise to these folk/pop stars. After all, the free exchange of musical materials is a good thing, isn't it? Distributions of power are rarely balanced. For most contemporary singer/songwriters, aesthetic choices and the economics of appropriation appear to be the primary issues at stake in the globalization of the folk. Indeed, in some cases—Christopher Waterman's chronology of "Corrine, Corinna," for example—the stages of mediation through which appropriations are framed blur the paths through which cultural material is assimilated into the folk repertoire, and seemingly by default, economy becomes the primary site for negotiating diverse cultural material. In other cases—the Small Potatoes song "Mad Mouth," for example—aesthetic considerations determine the only apparent boundaries in a decidedly postmodern politics of image.

However, to locate the American folk's world music appropriations in the grips of an "I like the way it sounds, so what's the problem?" argument is to attempt to redeem an innocence long past. Our musical history of love and theft has been laid bare, both within the ivory tower and in the popular press. There can be no more claims to a folk innocence. As singer/songwriters embrace their own mobility as cultural tourists, they must also adopt a critical stance regarding the subtle and not so subtle implications of these borrowings. As global citizens and as historically located subjects, American singer/songwriters should be duty-bound to consider the tenacious legacies of colonialism in the postcolonial present. Relative positions of power—and here I am referring to Michel Foucault's notion of the "omnipresence of power: not because it has the privilege of consolidating everything under its invincible unity, but because it is produced from one moment to the next, at every point, or rather in every relation from one point to another" (*The History of Sexuality*, 93)— ignored in the service of unself-conscious aesthetic choices, risk accusations of ventriloquism at best and contemporary minstrel performance at worst. I am not suggesting some sort of musical or cultural isolationism. Rather my hope is that the American folk discard the false innocence of our contested past and become aware of and attuned to the historical, economic, and cultural conditions of the world in which our tourism leads us.

He wore a suit and his favorite tie

He was a classically handsome guy

Her red dress had lace on the edge

A plunging neckline, a little cleavage

They sat in the corner where the lights are low

Heads together, talking real slow

This is not what it looks like

This is not what it seems

He's not looking for love

She's not the girl of his dreams

He's got a guy waiting at home

She wants a bride, not a groom

You gotta get the inside story

Never assume

—Jamie Anderson, "Never Assume," from *Never Assume* (1995)

Unnatural Acts
Sexuality, Gender, and a Folk Politics of Inclusion/Exclusion

Increasingly over the last decades of the twentieth century, critical discourses on sexuality and gender opened doors for widespread institutional implementations of related cross-disciplinary fields of inquiry. Women's studies, gay and lesbian studies, and so-called "queer theory" have become legitimate academic enterprises, reflecting large-scale, if inconsistent, societal shifts in ways of thinking about feminism, homosexuality, and homosexuals.[1] In his book *Homosexual Desire*, first published in English in 1978, Guy Hocquenghem cynically asserts: "There is a deeply rooted myth in contemporary society, the myth of a constant progress, in terms of bourgeois ideology, towards the liberalization of public morals and respect for the individual" (62). What Hocquenghem sees as "the myth of a constant progress" appears to be, in light of academic, juridical, and popular cultural changes over the past thirty years, more an erratic progress, a movement in fits and starts toward an increasingly tolerant, yet still stubborn, parochialism regarding homosexuality and, more generally, a politics of desire.

Among the many scholars who have been instrumental in the institutionalization of these disciplines, Michel Foucault is one of the most vocal and celebrated. His *History of Sexuality*, also first published in 1978, marks a critical disjuncture from the biological arguments that positioned homosexuality as genetically determined. His work suggests that "sexuality" in general is a cultural/historical construction. As cultural constructs, sexuality and not coincidentally homosexuality were freed from the stigma of "abnormality" or "aberrance." No longer tied to physical science or "nature," sexual relations generally, and same-sex relations specifically, could be claimed as legitimate manifestations of desire instead of "unnatural acts."

Yet there are fundamental differences between academic discourses on gender and sexuality and ways in which the folk negotiate those same slippery slopes. From the "ivory tower," the theoretical frames attempt to explain conceptual problems, define complex cultural processes, and posit solutions that resolve conflicting perspectives. Most musicologists who focus on these issues are less concerned with obvious textual references in music than with the possibilities in reading sexual or gendered discourses into nontextual musical settings. That is, music is the central concern and lyric text is of secondary interest.

For feminist, gay, or lesbian contemporary singer/songwriters, the lyric is the primary vehicle through which gender and/or sexuality are expressed. This central concern with text rather than with strictly musical considerations indexes legacies of folk's grand narratives: simplicity above complexity, "common-man" anti-intellectualism, and implicitly if not overtly stated conventions of "tradition." These ideals continue to hold sway over the often conflicted discourses of the contemporary folk. Issues of subjectivity so prominent in academic discussions of music and culture, while perhaps occasionally adding nuance to folk expressions of sexuality and power, are generally overlooked in favor of approaches that privilege the everyday experiences of the individual—a politics of the Ordinary. For the folk, surface analyses of the popular press play a more significant role than theoretical ponderings of philosophers and musicologists.

Queer as Folk—Queer and Fucked

On 18 August 2002, an article entitled "Queer as Folk" by David Hajdu appeared in the *New York Times* online magazine. Over the next few weeks, the responses posted to Internet folk music and community lists, newsgroups, and usergroups were almost uniformly negative. Hajdu was attempting to shed some critical light on what he saw as the folk community's celebration of lesbian singer/song-writers. However, for some readers his assertions regarding folk music's preoc-cupation with lesbians—gay male folksingers were not mentioned—bordered on homophobic paranoia. His initial premise suggests, "The audience for artists like [Christine] Lavin, like that of folk music in general, is predominantly female and increasingly gay." In addition to his claims that folk had become "the sound of lesbian culture," Hajdu further incited critics by saying, "Across the lines of gender and sexual orientation, moreover, there are concerns that the folk scene, in its tightening links to lesbian culture, is becoming exclusionary, limiting its audience and freezing the music in orthodoxy."

This initial set of assumptions and observations, while highly suspect in terms of accuracy,[2] brings up questions and issues regarding contemporary singer/songwriters, the American folk, folk/mainstream music markets, and a non-genre-specific musical politics of sexuality. Is the folk audience really "pre-dominantly female and increasingly gay"? Maryl Neff's 1996 statistics indicate an almost equally divided male/female folk demographic. My own fieldwork experiences and observations indicate no substantial imbalance between num-bers of female and male listeners. However, in his article Hajdu is reacting, or perhaps overreacting, to what might appear to be a recent tidal wave of lesbian singer/songwriter activity enveloping the folk landscape.

At the Falcon Ridge Folk Festival the roster regularly includes some openly lesbian performers. If a new listener were to attend the festival for only a few well-planned hours, the main stage performances could lead to the assumption that lesbians are ubiquitous on folk music landscapes. However, a glance at the schedule of performers for the entire festival indicates a majority of the per-formers are not only heterosexual (perhaps) but male as well. Also noteworthy is that the festival's producers book more female performers than many other festival presenters. The Kerrville festival's schedules for the past several years, for example, are weighted much more heavily toward male performers. Hajdu's initial agenda, to suggest that folk music is being overrun by lesbians, appears flawed from the outset.

Yet today's folk landscape does provide a relatively friendly site for non-heterosexual, and particularly lesbian, artistic expression. In moderately un-fettered articulations of individual sexualities within the folk community, gay and lesbian performers—like all performers who derive part or all of their in-come playing folk venues—interact with the marketplace in various ways. Like African drumming ensembles and Celtic bands, gay and lesbian folkies may, either inadvertently or by design, index the play of difference and sameness as measures of exchange.

Otherness has become a commodity. Sexuality, like ethnicity and perhaps eccentricity, serves to provide codes through which performers may be readily identified and remembered. This comes as no real surprise as music industries' marketing of these characteristics is ubiquitous and long-lived. Here I am not suggesting that lesbians are "outing" as a marketing ploy. Rather, as music impresarios perceive a market for what has become generally categorized as women's music, performers, both lesbian and not, are caught up in the dialectical frame of that labeling process: the definition and distinction of common interest groups and the consequent implications of cultural homogeneity within that category.

One of the more articulate responses to Hajdu's claims regarding that perceived homogeneity came from Amy Ray, a member of the pop group the Indigo Girls,[3] whose response was entitled "Queer and Fucked." Ray addressed many of Hajdu's assumptions regarding the folk, among them the discrepancy between agency and markets. Ray's exception to the idea that lesbians are defined as a market rather than individual cultural contributors suggests a dilemma of similarity and difference. For performers whose work situates them within the context of the women's music movement, if it can be so designated, the process of othering is innately linked to its obverse, what Naomi Schor, in her essay "This Essentialism Which Is Not One," has called "saming." By acknowledging a labeled sexual otherness, either enacted, endorsed, or simply addressed, lesbian artists face the consequences of association with the marginalized Other, while effectively galvanizing groups whose identities, or at least elements thereof, rely on that association. Ideologically the plays of power and resistance in this dance of difference and sameness reflect a generally increasing presence and potency of women in the music industry. That the American music industry, in terms of both artists and power brokers, has been dominated by men is obvious. That for the industry women have become a presence to be reckoned with artistically and economically is equally apparent. In the past few decades, artists playing music that expresses resistance to conventional patriarchal attitudes and sexual discrimination have effectively created a cross-genre artistic/social movement that has become significant not only for its message, but also in the marketplace.

Hajdu's conflation of women's music with folk is a relatively common and historically understandable misconception. Judith Peraino states, "In popular usage, the term 'women's music' refers either to music whose lyrics convey an explicitly lesbian or feminist message, or to recorded music commercially released by a women-owned and operated label such as Olivia Records" ("Rip Her to Shreds," 21). The definition is devoid of any musicological stylistic implications. In its performative practice, women's music is as diverse stylistically as the artists who embrace the label or who are ideologically and aesthetically situated under that umbrella. However, Peraino asserts that historically women's music is definitely associated with the folk, drawing as its initial stylistic inspiration "the leftist urban folk music genre epitomized by the songs of Woody Guthrie and Pete Seeger" (23). She suggests that the political nature of what Serge Denisoff called "urban folk music" provided a common ideological position for feminist and lesbian artists who also found in folk's acoustic instrumental setting a stylistic alternative to electric, highly rhythmic, and unquestionably male-dominated pop and rock musics, "whose mass consumer success had diluted their political potency" (ibid.). Yet those assertions have become problematic since the early 1990s when Peraino wrote them. As the folk have changed, so has the nature of women's music.

For a new generation of artists who grew up listening to pop and rock music, the folk associations may be less salient than early forays into women's music landscapes. As Amy Ray states in her response to Hajdu's article, "I know more gay women punkers than folkies. The Riot Girrl punk movement did more to change and propel the women's music scene than anything in recent history; it inspired a whole host of young artists in every tradition. Young lesbians know the Butchies, not Cris Williamson."

Regardless of its historical and ideological underpinnings, it is doubtful that an argument could be made against the existence of a market for women's music, no matter how one chooses to define it. For folk artists, as well as performers in any number of popular genres, associations with women's music may translate into increased public exposure to an ideologically receptive audience and subsequently into increased record sales. In the process of locating the women's music phenomenon in the context of markets, Hajdu implies that some heterosexual folksingers have posed as lesbians, or at least concealed their heterosexuality, in order to exploit that market. Specifically he alluded to Dar Williams, who responded with a diplomatic renouncement of the assertions and a vote of support for her gay fans.

Williams's response, as well as Ray's critique, indexes the contested relationship between women's music (and folk music in general) and music as commodity: intersections of ideology and capital. Somehow recognizing a potential market and playing to that market is perceived as a betrayal of trust rather than admirable business acumen. The music industry, and folk music is no exception, is inextricably tied to capital exchange. Folk's utopian egalitarianism coexists in an awkward alliance with its economic realities.

The audience for women's music, and specifically the audience for lesbian contemporary songwriters, has made a significant contribution to the general interest in folk music over the past decade. Listeners who might not otherwise have been exposed to folk's current generation of artists are increasingly attending festivals and venues featuring not only lesbian performers but also folkies in general. Folk's ideology of inclusion has provided a relatively affable environment for political/sexual expression and women's music has reciprocated.

July 2002: Youth, Ani, and the Liberation of Desire

The crowds at the Falcon Ridge festival have been increasing incrementally over the past few years, but this year was busier than ever. The usual audience demographic—white, thirty-five- to fifty-five-year-olds—appeared to be giving way to a significantly younger contingent of attendees. Not only were there more young people, but also they looked different than the sons and daughters of the usual suspects who came to the festival by default because they were too young to stay home unattended while mom and dad spent the weekend reinventing their misspent youth. The twenty-somethings who were so prominently represented that year were considerably worldlier in appearance than their somewhat younger counterparts among the folk progeny. Many if not most of them were sporting multiple body piercings. Tattoos were clearly part of the uniform du jour, and gender-bending clothing was common.

The new folk audience, as it turned out, was attending the festival primarily to support a performance by *Ani DiFranco* on Sunday night. Yet despite the fact that DiFranco's was the final performance of the festival, much of her audience arrived early in the weekend and stayed through the final act. The influx of youth was both tolerated and welcomed by the traditional audience for the festival. The general attitude toward the young and trendy DiFranco fans was cautious welcome. What was most intriguing was the sexual ambiguity that accompanied this decidedly non-folkie folk music audience. Many of the couples who wandered through the maze of concession booths were same-sex couples, almost exclusively women. Occasionally male couples held hands while strolling though the crowded public space, but these public intimacies were comparatively rare. In keeping with the public persona of DiFranco, a sense of sexual interrogation and experimentation was very much in evidence.

Ani DiFranco is an artist whose public persona plays an integral role in her cultural production. In the industry she is an enigma, considered a folk star, or punk folk star as the case may be, yet transcends the economy of folk and traverses the margins of the popular music industry. As a performing artist, she has a reputation for being demanding and somewhat impatient. Her presence in the microindustry—as well as the popular music industry at large—is legendary owing to sales in the millions of her independently produced recordings. She is an engaging performer whose lyrics are particularly germane for her target audience. Fans have suggested that DiFranco's music echoes their general sense of "anger and betrayal."[4] Yet her attraction does not seem particularly transgenerational. However, for her fans DiFranco has an almost evangelistic appeal. Accordingly the choices she makes in her private life—at least those she chooses to make public—have immense implications for her avid followers.

Some time ago DiFranco "came out" publicly as bisexual. The somewhat ambiguous sexuality the artist conveyed through performance and media exposure prior to her public outing was apparently problematic in terms of image. For whatever reason, it became important to publicly define DiFranco's sexuality. For stars of popular culture, whether they are pop stars like DiFranco, or movie stars, or television sitcom idols, publicly defining themselves in terms of sexuality has the advantage of addressing formerly taboo topics within the context of a national and world forum, yet also positions sexuality at the locus of constructions of self. For example, television sitcom star Ellen DeGeneres, in foregrounding her sexuality in a weekly sitcom on which she portrayed a lesbian, becomes embedded in popular memory not as DeGeneres the actor but as DeGeneres the lesbian actor. The danger in this sort of construct is that the diversity of the artists involved in cultural production becomes lost in the definition of categories and markets into which they can be neatly filed.

For pop music stars, these public declarations of sexuality are particularly potent. Their association with the world of fashion—Elvis's "ducktails," the Beatles' "mop tops" and Carnaby Street outfits, the Seattle grunge look, the retro punk of DiFranco and others—positions popular music stars in powerful social roles. Fashion extends beyond the clothing, body piercings, and outward trappings of uniform to behavior. For Ani DiFranco, many of whose fans are moved by her musical message to emulate her social behaviors, the pronouncement of her sexuality amounted to an endorsement of sexual freedom of choice. For the folk at large, perhaps DiFranco's declaration had little apparent consequence. Yet for her legions of fans it encouraged a general attitude toward sexuality that reflected a clear departure from conventional assumptions of heterosexuality as a definitive norm. Through her and her audiences' association with the folk, that freedom of choice became more visibly intertwined with the community's expressed ideology of diversity, inclusion, and equality.

Ani's Folk: Sexual Choice and Cultural Capital

As I set up my camping spot on the large hill overlooking the main stage and concession area I struck up a conversation with two of my neighbors. Both men were in their late teens or early twenties and were dressed in shorts, T-shirts, and tennis shoes, the standard summer camping attire. Neither of them sported the piercings, tattoos, or other fashion accoutrements that may have identified them with conventional retro punk fashion. They seemed typical undergraduates and were pleasant and helpful.

After setting up camp, I joined the men at their campsite. A half hour or so later, a young woman, obviously a classmate of the two men, approached the camp, greeted her two friends, and joined us under the elevated tarp that shaded the area. Except for a few facial piercings, the young woman's appearance was unremarkable. She sang a song or two, chatted amiably about music—Ani DiFranco was mentioned in reverent terms—and made herself comfortable on one of the camp chairs. In the course of her dialogue with her friends—I was an outsider in this exchange, addressed only peripherally—she mentioned expecting to be joined by a girlfriend that evening. When she spoke of the girlfriend, her sexual attraction was explicitly stated. She described the woman's beauty and personal warmth and her own anticipation of their imminent physical contact. The exuberance and enthusiasm of her description were infectious and seemed intentionally situated in a context of social convention. That is, an environment of sexual acceptance provided the opportunity for unproblematic expression of desire. Yet the expression seemed also to belie a certain self-conscious awareness of the social and contextual shifts through which that expression was considered acceptable. That is, the overt expression of same-sex desire appeared as conscious resistance to a conventional American heterosexual hegemony.

As the woman shifted into monologue about her anticipated tryst, it seemed that her effusive pronouncement of desire carried with it a degree of cultural capital. The hipness of sexuality unencumbered by the repressive constraints of the past was unmistakable. This is not to say that the woman's pronouncements were not sincere. Rather, where homosexuality and bisexuality were once, and in some quarters still are, cause for social stigmatization, for many of the young and the hip it has become viable cultural currency due in no small part to artists such as Ani DiFranco.

The historically situated legacy of sexual stigmatization that has marked American society continues to be manifest in (American) society at large and in the folk world as well. As much as communities of folk claim indifference regarding individual sexuality, the tenacity of sexual prejudices, like the tenacity of racial prejudices, is often at issue. One prominent church basement concert series was forced to find a new performance space after presenting a particularly outspoken lesbian singer/songwriter. The church administrator stated that the presenter's agenda did not coincide with church doctrine. Another "out" performer with whom I spoke has been turned down by several venue operators, all of whom either intimated or flatly stated that their audiences simply are not ready for her "lesbian message." Yet by and large the folk world is more lesbian friendly than American society as a whole. For "women's music" performers generally and lesbian folksingers specifically, an increasingly vocal presence on folk landscapes marks a certain contrast with gay male performers, whose industry profile is considerably less conspicuous.

Bear Music

In 2000, *Martin Swinger*, a folksinger from Augusta, Maine, released a CD entitled *BearNaked*. Like the vast majority of folk/acoustic singer/songwriter releases over the past decade, *BearNaked* was independently produced, released, and marketed. The recording includes several Swinger compositions as well as some familiar popular and children's songs, the presence of which on the CD are remarkable for shifting meanings within the context of the production. Swinger chose to express a male homosexual perspective through the familiar tunes, most of which reference bears, a culturally specific encoded term for gay men.

The opening song on the recording is the familiar children's song "Teddy Bear's Picnic," written by John Bratton and James Kennedy. The musical setting Swinger provides begins with a simple guitar and solo voice accentuated at the end of the phrase with a muted cymbal, after which the guitar, doubling a staccato moving bass line, provides a sense of temporal movement. After the first two verses of the song there is an instrumental interlude in which a kazoo takes the solo. During the second interlude following the chorus, or B section, a male chorus singing percussionistic vocables, in which tenor antecedent phrases are answered by falsetto consequent phrases, contributes to an overall sense of whimsy.

The potential for "high camp" in this adaptation is great. However, Swinger manages to avoid any overt sense of parody and produces a lively, entertaining piece that utilizes a conventional Western musical developmental framework that accentuates a feeling of sincere enjoyment in the act of making music. How much of that interpretation relies on my personal knowledge of the artist and the obvious joy he invests in his musical production is debatable. This particular song and Swinger's setting and performance would not seem out of place on a recording marketed to the lucrative children's market except for minor changes to the original lyric and specific phrasings he chose to accentuate the cultural context of the production as a whole.

The original lyric that ended the chorus section read as follows:

But at six o'clock their mommies and daddies will take them home to bed
Because they're tired little teddy bears

Swinger eliminates the word "mommies" and augments the duration of the word "daddies," highlighting the sexual politics behind the album's conceptual project. Likewise, a leap to F while singing the word "gaily" in the line, "see them as they gaily gad about" provides an obvious code to the context.

While Swinger's project presents contextual juxtapositions that shift meanings of traditional repertoires, he also includes straightforward, though clearly not "straight," love songs, which are emotionally charged and convincingly performed. His song "Teddy Bear's Lullaby" illustrates the emotional and physical attachments between two people, the only clue to the gay thematic is the clear male tenor voice singing the lyric. *BearNaked* is clearly a statement by a gay man that presents homosexuality not as a symbol of otherness, but rather as an intersection at the crossroads of the ordinary. Yet Swinger's project is an exception to the rule in the folk world. Where lesbian folkies have exerted a forceful presence within the folk community in the past decade or so, gay men have been less successful in galvanizing mass audiences for their work. The reasons for this discrepancy are worth interrogating.

In Jeffrey Weeks's preface to the 1978 edition of Guy Hocquenghem's classic of queer theory, *Homosexual Desire*, he says, "In a patriarchal society, female sexuality is defined in relationship to the male" (38). While Hocquenghem has been soundly criticized for framing his analysis exclusively in the context of male homosexuality, Weeks's statement is consistent with that approach but can be seen as situating it within contexts of power. Brian Pronger in *The Arena of Masculinity: Sports, Homosexuality, and the Meaning of Sex* (1990) suggests, "It is more socially acceptable for a woman to be masculine than for a man to be feminine because it is more acceptable to take power than it is to relinquish it" (59). Of course this is not to say that all lesbians are masculine or that all gay men are feminine. Rather what it suggests is a decidedly patriarchal perspective on conventional attitudes about relative acceptability of nonheterosexual relations.

Hocquenghem's notion that phallocentrism and the privatization of the anus lie at the root (no pun intended) of the homoerotic attraction/revulsion dialectic privileges maleness and subordinates the female. In terms of the potency of attraction/revulsion, what this position implies is a certain benign indifference to same-sex female relations due to the absence of the phallus. If the market in soft- and hard-core pornography is any indication, the male perspective on lesbianism goes well beyond benign indifference and is a compelling sexual stimulant for many heterosexual men. Internet spam indiscriminately sent to e-mail accounts frequently advertises graphic pictures of women having sex with other women as well as "streaming video lesbians."

The "phallocratic" (to use Hocquenghem's term), patriarchal, historical backdrop that underscores the current conditions through which the folk negotiate public selves suggests a convoluted dialectics of power, resistance, and irony. Lesbian women subordinated by gender and marginalized by sexuality have come together in remarkable numbers to resist conditions of patriarchal dominance. Their numbers have had a noticeable impact on the economics of the folk landscape. Gay male folkies have found a considerably less friendly atmosphere for resistance to conventional attitudes regarding homosexuality.

As a result the market for folk music that specifically addresses gay male themes is tiny when compared to the women's music market. This brings to the fore the argument that women's music does not necessarily index lesbian issues. A great number of nonlesbian women performers, as well as male performers perceived as friendly to women's issues, are situated under the rubric of the women's music movement. Music that directly addresses gay male issues by its very nature speaks to a much more specific audience of consumers. In the past five years I have interviewed only two gay male folk singer/songwriters who regularly perform material that openly references their homosexuality. It seems dangerous ground to travel for performers who aspire to make a living playing music. On Martin Swinger's Web site there is, as of late in 2005, no mention of the *BearNaked* project nor any reference to anything gay. The man is trying to derive his income from making music. He performs in restaurants, coffeehouses, concert series, and is an accomplished teacher, conducting music and songwriting seminars in schools for elementary through high school aged students. While Swinger is clearly "out," he also recognizes the stigma attached to homosexuality that retains its tenacious grip on the popular sexual imagination.

The second singer/songwriter with whom I have spoken whose material addresses the experience of being a gay male is *Mark Weigle*. Weigle has achieved a level of notoriety that is exceptional considering his explicitly gay male perspective. At the time of this writing, Weigle is on tour in Germany where he apparently has a substantial audience. *Billboard* magazine, the popular music trade journal, wrote an exceptional review of his music, and other publications have followed suit with reviews of his material. Yet despite an unprecedented level of success in presenting a gay male musical perspective, Weigle is virtually unheard of in most East Coast and southern folk music circles.

Since the early 1990s the folk landscape has become more a site for the expression of individual and group sexual identity than it has ever been before. The integration of conventional folk aesthetics and messages with gay-specific themes has been celebrated as a continuation of folk's traditional topicalism, and the conflation of those elements has been embraced (albeit begrudgingly at times) at various levels by folk communities. That some relative positions of power represented by male, as the symbol of patriarchal dominance, and female, as the symbol of the subordinated, have been reconfigured in terms of marginalized groups defined by sexuality and the markets through which their voices are articulated, is an inescapable element of the contemporary American folk landscape.

Folk's politics of sexuality is constituted by multilevel and complicated interrelationships involving individuals, institutions, interest groups, and the marketplace, as well as by an expressive poetics of experience and publicly articulated and enacted expressions of present and past love and lust, celebrated or unrequited, lost and longed for. In short, sexuality for the folk is remarkably similar to sexuality in America and the West more generally. This politics is negotiated at conventional interactive levels as well as at the level of the symbolic: a level at which power and resistance, as well as constructions of personal and public selves, intertwine with the wiles of capitalism in both contested and synergistic relations.

One optimistic aspect of the folk's often contested relationship with what Herbert Marcuse might call the "liberation of desire," is the open addressing of more pressing problems that face us all. Gay and lesbian singer/songwriters confront issues that extend beyond the personal and social consequences of their sexuality, yet the messages are often couched in contexts of individual experience.

"Goddamn HIV" by Mary Gauthier (excerpt)

My name is Michael Joe Alexandry
I been a queer since the day I was born
My family they don't say much to me
My heart knows their silence as scorn
My friends have been dying
All my best friends are dead
I walk around these days with their picture in my head
Spend my time thinking about some things they said

And I don't know what's happening to me
Goddamn HIV

And I don't know what all of this means
I don't think it means what it seems

Mary Gauthier's lyric illustrates the stark perspective of a gay male for whom HIV has become an omnipresent and unwelcome companion. As an openly lesbian performer writing from a gay male perspective, Gauthier situates herself within a community of actors for whom nonheterosexuality has become the unifying element. That the devastation of HIV and AIDS has contributed to the sense of unity among gay and lesbian communities is both ironic and tragic.

We used to party all night till the dawn
I can still see the pretty boys with their tight leather on
In the downtown bars where it always is night
I could hang with my friends and feel all right
I was thirty years old when the sickness first came
And it rolled through my world like a wind driven flame
Leaving ashes, memories, funerals, and pain
And I don't know what's happening to me
Goddamn HIV

The musical setting for Gauthier's song speaks to the conceptual rift between the academic perspectives of the feminist scholars mentioned previously and the contemporary folk. The harmonic structure of the tune is tonally conventional and unremarkable in terms of development. The song is strophic, as is much of folk's musical production, and melodically limited. That is, the melody does not take any dramatic or unusual turns, and the pitch range is narrow. Gauthier's delivery is relaxed, and her vocal quality draws upon characteristics of older country music styles. She sings with a southern drawl, and the combination of musical simplicity and vocal twang are reminiscent of John Prine, an artist from whom generations of singer/songwriters have drawn inspiration.[5] There is no attempt to transgress what Renée Cox describes in "Recovering *Jouissance*: An Introduction to Feminist Musical Aesthetics" as "musical hierarchies," or the "musical semiotics of gender" theorized by Susan McClary. If anything the setting is more traditionally folkie than most contemporary folk production. Gauthier, like most of her contemporaries, is primarily concerned with song lyrics, and it is through these texts that messages—sexual and otherwise—are most prominently expressed in performance.

Conclusion

As gender and sexuality become more frequently and publicly addressed in folk discourses, the community's responses have been decidedly mixed. While a general liberalization of attitudes marks the surface of the folk landscape, undercurrents of difference and distance continue to exert constraints on writers and performers. In extreme cases institutionalized ideologies play the primary role in reinscribing sexual stigma.[6] The more subtle manifestations of long-held homosexual prejudices have yet to be reconciled for today's folk and the American public at large. It remains to be seen how the philosophical strides taken by the likes of Michel Foucault, Philip Brett, Guy Hocquenghem, and the scores of feminist, gay, and lesbian scholars currently writing on gender, sexuality, and music, will affect public perceptions of these contested issues. Like deeply rooted constructions of race, constructions of sexual difference are tenacious, and their excision from public imagination promises to be a long-term project.

Last night I found Jesus Christ washing my windshield
with a crumpled up page of the Los Angeles Times
and the headlines they read we'd be better off dead
or lucky just to make it to Christmas
—Alan Whitney, "Crucifixion Waltz," from *The Borderland*

9   A Last Word

The landscapes of the American folk changed dramatically in the last decade
of the twentieth century and the beginning of the twenty-first. Since beginning
this writing in the late 1990s, various elements of the folk have metamorphosed
further, causing celebration by some and concern in other camps. Undercurrents in the trajectory of the folk community at large suggest the possibility of
musical stasis. That is, many folkies argue that presenters seem to hire the same
collection of artists repeatedly, a practice that allegedly serves to standardize
general aesthetic parameters. Yet at the same time, world music is playing an
increasingly visible role on the folk landscape, introducing audiences to unprecedented varieties of unfamiliar sounds. The hierarchies that define levels of
success appear more clearly defined in terms of exchange value than they were
even a decade ago. Yet folkies with no aspirations for professional involvement
continue to gather in countless home-based song circles to make music with

friends and families. If, as some claim, the folk is becoming incestuous in its institutions, the people who make up the folk are often vocal in their message of public outreach and egalitarianism. These multiple and seemingly conflicting discourses point to a contemporary landscape in which defining what it is to be "folk" has become more complicated than simply associating with a specific musical style or a fixed set of performance practices. Folk is no longer a type of music. Rather, it is symptomatic of a dynamic confluence of ideas, ideals, and ideologies within which historical mythology, musical hybridity, tradition, lived experience, community, economy, tourism (both literally and figuratively), and technology intertwine in convoluted webs of signification.

The folk continue to grasp at the straws of memory and myth while simultaneously embracing the idea of folk music as dynamic process along with all that entails. For some the incursion of popular musics on folk landscapes and the escalating exchanges between these once antithetical realms signals an increasing commodification of folk music: that folk is rapidly being colonized by the popular—the commercial—and a sameness in musical/cultural production is the result. For others the ideological rift that once separated popular and folk has been replaced by a sporadic cycle of reciprocity in which those classifications cease to be relevant as both are subsumed under the logic of exchange value.

> Then I saw Rome burning in all of its glory
> and "We'll be right back after this word from Pepsi."
> and there was no benediction or a page in the papers
> I guess that nobody really gives a damn[1]

Unquestionably in the past two decades the business of folk has become considerably more businesslike and, not coincidentally, more dependent on technology. Like everything else, the American folk have been swept up in the global projects of late capitalism. To suggest that it has lost its ideological purity as a result would be disingenuous. Indeed at least since the early days of the twentieth century (and perhaps since the mid-nineteenth century) folk music has been inextricably tied to the marketplace and peripherally to technology. Does this make it somehow less folklike, less authentic, or less emotionally evocative? For people whose identification with folk plays a central role in their lives, the answer is an unequivocal no. However, that this relationship with capital and technology implies exclusivity based upon positions of privilege, remains one of folk's seemingly insolvable paradoxes.

> Then I dreamed of the ones so lost in their color
> and stoned by the distance and the deaths of their brothers

Its like this small world is coughing to shake off the ravage
of the first breath of the backside of an overdose

In many ways, my personal involvement in the folk and folk music over the years mirrors the dramatic changes in attitude, ideology, and perspective that have come to characterize the disjunctures between past and present that lie at the root of today's "folk concepts." As a white, middle-aged, well-educated folkie, I am the demographic norm. As such, the innate contradictions and paradoxes that exist at so many levels for today's folk have become inevitable constituents of my own engagement with folk music and community, a community that often wears the mantle of folkness like an ill-fitting suit. Like the folk at large, my personal politics of experience determines my musical production. The indexes of authenticity through which associations with the folk are enacted in performance are based upon that experience. As the early twentieth-century constructions of folk authenticity become further distanced by time, the traditional indexes of a folk authentic have begun to fade. Modernity and the information age have tempered the contemporary folk's notions of tradition. Likewise they have contributed to a changing folk aesthetic. While popular music was once the antithesis of folk music, the two are often indistinguishable as younger folkies bring the baggage of their popular musical backgrounds to the folk community. What was once considered practically sacrilegious—additions of electric instruments, drum sets, and so forth—has become commonplace.

Recording technology and particularly the Internet have altered the playing fields upon which the folk enact their performance of the past and present.[2] While engagements with technology seem at odds with lingering ideological claims to folk simplicity, they have been and continue to be eagerly and widely embraced by increasing numbers of folkies who see the emerging technologies as vehicles through which they might more fully and conveniently engage capitalism. This engagement is rarely seen as problematic in terms of folk's past associations with political movements, specifically communism. The contemporary folk has, for the most part, succumbed to the hegemony of late capitalism.

Yet the microindustry that has arisen around folk's current resurgence maintains a distinct countercultural self-image, an image that pits it against the popular music industry in a sometimes awkward dance of imitation and disdain. The contest of folk versus the popular has shifted from the realm of the aesthetic to the transactions of industry. The folk microindustry has played a pivotal role in the development of spoken and unspoken hierarchical positions of power, which are ultimately determined by a politics of economy. Many folk entrepreneurs espouse the egalitarian idealism that is so thoroughly ingrained in folk discourses, while at the same time inscribing and reinscribing the hierarchies that have come to characterize the contemporary folk landscape.

As that landscape has become more viable economically, the venues in which folk music is presented have become more plentiful and varied, creating a new class of folk intermediaries: the presenters. These contemporary power brokers, like their forebears in the early twentieth century, have contributed to the paradoxical nature of current notions of a folk concept. The proliferation of folk venues has presented new opportunities for legions of musicians with aspirations of becoming professional folksingers. Yet inevitably a venue's success is dependent upon filling seats. As such, many folkies have complained that it is primarily the better-known and thus salable artists who are the principal beneficiaries of this increased exposure. In coffeehouses, as well as concert series, house concerts, and festivals, hierarchies are reinforced through booking decisions based upon the drawing power of specific artists. Numerous folk festivals reflect these tiered artist designations within the context of complex fields of social interaction and ideological contradiction.

Festivals present opportunities for mass enactments of a folk idealism punctuated by the intersections of power relations and economics. As a site for enacting community, the festival is a microcosm of the folk landscape. At the festival the communal egalitarianism that underscores codes of behavior for contemporary folkies is a pervading theme that highlights the paradoxical economic and hierarchical power relations that flow beneath the surface of folk's idealized ethics. It is also the site for decidedly unself-conscious reinscriptions of the racial imagination. The dramatic underrepresentation of nonwhites at folk festivals mirrors the same phenomenon on the folk landscape at large: a situation that is lamented by folkies but which also may suggest itself as protection from the racial Other. Yet otherness is also exoticized and, in terms of world music, eagerly embraced.

For the contemporary folk, like the international music industry at large, the exotic has become a salable commodity. The idea that the folk extends beyond the West has allowed for musically diverse elements to become integrated into American folk idioms at an unprecedented rate. African percussion instruments, Celtic strings, and Latin American flutes are frequently used in conjunction with traditional folk instruments, creating a sense of sonic hybridity that would have been considered aberrant to folkies a few decades ago. Likewise American folk conventions have been adopted by non-American performers further muddying the waters of signification, history, and the production of musical meanings for folk's relatively homogeneous audience.

The fictions of folk's past—particularly the rural ideal and the common man—coexist in uneasy counterpoint with mostly white middle-class suburban spheres of experience. The persisting claims to inclusion and diversity that mark contemporary folk concepts have opened doors for gay and lesbian performers and audiences but have fallen short in winning over the racial or "ethnic" Other. The persistent inequities of power and privilege that have proven so divisive in the past and present have yet to release their global stranglehold. If the folk's overt messages of inclusion seem impotent, perhaps they will become less so through repetition. If folk's dominant aesthetic speaks only to its tradition-ally white, middle-class constituency, the next generations of singer/songwriters have their work cut out for them.

Epilogue
Peeling the Orange: The Future of Folk

In some ways, this project has been like peeling an orange. Bit by bit the bitter skin has been stripped away with the promise of sweet reward always lingering somewhere beneath the surface—redemption. When Charles Keil stated, "Can't we keep 'the folk' concept and redeem it? No! and no! again" (quoted in Middleton, "Editor's Introduction"), he was both right and wrong. As I have argued, the "folk concept" with its conceptual roots in the Herderian notion of *volk* and its subsequent reconstruction and reinvention by Francis Child, Hubert Parry and various nineteenth-century collectors and ideologues is clearly beyond redemption. Its reinscription and adaptation by early twentieth century cultural intermediaries in the project to construct an American folk authentic is equally untenable. As folk music has changed, so has the "folk concept."

While lingering ideals of folkness continue to index persistent mythologies, those myths are becoming more like sepia-tinged photographs of unrecalled pasts. As new generations of singer/songwriters construct new folk identities, the "folk concept" is filtered through the lens of the present and the recent experiential past. Most contemporary folk singer/songwriters have adopted the long-held ideal of communalism, a trend that seems, if anything, to be increasing as the world becomes a more dangerous place. While many still pay homage to the myths of rural simplicity and the common man, much of the historical baggage of authenticity and fetish for tradition appears to be losing its currency. As the "old" folk's signifiers become less familiar, I anticipate that they will cease to remain meaningful. As younger folkies' personal histories grow further apart from the fictive pasts upon which Keil's "folk concept" was based, they create new images, indexes of authenticity, and traditions—new folk concepts. Folk music has changed. If it sometimes seems to have lapsed into a period of sameness, we can only hope that will also change as future generations of singer/songwriters continue to peel the layers off the past and find that the orange beneath tastes pretty good.

> Then I saw my lover's eyes so filled with forgiveness
> there was no hesitation no papers to sign
> Now I'm asking myself what was it I missed here
> and why did I steal this when no one was looking?
> Then Jesus said, "Saving the world is a lost occupation
> like barnstorming, or witchcraft, or rock and roll,
> but, if you're waiting for someone to give you the signal,
> Son, if you hear the singer there must be a song."
> —Alan Whitney

NOTES

Introduction

1. Because of the ambiguities of the term "folk music," some scholars, Benjamin Filene among them, have opted to substitute the term "vernacular music" in their work. Despite the problematic nature of the terminology, I will use "folk" as a descriptor because of its popular use among people who make and consume this music. To not do so would, in my opinion, constitute academic ventriloquism.

2. I have long found my father's infatuation with folk music to be somewhat incongruous with his chosen career. Particularly in the 1940s and '50s, folk's connections with organized labor and the Communist party were common knowledge. These ideological connections did not seem to make much difference to my parents despite their otherwise fairly conventional anticommunist political worldviews. Both my mother and father enjoy folk music as an aesthetic experience, devoid of ideological underpinnings.

3. House concerts, church basement concert series, new folk festivals, and coffeehouse concert series mark the most recent proliferation of what I will call folkspace, which will be addressed at length in chapters 5 and 6.

4. Younger artists were not entirely excluded from the more desirable venues. Yet there were very few younger artists achieving wide popularity with folk audiences. The exceptions were, for the most part, artists who played music that fit into various established and generally accepted folk "traditions."

5. My bachelor's and master's degrees are in music composition.

6. The advertising slogan was from General Motors: "This is not your father's Oldsmobile."

7. This phenomenon is not limited to a single genre of popular music. Rather it is a more generalized trend that can be applied to any form of popular music, art, or entertainment in industrialized and, more importantly, "technologized" capitalist societies. Generation Xers are the first in the history of the planet to have been raised in an environment so completely saturated with technological mediation that it is almost impossible not to engage with it at some level.

8. And a very popular modernist nostalgia at that, not only for academics but also for the "folk."

9. In suggesting that a postmodern reading of the contemporary folk may have some validity, the thoroughly "modern" notion of Frankfurt School dialectics may seem a strange bedfellow. Where Adorno and Horkheimer's work suggests an absolute ethics grounded in some of the most contested grand narratives of modernism—specifically the sort of good/evil dualities attached to various moral imperatives, which shape the fundamental basis of their Dialectics of Enlightenment—a strictly postmodern approach would find that assumption mired in impotent modernist subjectivities. Perhaps the rec-

onciliation of these approaches lies not in a blanket acceptance of either as the gospel, but in the practical application of each as it applies to a politics of experience.

10. "Retrospective imagination" refers specifically to the ways that history and memory interact in a process by which pasts are interpreted, reinterpreted, and reconfigured through the lens of the present. In the context of the "folk," the retrospective imagination also bears resemblance to what Veit Erlmann has called the "global imagination . . . the means by which people shift the contexts of their knowledge and endow phenomena with significance beyond their immediate realm of personal experience" (*Music, Modernity, and the Global Imagination*, 4).

11. Specifically I am referring to Pierre Bourdieu's critique of the high/low cultural distinctions in European society. However, other scholars including Lawrence Levine, Simon Frith, and a host of others have since presented convincing arguments bolstering Bourdieu's critique.

12. I do not mean to suggest that Peter Manual has blindly celebrated technology's potential for redemption.

Earlier critical thinkers who issued warnings include Herbert Marcuse, who wrote in 1941: "Technics by itself can promote authoritarianism as well as liberty, scarcity as well as abundance, the extension as well as the abolition of toil" (quoted in Arato and Gebhardt, *The Essential Frankfurt School Reader*, 139). While Marcuse's comments were made in the context of antifascist sentiments shared by his Frankfurt School colleagues, they seem apropos to present-day concerns regarding technological advances in communication and aesthetic production.

13. In the past thirty years the American public has generally become more tolerant of homosexuality, as evident in legislation designed to assure equal rights, not to mention often sympathetic portrayals of homosexuals on prime-time television.

14. Perhaps due to its commercial success in the late 1950s and early 1960s, "Anglo-American folk music" of the type played by the Kingston Trio; the Weavers; Peter, Paul, and Mary; and other popular groups of the period, was perceived as a sort of folk paradigm, defining the term in the popular consciousness.

15. Ken Gourlay's 1978 article "Towards a Reassessment of the Ethnomusicologist's Role in Research" was instrumental in illustrating the inevitability of the researcher's effect on the ethnographic project and also raised questions about ethnographic objectivity. How can there be any "true" objectivity when the perception of everything we experience is mediated by our own cultural loading—our worldviews?

1. Folk Music Has Changed

1. The notion of a "folk ideal" encompasses a wide variety of familiar populist themes including staunch individualism, the superiority of rural simplicity over the urban rat race, and the primacy of the land.

2. A project doomed to failure due to its overly ambitious scope.

3. Including the notation "additional words and music by . . ." has long been an apparent loophole in the copyright ordinances, allowing interpreters of preexisting songs

to make legal claims to ownership of that material. John Lomax made free use of this aspect of copyright law, either directly or by stretching the intent of the law, in his book *Cowboy Songs and Other Frontier Ballads*, first published in 1910. According to Filene, Lomax omitted attributions for various songs, edited material by several contributors combining various parts of different versions to result in final versions to his liking, and neglected to mention that he had a hand in the reinvention of these tunes. Veit Erlmann addresses the same sort of process regarding the song, "Wimoweh" in his book *Music, Modernity, and the Global Imagination*.

4. Lawrence Levine describes the process of inculcating the notion of high/low aesthetic distinctions into American popular perceptions in the late nineteenth and early twentieth centuries in his engrossing *Highbrow/Lowbrow: The Emergence of Cultural Hierarchy in America*.

5. Bill Malone describes this sort of process in his book *Country Music, U.S.A.*: "Before World War I, the music industry—then represented chiefly by vaudeville, the sheet music business, and the phonograph interests—concentrated on urban America because of its population density and easy accessibility. The rural market was not totally neglected, but it received the same entertainment material that was directed to the cities. Rustic types were staples of American entertainment, but these were usually sophisticated entertainers, such as Josh Denman and Cal Stewart, who merely acted the parts of hayseeds or rubes" (31).

6. Hawaiian style guitars, played exclusively with a glass or metal slide, were a favorite among bluegrass groups and have been regular additions to country and popular musics at least since the 1920s.

7. Dobro is a brand of resonator guitar that is popular among folk, blues, and bluegrass players. John Dopyera established the company with his brothers in 1928. Dobro stands for DOpyera BROthers. The term "dobro" is now commonly used as a generic descriptor for resonator guitars in general. For a detailed explanation and history of resonator instruments see Bob Brozman et al.'s *The History and Artistry of National Resonator Instruments* (1993), cowritten by John Dopyera and others.

8. A capo is a clamp that raises the pitch of the instrument depending upon where it is placed on the neck of the guitar. DADGAD indicates the tuning of the guitar strings beginning from the lowest pitched string. In DADGAD, playing without a capo would generally indicate that the song's tonal center is D. Placed on the second fret, the capo raises the pitch of the tonal center to concert E.

9. Guitar strings vibrate for a longer duration and with more resonance when not fretted.

10. "Folkie" refers to a folk music aficionado.

11. Here I mean "media" to be the broadcast, recording, television, and publishing industries.

12. During South Texas summer days the weather gets stifling, and most veteran "Kerrverts" meet under various such tarp arrangements to stay out of the sun.

13. In one version Wilfrid Mellers states, "There is an apocryphal legend that when Louis Armstrong was asked whether he considered his music to be folk music he replied:

'Wal, yeah, I guess so: leastways, I never heard no horse makin' it' " ("God, Modality, and Meaning in Some Recent Songs of Bob Dylan").

14. Since around 1990 the proliferation of folk-music-related Internet resources has sparked a huge resurgence of popular and scholarly debate on the definition of folk music. The Internet allows an unprecedented level of communication and mediation that has profoundly affected processes of folk identity and (unbounded) community formation, a subject to which I devote particular attention in chapter 3.

15. Fair4us@aol.com, posted in November 1998 on Internet folk music list.

16. Guthrie Thomas, posted reply in November 1998 on Internet folk music list.

17. These enactments are manifest and immediately apparent in most of the venues at which the folk gather as a community.

2. Popular Imagination, the "Common Man," and Shifting Authenticities

1. The term "revival" used to describe folk music's commercial popularity is, in some critics' view, a misnomer. The argument is that folk music has always been important to a great many people and was "revived" only in terms of its commercial potential as an exchange commodity.

2. For the performance Dylan played an electric guitar and appeared on stage with the Paul Butterfield Blues Band, an electric ensemble. The crowd at the Newport Folk Festival, which was considered a "traditional" folk venue, booed Dylan, who was the undisputed champion of the '60s revival, for abandoning the acoustic guitar and harmonica in favor of the new electric sound.

3. The notion of origins with regard to folk and rock is a particularly slippery slope, one for which Cantwell implies simplistic explanations.

4. The Lomax manipulations of repertoire, aspects of performance, and image are well documented in several accounts, including Charles Wolfe and Kip Lornell's *The Life and Legend of Leadbelly*. In 1998, I interviewed Israel (Izzy) Young, the original proprietor of the Folklore Center in Greenwich Village, who also asserted the Lomaxes' culpability in related ideological projects.

5. The demographics of the folk suggest a primarily white, middle- to upper-middle-class, well-educated audience most of whom are between the ages of thirty-five and seventy-seven.

6. These themes, as I have explained previously, are growing less prevalent as contemporary singer/songwriters address more current topics in their songs. However, they still retain an imaginative appeal for the premodern simplicity that once defined the folk and continues to exert varying degrees of influence.

7. Richard Peterson discusses similar contexts of authenticity in *Creating Country Music: Fabricating Authenticity* (1997).

8. For a cogent discussion of the philosophical history of the contested notion of authenticity, see Regina Bendix's *In Search of Authenticity: The Formation of Folklore Studies* (1997).

9. This information comes from a variety of sources, most notably Charles Wolfe and Kip Lornell's *The Life and Legend of Leadbelly* (1992).

10. Poole was a hillbilly music performer who gained notoriety in the 1920s.

11. Among them, Eric Lott's *Love and Theft: Blackface Minstrelsy and the American Working Class* and Peter Stallybrass and Allon White's *The Politics and Poetics of Transgression*, present particularly trenchant examples.

12. The version to which this refers is by Luke Jordan.

13. This statement is based on personal observation and experience in the folk world over the past few decades as well as on corroborating data gathered by Maryl Neff for her 1996 doctoral dissertation, "Media Usage among Folk Music Communities."

14. The Oriental opium den, portrayed by Western popular culture as the quintessential den of iniquity, is still a powerful symbol of the Oriental Other and has been resurrected by Hollywood as recently as 1994 in the movie *Legends of the Fall*.

15. The romantic notion of the tortured artist has been with us at least as far back as the nineteenth century when figures like Vincent van Gogh and Henri de Toulouse-Lautrec paved the way for future generations of suffering artists. Long before Charlie Poole set the country music standard for fast living, the die was cast.

16. Stuart is best known as an accomplished accompanist for his wife, Stacey Earle.

17. Jameson continues, asserting "that content, those initial raw materials, are, I will suggest, to be grasped simply as the whole object world of agricultural misery, of stark rural poverty, and the whole rudimentary human world of backbreaking peasant toil, a world reduced to its most brutal and menaced, primitive and marginalized state" (*Postmodernism*, 7). He goes on to contrast that interpretation with Martin Heidegger's contention, "[T]here vibrates the silent call of the earth, its quiet gift of ripening corn and its enigmatic self-refusal in the fallow desolation of the wintry field" (quoted in ibid., 8).

18. There are remarkable similarities in the drawing of emotional response in this sort of performance to the German political scientist Dolf Sternberger's notion of genre and genre painting. Like the genre painting, Shore's (and most other artists') fundamental task is to invite the audience to participate in the emotionality of the song and, ideally, to situate the "living pictures" of the narrative within the bounds of generalized personal experience.

19. "Race records" were recordings by black and other "ethnic" performers marketed primarily to growing populations of consumers during the 1920s through the 1940s.

20. Of the considerable number of country-blues players I can think of, only three are African American—Guy Davis, Jerry Ricks, and Keb' Mo'—and none of the three play exclusively old-style country blues. Surely there are more black country bluesmen, and I apologize to them for not including their names. I simply have not come into contact with them in the course of my investigation.

21. The independent thumb technique is characterized by a root/octave or root/fifth ostinato moving through the song's progression while chords, arpeggios, and melodic lines are played above it. In bottleneck playing the player uses a glass or metal tube,

which fits onto one of the fingers of the left hand, to slide from one note to another in a portamento style.

3. Wired Folk

1. Of course this does not suggest that Dylan single-handedly killed the folk revival. His Newport performance is simply a convenient historical marker of the inevitable decline of folk's commercial heyday. Dylan was certainly in the right place at the right time, as he has been many times in his career.

2. According to Nolan Porterfield, the Lomaxes began their 1933 field excursion with a spring-driven cylinder dictating machine from the Dictaphone Corporation of Philadelphia (*Last Cavalier*, 297). The machine was operationally temperamental and the sonic quality was reputed to be marginal at best. During the course of this field trip, the machine was replaced by an acetate disk recorder provided by Walter Garwick, a former engineer for the Fairchild Corporation (301).

3. When Lomax wrote "Saga of a Folksong Hunter," the implied paternalism would have been laudable in the eyes of most who read it. The notion of "giving voice to the voiceless" has since fallen out of favor among scholars. However, in some nonacademic circles it retains its Lomaxian currency. In chapter 4, I discuss a 1999 Folk Alliance workshop at which the "voice to the voiceless" theme was unproblematically celebrated by the discussants.

4. According to Steve Schoenherr's "Recording Technology History," the Magnecord company created "one of the first open reel stereo tape recorders" in 1949. By 1954, RCA Victor had begun marketing prerecorded music on reel-to-reel tape. David Morton's "A Chronology of Magnetic Recording" suggests that the first catalog of taped music was marketed by Recording Associates as early as 1950.

5. The merits of the situation were highly debated among professional recording engineers. At the time of this writing, analog versus digital debates still rage at industry trade shows and on Internet newsgroups. Analog devotees insist that magnetic tape sounds better than digitally reproduced sound. Those in favor of the digital machines suggest that devotion to analog tape is a nostalgic claim to authenticity. Of course technical arguments regarding tape saturation, possible on analog tape and impossible on digital tape, poor quality digital I/Os on the ADAT, the 44.1 kHz CD standard for digital, and countless other topics, many of which are beyond my own understanding, accompany the more subjective aesthetic comparisons. In a display of disdain for semipro and digital gear in general, one dyed-in-the-wool analog proponent at a recent NAMM (formerly National Association of Music Merchants; now International Music Products Association; but universally known as NAMM) trade show impaled a low cost Mackie mixing board and an ADAT on a long stick and attached a sign to the sculpture that read SHIT ON A STICK.

6. The sound files created by these systems are generally quite large, and their transmission through Internet networks can be time-consuming. However, in comparison to transporting tapes by conventional means, the possibility of Internet file transfers

presents a situation whereby the potential for international recording sessions simultaneously occurring in widely disparate locations is not inconceivable.

7. According to David Halberstam, as early as 1952, nineteen million American homes had televisions.

8. "Usenet newsgroup" is defined by the Florida State University Internet glossary as "a widely used Internet service that organizes people's comments by topics, called newsgroups. These newsgroups have their own structure, with people commenting on previous comments, starting new discussions, etc. Some groups have a readership of over 100,000 people worldwide. There are more than 12,000 newsgroups in existence." The same source defines "listservs" as "discussion groups on many different topics conducted by e-mail. Participants subscribe to a certain list and receive all the messages posted to the list. Subscribers may post a query or present an issue to the group to get an answer to a question or to stimulate discussion. Lists often have a moderator who manages the information flow and content."

9. A "thread," in the context of the newsgroup, means a conversation regarding a specific topic. A thread begins when one participant asks a question or comments on a particular subject, to which others respond. The initial comment and the responses constitute a thread. There may be hundreds of separate threads occurring simultaneously in a group, and it is not unusual for several long-lasting threads to reference the same issues and involve many of the same participants.

10. Karl Marx's notions of privatization of life and particularly of the isolated individual, while directed toward a specific temporal location and particular cultural circumstances, translate well to the virtual communities of the Internet. However, the isolated individual has, through these interest groups, joined with other isolated individuals to create social bonds that may exist only in the virtual domain, or may transcend the ether at real life events planned in the course of the group's discussions.

11. Most of the threads generated by Tyrone's inquiry are, at the time of this writing, listed at the following URL: http://groups.google.com/groups?q=Tyrone+group:rec .music.makers.guitar.acoustic&hl=en&lr=&ie=UTF-8&start=30&sa=N (last accessed 10 September 2005).

12. Race and its bearing on the demographics of folk musicians and audiences is an issue that surfaces throughout this project and is addressed at length in chapter 6, which deals with folk festivals.

13. To my knowledge, at the time of this writing Rowoth is still the moderator of the folkmusic list but not of FolkBiz.

14. Other products may include instructional, poetic, or informational books; keychains, T-shirts, or refrigerator magnets emblazoned with the artist's name or logo; or any number of folk-music-related or non-folk-music-related items.

15. Musician press kits are usually folders containing eight-by-ten photographs of the artist, short biographies, compact discs or tapes, and contact information.

16. Although Benjamin Filene has made a convincing argument that the construction of a folk "authentic" underscored much of American folk music promotion in the 1930s and '40s.

17. While lyrics referencing computer use and terminology have become commonplace at song circles and folk festival campfires, by and large contemporary professional touring folk musicians avoid the topic, apparently considering it to be a topic for amateur players and would-be comedians.

18. I must admit that the lyrics may have been exceptionally innovative, but given their context within the sonic structure I was unable to concentrate on lyric content.

4. The Business

1. None of these terms are mutually exclusive. That is, performers may also be presenters or may wear any number of different hats within the context of the microindustry.

2. In 1996, Robert Burnett listed the big six as Time Warner, Sony, Philips Electronics, Bertelsmann, Thorn EMI, and Matsushita (*Global Jukebox*, 2).

3. Folk venues, including house concerts, coffeehouses, and "church basement" concerts, are discussed at length in the following chapter. The limited physical space of most of those venues allows for relatively intimate performer/audience proximity.

4. This is the same historical/epistemological thread that Marshall McLuhan draws upon in his classic *Understanding Media* (1964), when describing the artist as "the man of integral awareness" (65).

5. Tim Drake suggested that high-end performers in contemporary folk often made incomes in the "six-figure" range. Apparently, for most of these performers low in the "six-figures" best describes their income. By comparison, in *The Global Jukebox*, Robert Burnett documents mid-1990s recording contracts of Michael Jackson and Madonna worth multiple millions of dollars (24–25).

6. Prior to the U.S. invasion of Iraq on 20 March 2003, the folk responded to the threat of war through antiwar songs old and new and with active protests.

7. In this sense the folk microindustry is like any other market-driven business: the CD as advertisement is one element in a chain of signifiers inevitably leading to the next commodity.

8. The term "product" has come into common use in the industry at large and usually refers to CDs and cassettes, which are, for the contemporary folk singer/songwriter, marketed largely through direct sales at performances.

9. Occasionally artists who are considered either directly or peripherally associated with folk music assert a public position in which they criticize the "guardians of the folk": those whose insistence upon traditional musical elements as criteria for folk inclusion reinscribe ideological disjunctures between folk and the popular.

10. Crosby, Stills and Nash, the Eagles, and other groups of that era popularized this thick vocal texture for rock and folk-rock audiences.

11. Even within the short lists of popular folk artists there are different levels and degrees of popularity based upon largely extramusical factors, all of which eventually constitute the performer's drawing power.

12. "Food chain" in this context is a term used by presenter Glenn Drinkwater in a conversation.

13. Although the "mass audience" for contemporary folk music appears to be growing, it is still tiny when compared to the mainstream popular music audience.

14. I observed one particularly striking example of this practice at the Falcon Ridge Folk Festival in Hillsdale, New York, in July 2001. Greg Brown, who is one of folk's top draws, was performing on the main stage dressed in cutoff jeans, Wellington style work boots, a colorful vest, and a leather floppy hat reminiscent of 1960s youth culture. Initially it struck me that Brown's appearance was a retro hippie affectation of the type popular among contemporary youth. However, upon sober reflection it occurred to me that Brown began his career in New York's Greenwich Village in the 1960s. For Greg Brown the attire was likely not a retro fashion statement but rather a reconstruction. This relationship between past and present, or perhaps intent and perception, seemed ultimately appropriate in the context of an engaging aspect of folk's politics of image.

15. As far as I am aware, the only large-scale statistical study of folk music audiences is Maryl Neff's 1996 doctoral dissertation. My personal observations of folk audiences over the past decade indicate that an overwhelming majority of folk's active audience is over the age of forty. Neff's study supports my observations, which are also largely taken for granted by performers and presenters.

16. Except perhaps when the relationship with the mainstream is long past. Quite a few of the pop folk stars of the 1960s, whose popularity waned following the decline of the "revival," are regular performers on the contemporary folk scene.

17. The relative autonomy of the Texas acoustic/folk industry mirrors the prevalent ideology of independence and individualism that has come to represent a Texan identity. The image of the autonomous Texan has a long history and involved folklore. To this day television and magazine advertisements for Texas travel destinations exploit the notion of Texas as "almost a different country" (from a Texas Travel Bureau advertisement).

18. I am reasonably familiar with the Texas and Northeast folk music scenes, having lived in both areas, but have spent little time in the Northwest.

19. In the years that have passed since then, I have heard nothing else about any of them, and to my knowledge none have played again in Texas. A recent World Wide Web search revealed that at least one is touring regularly and even playing occasionally on the East Coast. All maintain personal Web sites with information about themselves and on which their CDs can be purchased.

20. Publicists and road managers may be employees of management companies or may be independent.

21. The number 150 as a measure for agency consideration came up time and again in interviews and casual conversations with artists' representatives. It seemed as if they had all come together and decided that 150 was the turning point between levels of economic credibility.

22. Zollo is the author of *Songwriters on Songwriting* (1991), an extensive collection of interviews by some of the best-known popular songwriters of the last fifty years from Sammy Cahn to Frank Zappa.

Ian, a regular columnist for *Performing Songwriter*, is a singer/songwriter whose songs "Society's Child" and "At Seventeen" were radio hits in the late 1960s. She has received multiple Grammy Awards and is a popular performer at folk festivals, theaters, and various high-profile folk/acoustic venues.

23. Today it measures some 7¾-by-10 inches as compared with *Dirty Linen*'s 8⅜-by-10, and *Performing Songwriter*'s substantial 9-by-11. While such observations may seem insignificant, they speak to certain assumptions regarding each magazine's economic stake in the microindustry and their general ideological directions. Clearly the publication's not-for-profit status has bearing on its more proletarian appearance.

24. The number of stations programming folk music is changing rapidly, if not daily. The economy of radio broadcasting, as well as continually changing personnel at university stations, has direct bearing on programming decisions. Thus programs with declining or simply small audiences may disappear without notice.

5. Folkspace

1. An open-mic is a popular event at bars, restaurants, and miscellaneous venues, at which anyone can sign up to play a song or two.

2. In another sense, place has long been an index of recognition for popular music audiences. Since the early twentieth century, songwriters have used place names in their song lyrics to garner favor with audiences familiar with a specific locale: the idea being that listeners will transfer their own local experience of place to the reception of the song. A song like W. C. Handy's "Beale Street Blues," for example, would presumably sell a significant number of units in Memphis simply because the audience can relate a personal knowledge of that storied area of town to the meanings derived from the lyric. This technique is occasionally exaggerated, as in Chuck Berry's "Sweet Little Sixteen" and the Beach Boys' "Surfin' USA" in which as many city names as can possibly be worked into the lyric scheme are mentioned in rapid succession. Whether this invocation of place indeed promotes record sales is difficult to say. Yet the idea suggests that a song's commercial success relates directly to its efficacy in evoking personal and public memory. Presumably in hearing the name of one's hometown in a song the listener might imagine a sense of common experience with the performer.

3. In *Listening in Paris: A Cultural History* (1995), James H. Johnson suggests, "Audiences reasoned on some level that if politeness was necessary to succeed, its absence signaled inferiority. Policing manners thus became an act of self-reassurance. It confirmed one's social identity by noticing those who didn't measure up, whether through (choose your label) ignorance, laziness, bad upbringing, insensitivity, or overall dullness" (232).

4. This is not to suggest that folk audience behavior is modeled after the Parisian opera audiences of the nineteenth century, merely that there are behavioral similarities between the two. Lawrence Levine documents the changes in audience behavior in the nineteenth and early twentieth century in terms of the emergence of an American high/low cultural hierarchy: concert music on one end of the spectrum and the reviled popular on the other. The folk's traditional aversion to the popular situates it within a similar high/low dialectic frame: folk as high and popular as low. While popular music audiences are almost expected to scream for pop stars, to dance, and to express them-

selves actively at performances, the folk demand a certain level of decorum and reverence to the primacy of the lyric.

5. The "suggested donation" is often a way around paying performance royalties to performing rights organizations.

6. "Product" generally refers to compact discs and cassette tapes, although the term may extend to various promotional items such as T-shirts, caps, and key chains emblazoned with the performer's name, logo, or other identifying artwork.

7. I first met Dave Carter at the Woody Guthrie Folk Festival in July 2000, where we swapped songs at a song circle in the campground and enjoyed each other's company. When I heard Pilant would be hosting Dave and Tracy, I asked to open the show primarily to have an opportunity to visit with Dave.

8. Dave Carter and Tracy Grammer subsequently went on tour with Baez, who proved to be a champion of their music, but on 19 July 2002, three weeks before his fiftieth birthday, Dave died suddenly of a heart attack.

9. At the Folk Alliance conference in 1999, at least one well-attended workshop concerned maintaining one's health while touring. Nutrition and exercise as well as sleeping habits and remedies for colds and other ailments were shared among the participants.

10. With only one exception, all of the concert presenters I have come into contact with through interviews, casual conversations, or e-mail correspondence have been male. Sometimes married couples present concerts, but invariably it is the male partner with whom the series is publicly identified.

11. These are the only two categories of venues that I have heard mentioned. Presumably below a B rating would suggest that the series is not important enough to be concerned about. The A-list includes the top-tier artists such as Cheryl Wheeler, Patty Larkin, John Gorka, Richard Shindell, and others who have achieved a comparatively high level of national and sometimes international recognition.

12. In *Distinction: A Social Critique of the Judgement of Taste* (1984), Bourdieu says of these intermediaries: "Assigning themselves the impossible, and therefore unassailable, role of divulging legitimate culture—in which they resemble the legitimate popularizers—without possessing the specific competence of the legitimate simplifiers, they have to make themselves, as Kant puts it, 'the apes of genius' and seek a substitute for the charismatic *auctoritas* of the *auctor* and the lofty freedom in which it asserts itself. . . . [A]nd all this must be done while living in the unease of the inherently contradictory role of a 'presenter' devoid of intrinsic value" (326).

13. I played an opener spot for a concert series recently where the featured performer made almost three times her minimum fee, which amounted to over $2400. Selling an additional twenty to thirty CDs at fifteen dollars each makes for a profitable evening in the folk music world.

14. As discussed previously, Bob Dylan is often credited with the demise of the folk revival. However, Dylan's electric performance at Newport in 1965, rather than being the impetus for folk music's commercial decline, simply provides an opportune marker in a predictable trend in American popular music markets. Popular music audiences are fickle. What was once exciting and innovative shortly becomes yesterday's news. Popu-

lar audiences were simply ready for different sounds. In some ways rock and roll was a more successful vehicle for expressing a growing anger and frustration with the American political system, in which young people felt they had little or no real voice. In any case, folk music ceased to be the popular music du jour through a relatively predictable process of attrition. The popular music audience's shortened attention span may be situated in a postmodern politics of image, or a less prosaic modernism. The quest for the new and innovative in music and art has long been a project of modernism and various avant-garde movements. Certainly arguments either way can be convincing. However, neither the dyed-in-the-wool postmodernist nor the entrenched modernist approach can definitively take credit for the whims of the popular audience.

6. The Folk Festival

1. The number of local and regional festivals in which folk music plays some part is considerably larger. These figures represent only festivals in which music, dance, or some combination thereof play the central role.

2. "Fieldwork" is a term with which I am uncomfortable. The word implicitly reinscribes the paternalistic relationship between subject and observer that anthropologists have wrestled with for so long. The "field" is a potentially insurmountable boundary that separates those studied from those doing the studying.

3. The song circles at camps are called "campfires." Some actually have campfires, although generally the disadvantages of smoke blowing into performers' faces seems to outweigh the aesthetic benefits. Thus many, if not most, "campfires" are campfires only in name. During droughts open fires are prohibited at Kerrville, and the moniker becomes entirely symbolic.

4. The "folk strum" is a common rhythmic strumming pattern that Mary Melena suggests is "hard wired" into all beginning guitarists' DNA.

5. "Kerrvert" is a common term at the festival meaning someone who has been to the festival more than once. First-time attendees are called "Kerrvirgins."

6. Since the previous year I had purchased a reasonably sized tent and other gear in anticipation of spending extended periods of time in "the field."

7. Norman Cohen wrote the article "Tin Pan Alley's Contribution to Folk Music" in 1970. The associations between folk music and Tin Pan Alley have, with the advantage of passing time, become more integrated. Indeed many Tin Pan Alley songs are popularly considered as unproblematic parts of folk repertories.

8. West African and Middle Eastern drums have become popular accompaniment instruments for the contemporary folk. The term "ethnic" is a commonly used general descriptor for any drum of non-Western origin.

9. My friend Wendy Wentworth erroneously told several people that I was pursuing a degree in rock and roll. When I correctly explained my work, which was necessary several times a day, I became somewhat of a curiosity among long-time Kerrverts.

10. At this point these invitations have less to do with symbolic capital than simply friendliness born of increasingly close relationships.

11. Some Stupidians favor the alternative spelling "Stoopid."

12. This is paraphrased from a conversation I overheard while waiting in the checkout line of the local grocery store.

13. The only exception I can recall concerns the Billy Bragg/Wilco collaboration in which previously unrecorded Guthrie lyrics were set to music composed by Bragg and released on a CD entitled *Mermaid Avenue* (1998). Some folk purists were incensed by the project and considered the adaptation of Guthrie's lyrics a near sacrilege.

14. There is always an element of risk in making such assumptions. There is a large and vocal gay folk community, and many gay folkies are Falcon Ridge regulars.

15. Presenter Glenn Drinkwater and I discussed the underrepresentation of African-Americans playing the national folk circuit. We could list fewer than twenty black performers who actively play house concert, coffeehouse, and church basement circuits in the United States.

16. The meanings of the terms "race" and "ethnicity" have been hotly contested at least since the beginning of the twentieth century. Marcus Banks in *Ethnicity: Anthropological Constructions* (1996) provides an adept account of the primary terminological arguments and a synopsis of changing perspectives in the scholarly literature. In my discussion of race I see no need to revisit biologistic and cultural constructivist arguments. Rather I use the terms as markers—as signs, if you will—for the perception of otherness and sameness that they imply specifically within the context of folk's past and present.

17. While many black gospel groups perform outside of the church, generally their performances remain religious in nature. That is, they serve as evangelical vehicles.

18. Thomas Dartmouth Rice is often credited with "inventing" blackface minstrelsy after observing a crippled black street performer dancing and singing a tune with the chorus, "Weel about and turn about and do jis so. Eb'ry time I weel about I jump Jim Crow." Rice's Jim Crow characterization was a tremendous success and garnered national attention.

19. In the 1940s sales of race records, primarily to black urban labor migrants, reflected an increasing market for recordings by urban-based blues ensembles. The development and commercial availability of electric guitars, amplifiers, and relatively portable public address systems enabled musicians not only to play louder and in larger ensembles, but allowed for tonal experimentation. These were technological innovations that black musicians appeared to welcome. As the technology became available the old-fashioned acoustic instruments and solo singer/songwriters, or songsters, lost their popular appeal. For African-American audiences the electric blues and later rhythm and blues must have resonated with their urban spheres of experience more immediately than older rural-based acoustic styles.

20. Both Benjamin Filene and Charles Wolfe and Kip Lornell provide detailed historical accounts of the construction of a folk heritage and the complicated roles race played in that construction.

21. Here I do not mean to imply that the presenters have appointed themselves gatekeepers in an active attempt to guard their audience from some perceived black threat.

However, several festival attendees noted a degree of reluctance on the part of presenters to hire black performers or groups considered "too black."

7. Music for Export

1. Solomon Linda was a black South African recording artist whose song "Mbube" not only became "South Africa's first 'hit' and Linda's choir isicathamiya's uncrowned kings, but also the word mbube became synonymous with the whole genre of male a cappella choral singing" (Erlmann, Music, Modernity, and the Global Imagination, 204). In early 2006 a financial settlement (for an undisclosed amount) was reached between the Solomon Linda estate and the song's copyright holder, apparently putting to rest the history of inequity surrounding the economics of "Mbube/Wimoweh."

2. South Africa continues to be a troubled place. Katz's rhetoric did nothing to enhance the upstate New York audience's knowledge of that country's continuing problems. Rather she chose to accentuate the uplifting events surrounding Nelson Mandela's election to the presidency, the band's performance at that event, and the positive steps that have been undertaken in the pursuit of equality and equity in South Africa.

3. This is not to say that some highly skilled contemporary bluesmen bring nothing new to the style. On the contrary some players, including Steve James and Roy Bookbinder among others, have managed to integrate their personal technical and aesthetic elements into the older, fixed styles, resulting in what Ulf Hannerz calls in "The World in Creolization" "new diversities." However, the fundamental stylistic characteristics of country blues were fixed in the early twentieth century.

4. This Anglo-European heritage may be "imagined" in terms of its experiential currency. That is, the personal connections to these histories are most often imagined.

5. In Global Pop: World Music, World Markets (1997), Timothy Taylor describes this sort of criticism of Youssou N'Dour from Senegal and Angélique Kidjo from Benin, who "face constant pressure from westerners to remain musically and otherwise premodern—that is, culturally 'natural'—because of racism and western demands for authenticity" (126).

8. Unnatural Acts

1. Colleen Lamos, in her essay "The Ethics of Queer Theory," examines the conceptual similarities and differences between gay and lesbian studies and queer theory. In my analysis I do not make clear distinctions between the two. This does not mean that there are none. Rather I am more interested in examining general trajectories in studies of sexuality and how, or if, those ideas have clear consequences for the folk.

2. Of the performers Hajdu lists, several, including Melissa Etheridge, Nanci Griffith, and K. D. Lang, are only peripherally associated with the folk music scene. Griffith was once a folk circuit regular, but after achieving national prominence and major label representation, her "big-time" status positions her within decidedly mainstream markets.

3. Oddly the Indigo Girls are not considered a folk group per se. They do have ties to the folk but long ago transcended the economic limits of that circuit.

4. Anger and betrayal are common themes among DiFranco's fans. The sources of the anger seem ambiguous, but as I understand it in terms of a generational phenomenon, it focuses on a general social sense of unfulfilled promise: promises of a better world made during the 1960s; promises of marital stability versus high divorce rates; the abandonment of social and environmental concerns in favor of individual and corporate greed.

5. One presenter once said to me, "If John Prine was an irritable lesbian, he'd be Mary Gauthier."

6. The previously mentioned case in which a lesbian performer was excluded from the concert roster of a church basement series is one example.

9. A Last Word

1. The lyrics quoted in this chapter are all from "Crucifixion Waltz" (Whitney, *The Borderland*).

2. The Internet has also dramatically changed the nature of fieldwork. Through Internet forums for discussion and the immediacy of e-mail communications, it is now possible to streamline the fieldwork process and to conduct interviews, listen to musical performances, and even communicate via live streaming video. The net has reconfigured possibilities for conducting fieldwork research, at the same time suggesting a reconfiguration of notions of alienation.

BIBLIOGRAPHY AND DISCOGRAPHY

Aberjhani. "Rent Party." In his *Encyclopedia of the Harlem Renaissance*, cowritten by Sandra L. West, 279–280. New York: Facts on File, 2003.

Abrahams, Roger D., and George Foss. *Anglo-American Folksong Style*. Englewood Cliffs, N.J.: Prentice Hall, 1968.

Adorno, Theodor W. *The Jargon of Authenticity*. Translated by Knut Tarnowski and Frederic Will. Evanston, Ill.: Northwestern University Press, 1973.

Alesis. "About Us." http://www.alesis.com/index.php?id=8,2,0,0,1,0 (accessed on 10 September 2005).

Anderson, Jamie. *Never Assume*. Tucson, Ariz.: Tsunami Records, 1995. Sound recording.

Arato, Andrew, and Eike Gebhardt, eds. *The Essential Frankfurt School Reader*. New York: Urizen Books, 1977.

Attali, Jacques. *Noise: The Political Economy of Music*. Minneapolis: University of Minnesota Press, 1985.

Averill, Gage. *A Day for the Hunter, a Day for the Prey: Popular Music and Power in Haiti*. Chicago: University of Chicago Press, 1977.

Avildsen, John G. *The Power of One*. Burbank, Calif.: Warner Home Video, 1992. Video-recording.

Banks, Marcus. *Ethnicity: Anthropological Constructions*. London: Routledge, 1996.

Barthes, Roland. "The Death of the Author." 1968. Reprinted in *Image, Music, Text*, translated by Stephen Heath. New York: Hill and Wang, 1977.

Baudrillard, Jean. "The Melodrama of Difference." In *The Transparency of Evil: Essays on Extreme Phenomena*. Translated by James Benedict, 124–138. London: Verso, 1993.

Bauman, Richard, Patricia Sawin, and Inta Gale Carpenter. *Reflections on the Folklife Festival: An Ethnography of Participant Experience*. Special Publications of the Folklore Institute, no. 2. Bloomington: Folklore Institute, Indiana University, 1992.

Bellah, Robert N., et al. *Habits of the Heart: Individualism and Commitment in American Life*. Berkeley: University of California Press, 1985.

Belz, Carl I. "Popular Music and the Folk Tradition." *Journal of American Folklore* 80, no. 316 (April 1967): 130–142.

Bendix, Regina. *In Search of Authenticity: The Formation of Folklore Studies*. Madison: University of Wisconsin Press, 1997.

Benjamin, Walter. "The Work of Art in the Age of Mechanical Reproduction." 1936. In *Illuminations*, edited by Hannah Arendt, translated by Harry Zohn. New York: Harcourt, Brace, 1968.

Blacking, John. "Making Artistic Popular Music: The Goal of True Folk." *Popular Music* 1 (1981): 9–14.

Bohlman, Philip V. *The Study of Folk Music in the Modern World*. Bloomington: Indiana University Press, 1988.

Booth, Gregory D. and Terry Lee Kuhn. "Economic and Transmission Factors as Essential Elements in the Definition of Folk, Art, and Pop Music." *Musical Quarterly* 74, no. 3 (1990): 411–438.

Borders Group, Inc. "About Borders Group." http://www.bordersgroupinc.com/about/index.html (accessed on 10 September 2005).

Bourdieu, Pierre. *Distinction: A Social Critique of the Judgement of Taste.* Translated by Richard Nice. Cambridge, Mass.: Harvard University Press, 1984.

Boyne, Roy. "Culture and the World-System." In *Global Culture: Nationalism, Globalization and Modernity,* edited by Mike Featherstone, 57–62. London: Sage Publications, 1990.

Brand, Oscar. *The Ballad Mongers: Rise of the Modern Folk Song.* New York: Funk and Wagnalls, 1962.

Brett, Philip. "Musicality, Essentialism, and the Closet." In *Queering the Pitch: The New Gay and Lesbian Musicology,* edited by Philip Brett, Elizabeth Wood, and Gary C. Thomas, 9–26. New York: Routledge Press, 1994.

Brozman, Bob, John Dopyera, Richard A. Smith, and Gary Atkinson. *The History and Artistry of National Resonator Instruments.* Fullerton, Calif.: CenterStream, 1993.

Burnett, Robert. *The Global Jukebox: The International Music Industry.* London: Routledge, 1996.

Cantwell, Robert. *Ethnomimesis: Folklife and the Representation of Culture.* Chapel Hill: University of North Carolina Press, 1993.

———. *When We Were Good: The Folk Revival.* Cambridge, Mass.: Harvard University Press, 1996.

Charlton, Katherine. *Rock Music Styles: A History.* Boston: McGraw-Hill, 1998.

Clifford, James. 1986. "On Ethnographic Allegory." In *Writing Culture: The Poetics and Politics of Ethnography,* ed. James Clifford and George E. Marcus. Berkeley and Los Angeles: University of California Press.

Cohen, Norman. "Tin Pan Alley's Contribution to Folk Music." *Western Folklore* 29, no. 1 (1970): 9–20.

Cohen, Ronald D. *Rainbow Quest: The Folk Music Revival and American Society, 1940–1970.* Amherst: University of Massachusetts Press, 2002.

———. *"Wasn't That a Time!": Firsthand Accounts of the Folk Music Revival.* Metuchen, N.J.: Scarecrow Press, 1995.

———. "Woody the Red?" In *Hard Travelin': The Life and Legacy of Woody Guthrie,* edited by Robert Santelli and Emily Davidson, 138–152. Hanover, N.H.: Wesleyan University Press, 1999.

Connor, Steven. "The Ethics of the Voice." In *Critical Ethics: Text, Theory, and Responsibility,* edited by Dominic Rainsford and Tim Woods, 220–237. New York: St. Martin's Press, 1999.

Cox, Renée. "Recovering *Jouissance*: An Introduction to Feminist Musical Aesthetics." In *Women and Music: A History,* edited by Karin Pendle, 331–340. Bloomington: Indiana University Press, 1991.

Crapanzano, Vincent. *Tuhami: Portrait of a Moroccan*. Chicago: University of Chicago Press, 1980.

Cusick, Suzanne G. "On a Lesbian Relationship with Music: A Serious Effort Not to Think Straight." In *Queering the Pitch: The New Gay and Lesbian Musicology*, edited by Philip Brett, Elizabeth Wood, and Gary C. Thomas, 67–83. New York: Routledge, 1994.

Denisoff, R. Serge. "Democratization of Popular Music." *Media Development* 1 (1982): 29–31.

———. "The Evolution of the American Protest Song." In *The Sounds of Social Change: Studies in Popular Culture*, edited by R. Serge Denisoff and Richard A. Peterson, 15–25. Chicago: Rand McNally, 1972.

———. "Folk Music and the American Left." In *The Sounds of Social Change: Studies in Popular Culture*, edited by R. Serge Denisoff and Richard A. Peterson, 105–120. Chicago: Rand McNally, 1972.

———. "Folk-Rock: Folk Music, Protest, or Commercialism?" *Journal of Popular Culture* 3 (1969): 214–230.

———. "Protest Songs: Those on the Top Forty and Those of the Streets." *American Quarterly* 22, no. 4 (1970): 807–823.

———. *Sing a Song of Social Significance*. 1972. 2nd ed., Bowling Green, Ohio: Bowling Green University Popular Press, 1983.

Eliot, Marc. *Death of a Rebel*. Garden City, N.Y.: Anchor Press, 1979.

Erlmann, Veit. *African Stars: Studies in Black South African Performance*. Chicago: University of Chicago Press, 1991.

———. *Music, Modernity, and the Global Imagination: South Africa and the West*. New York: Oxford University Press, 1999.

———. *Nightsong: Performance, Power, and Practice in South Africa*. Chicago: University of Chicago Press, 1996.

Evans, David. "Blues and Modern Sound: Past, Present, and Future." In *Folk Music and Modern Sound*, edited by William Ferris and Mary L. Hart, 163–176. Jackson: University Press of Mississippi, 1982.

Feld, Steven. "Notes on World Beat." *Public Culture Bulletin* 1, no. 1 (1988): 31–37.

Filene, Benjamin. *Romancing the Folk: Public Memory and American Roots Music*. Chapel Hill: University of North Carolina Press, 2000.

Folk Alliance: North American Folk Music and Dance Alliance. http://www.folkalliance .net (last accessed 14 September 2005). The quotations in the text can no longer be found in the same form on the Web site, though similar declarations are there.

Foucault, Michel. *The History of Sexuality*. Volume 1, *An Introduction*. 1978. New York: Vintage Books, 1988.

Frith, Simon. " 'The Magic That Can Set You Free': The Ideology of Folk and the Myth of the Rock Community." *Popular Music* 1 (1981): 159–168.

———. "Music and Identity." In *Questions of Cultural Identity*, edited by Stuart Hall and Paul Du Gay, 108–127. London: Sage Publications, 1996.

————. *Performing Rites: On the Value of Popular Music.* Cambridge, Mass.: Harvard University Press, 1996.

Fuchs, Barbara. *Mimesis and Empire: The New World, Islam, and European Identities.* Cambridge, England: Cambridge University Press, 2001.

Garfield, Simon. *Expensive Habits: The Dark Side of the Music Industry.* London: Faber and Faber, 1986.

Garofalo, Reebee. "Popular Music and the Civil Rights Movement." In his *Rockin' the Boat: Mass Music and Mass Movements.* Boston: South End Press, 1992.

Gauthier, Mary. *Dixie Kitchen.* Boston: In the Black Records, 1997. Sound recording.

Gillett, Charlie. *The Sound of the City: The Rise of Rock and Roll.* Rev. ed. New York: Pantheon Books, 1983.

Gourlay, Ken. "Towards a Reassessment of the Ethnomusicologist's Role in Research." *Ethnomusicology* 22, no. 1 (1978): 1–35.

Green, Archie. "Hillbilly Music: Source and Symbol." *Journal of American Folklore* 78, no. 309 (July 1965): 204–228.

Guilbault, Jocelyne. "Beyond the 'World Music' Label: An Ethnography of Transnational Musical Practices." *Beitrag zur Konferenz* Grounding Music, May 1996.

Hajdu, David. "Queer as Folk." *New York Times*, 18 August 2002.

Halberstam, David. *The Fifties.* New York: Villard Books, 1993.

Hall, Stuart. "Introduction: Who Needs 'Identity'?" In *Questions of Cultural Identity*, edited by Stuart Hall and Paul Du Gay, 1–17. London: Sage Publications, 1996.

Hannerz, Ulf. "The World in Creolization." *Africa* 57, no. 4 (1987): 546–559.

Hibbard, Don J., and Carol Kaleialoha. *The Role of Rock: A Guide to the Social and Political Consequences of Rock Music.* Englewood Cliffs, N.J.: Prentice Hall, 1983.

Hocquenghem, Guy. *Homosexual Desire.* London: Allison and Busby, 1978. Reprint, Durham, N.C.: Duke University Press, 1993.

Hubbard, Ray Wylie. *Crusades of the Restless Knights.* Cambridge, Mass.: Rounder Records, 1999. Sound recording.

Jameson, Fredric. *Postmodernism, or, The Cultural Logic of Late Capitalism.* Durham: Duke University Press, 1991.

Jensen, Joli. *The Nashville Sound: Authenticity, Commercialization, and Country Music.* Nashville: Vanderbilt University Press, 1998.

Johnathon, Michael. *WoodSongs: A Folksinger's Social Commentary, Cook Manual, and Song Book.* Lexington, Ky.: Poetman Records, 1997/1996.

Johnson, James H. *Listening in Paris: A Cultural History.* Berkeley: University of California Press, 1995.

Jones, Mr. *Waitin' for Me.* Pfarrkirchen, Germany: Dollar Bill Records, 2002. Sound recording.

Kaplan, Caren. *Questions of Travel: Postmodern Discourses of Displacement.* Durham: Duke University Press, 1996.

Kastin, David. *I Hear America Singing: An Introduction to Popular Music.* Upper Saddle River, N.J.: Prentice Hall, 2002.

Keil, Charles. *Urban Blues.* Chicago: University of Chicago Press, 1966.

Keil, Charles, and Steven Feld. *Music Grooves: Essays and Dialogues*. Chicago: University of Chicago Press, 1994.

Laing, Dave. "The Music Industry and the 'Cultural Imperialism' Thesis." *Media, Culture and Society* 8 (1986): 331–341.

Lamos, Colleen. "The Ethics of Queer Theory." In *Critical Ethics: Text, Theory, and Responsibility*, edited by Dominic Rainsford and Tim Woods, 141–150. New York: St. Martin's Press, 1999.

Lavin, Christine. *Getting in Touch with My Inner Bitch*. Self-published, 2000. Sound recording.

Levine, Lawrence W. *Highbrow/Lowbrow: The Emergence of Cultural Hierarchy in America*. Cambridge, Mass.: Harvard University Press, 1988.

Lomax, Alan. "Folk Song Style." *American Anthropologist* 61, no. 6 (1959): 927–954.

———. "Saga of a Folksong Hunter." *HiFi/Stereo Review* 4, no. 5 (May 1960). Also available online at http://www.alan-lomax.com/about_saga.html (accessed on 9 November 2005).

Lomax, John A., and Alan Lomax. *Cowboy Songs and Other Frontier Ballads*. Rev. ed. New York: Macmillan, 1938.

Lornell, Kip. *Introducing American Folk Music*. Madison, Wis.: Brown and Benchmark, 1993.

Lott, Eric. *Love and Theft: Blackface Minstrelsy and the American Working Class*. New York: Oxford University Press, 1993.

Lumer, Robert. "Pete Seeger and the Attempt to Revive the Folk Music Process." *Popular Music and Society* 15, no. 1 (1991): 45–58.

Lund, Jens, and R. Serge Denisoff. "The Folk Music Revival and the Counter Culture: Contributions and Contradictions." *Journal of American Folklore* 84, no. 334 (October 1971): 394–405.

Malan, Rian. "In the Jungle." *Rolling Stone*, 25 May 2000, 54–85. Reprinted online as "Where Does the Lion Sleep Tonight?" http://www.3rdearmusic.com/forum/mbube2.html (accessed 9 November 2005).

Malone, Bill C. *Country Music, U.S.A.* Rev. ed. Austin: University of Texas Press, 1985.

Manuel, Peter. *Cassette Culture: Popular Music and Technology in North India*. Chicago: University of Chicago Press, 1993.

McClary, Susan. *Feminine Endings: Music, Gender, and Sexuality*. Minneapolis: University of Minnesota Press, 1991.

McKeen, William. *Bob Dylan: A Bio-Bibliography*. Westport, Conn.: Greenwood Press, 1993.

McLuhan, Marshall. *Understanding Media: The Extensions of Man*. New York: McGraw-Hill, 1964. Reprint, Cambridge, Mass.: MIT Press, 1994.

Melena, Mary. *Something Passing Through*. Evanston, Ill.: Waterbug Records, 1997. Sound recording.

Mellers, Wilfrid Howard. "God, Modality, and Meaning in Some Recent Songs of Bob Dylan." *Popular Music* 1 (1981): 143–157.

Mészáros, István. *Marx's Theory of Alienation*. London: Merlin Press, 1970.

Middleton, Richard. "Editor's Introduction to Volume 1." *Popular Music* 1 (1981).

Morton, David. "A Chronology of Magnetic Recording." http://www.acmi.net.au/AIC/ MAGN_REC_CHRON.html (accessed on 10 September 2005).

Neff, Maryl. "Media Usage among Folk Music Communities." Ph.D. diss., University of Florida, 1996.

Nettl, Bruno. *The Study of Ethnomusicology: Twenty-nine Issues and Concepts.* Urbana: University of Illinois Press, 1983.

Peraino, Judith A. " 'Rip Her to Shreds': Women's Music According to a Butch-Femme Aesthetic." *repercussions* 1, no. 1 (1992): 19–47.

Peterson, Richard A. *Creating Country Music: Fabricating Authenticity.* Chicago: University of Chicago Press, 1997.

Porter, James. "Muddying the Crystal Spring: From Idealism and Realism to Marxism in the Study of English and American Folk Song." In *Comparative Musicology and Anthropology of Music: Essays on the History of Ethnomusicology,* edited by Bruno Nettl and Philip V. Bohlman, 113–130. Chicago: University of Chicago Press, 1991.

Porterfield, Nolan. *Last Cavalier: The Life and Times of John A. Lomax, 1867–1948.* Urbana: University of Illinois Press, 1996.

Pronger, Brian. *The Arena of Masculinity: Sports, Homosexuality, and the Meaning of Sex.* New York: St. Martin's Press, 1990.

Ray, Amy. "Queer and Fucked." 9 December 2002. http://www.indigogirls.com/ correspondence/2002/2002-09-12-a.html (accessed on 6 November 2005).

Recording Industry Association of America. "History of Recordings." http://www.riaa .com/issues/audio/history.asp#digital (accessed on 10 September 2005).

Reid, Harvey. *Steel Drivin' Man.* Portsmouth, N.H.: Woodpecker Records, 1991. Sound recording.

Rycenga, Jennifer. "Lesbian Compositional Process: One Lover-Composer's Perspective." In *Queering the Pitch: The New Gay and Lesbian Musicology,* edited by Philip Brett, Elizabeth Wood, and Gary C. Thomas, 275–296. New York: Routledge, 1994.

Santelli, Robert, and Emily Davidson. *Hard Travelin': The Life and Legacy of Woody Guthrie.* Hanover, N.H.: Wesleyan University Press, 1999.

Schacter, Daniel L. *Searching for Memory: The Brain, the Mind, and the Past.* New York: Basic Books, 1996.

Schoenherr, Steve. "Recording Technology History." http://history.acusd.edu/gen/ recording/notes.html#tape (accessed on 10 September 2005).

Schor, Naomi. "This Essentialism Which Is Not One: Coming to Grips with Irigaray." *differences* 1, no. 2 (1989): 38–58.

Seeger, Pete. *The Incompleat Folksinger.* Lincoln: University of Nebraska Press, 1992.

Shelemay, Kay Kaufman. "Recording Technology, the Record Industry, and Ethnomusicological Scholarship." In *Comparative Musicology and Anthropology of Music: Essays on the History of Ethnomusicology,* edited by Bruno Nettl and Philip V. Bohlman, 277–292. Chicago: University of Chicago Press, 1991.

Shore, Susan. *Book of Days.* Evanston, Ill.: Waterbug Records, 1997. Sound recording.

Stallybrass, Peter, and Allon White. *The Politics and Poetics of Transgression*. Ithaca, N.Y.: Cornell University Press, 1986.

Stuessy, Joe, and Scott Lipscomb. *Rock and Roll: Its History and Stylistic Development*. 3d ed. Upper Saddle River, N.J.: Prentice Hall, 1999.

Swinger, Martin. *BearNaked*. Augusta, Maine: BearNakedMusic, 2000. Sound recording.

Szatmary, David P. *Rockin' in Time: A Social History of Rock-and-Roll*. 5th ed. Upper Saddle River, N.J.: Prentice Hall, 2004.

"TASCAM Company History." http://www.tascam.com/Company.html (accessed on 10 September 2005).

Taussig, Michael T. *Mimesis and Alterity: A Particular History of the Senses*. New York: Routledge, 1993.

Taylor Guitars. "From the Beginning . . ." http://www.taylorguitars.com/history/essay .html (accessed 23 September 2005).

Taylor, Timothy D. *Global Pop: World Music, World Markets*. New York: Routledge, 1997.

Tomlinson, John. *Cultural Imperialism: A Critical Introduction*. Baltimore: Johns Hopkins University Press, 1991.

Wallerstein, Immanuel. "Culture as the Ideological Battleground of the Modern World-System." In *Global Culture: Nationalism, Globalization and Modernity*, edited by Mike Featherstone, 31–55. London: Sage Publications, 1990.

Walser, Robert. *Running with the Devil: Power, Gender, and Madness in Heavy Metal Music*. Hanover, N.H.: University Press of New England, 1993.

Waterman, Christopher A. "Race Music: Bo Chatmon, 'Corrine, Corrina,' and the Excluded Middle." In *Music and the Racial Imagination*, edited by Ronald Radano and Philip V. Bohlman, 167–205. Chicago: University of Chicago Press, 2001.

Weber, Max. "Science as a Vocation." 1919. In *From Modernism to Postmodernism: An Anthology*, edited by Lawrence Cahoone, 169–176. Malden, Mass.: Blackwell, 1996.

Weissman, Dick. *Music Making in America*. New York: Frederick Ungar, 1982.

Whitney, Alan. *The Borderland*. Rochester, N.Y.: Because We Can Records, 2000. Sound recording.

Wilgus, D. K. *Anglo-American Folksong Scholarship Since 1898*. New Brunswick, N.J.: Rutgers University Press, 1959.

Williams, Jack. *Across the Winterline*. Naperville, Ill.: Wind River, 1999. Sound recording.

Wolfe, Charles, and Kip Lornell. *The Life and Legend of Leadbelly*. New York: HarperCollins, 1992.

Zollo, Paul. *Songwriters on Songwriting*. Cincinnati, Ohio: Writer's Digest Books, 1991.

Zwick, Edward. *Legends of the Fall*. Culver City, Calif.: Columbia TriStar, 1994. Video-recording.

INDEX

civil rights movement, 55, 130
coffeehouse, xiii, xxii, 21, 82, 85, 135, 156;
   history and imagination of, 104–6, 111;
   new notions of, 95
Cohen, Ronald, xx, 124
colonialism, 136–38, 145
Colvin, Shawn, 17, 82
commodity: cultural, 58, 124; of difference,
   143, 148, 163; music as, xvi, xviii, 6–7,
   70, 131, 150
common man: and the artist, 65; the
   baby boomer as, 33, 106; and the
   Farm Couple, 26–27; fiction of, 119;
   folk association with, xxiii, 68, 71,
   87, 104; as folk paradigm, 19, 21–23;
   and folk radio titles, 91; as symbol of
   authenticity, 29; and Woody Guthrie,
   124
communalism, 65, 108, 123, 166
Communist Party, 6, 21
concert series, 35, 57, 80, 85, 89, 163;
   descriptions of, 96–98; historical
   precedent to, 95; radio show as, 91; and
   sexual prejudice, 153, 156; Sharon Katz
   show, 135; types of, 100–106
Connor, Steven, 7, 43
Cotton, Elizabeth, 131
country, notion of, 24
country music, xii, 24, 30, 76, 87; at the
   Folk Alliance, 69; and Mary Gauthier,
   158; and Steve Earle, 71
Cox, Renée, 158
Crapanzano, Vincent, xxiv
cultural intermediary. See power broker

Darling, Eric, 68
DAT, 46, 75
Davis, Rev. Gary, 77, 126
Davis, Guy, 126, 171
DeGeneres, Ellen, 152
demographics, xxi–xxii, 30, 33, 62, 68, 151,
   162; and industrialization, 10; Maryl
   Neff's study of, 125–26, 148; of the

1960s folk revival, 23; and RMMGA,
   51, 54
Denisoff, Serge, 5–6, 16, 70, 150
dialectics: of attraction and revulsion,
   30–31, 122; of exoticism, 136–37; of folk,
   xvi–xviii, xxi, 9, 12; of the folk festival,
   120; of labeling and sexuality, 149,
   155–56; negative, 59; and otherness,
   55; of past and modernity, 16; and
   technology, 44; of urban and rural, 24,
   28
difference: commodity of, 143, 148, 163;
   mythology of, 134. See also Other, the
DiFranco, Ani, 82–83, 125–26, 151–53
Dirty Linen, 41, 74, 86–88
dobro, 11, 69
Dorff, Stephen, 137–38
Drake, Tim, 81, 83–85
Drinkwater, Glenn, 130
drug use, 30–32, 99
Dylan, Bob, xiii, 3–4, 16; in Broadside, 85;
   influence of, on the Beatles, 120; at the
   1965 Newport Folk Festival, 20, 42, 59

Earle, Steve, 39, 71, 79
Eberhardt, Cliff, 79
Edwards, Don, 116–17
egalitarianism: as contrary to individual
   stardom, xv, 65; and the folk festival,
   108, 112, 114, 122, 131; and folk idealism,
   xxiii, 120, 161–63; and folk music
   organizations, 50, 73; and Graceland,
   136; and the music business, xxi, 91, 92,
   106, 150; and perceptions of folk, xv,
   xxi, 59
Eklund, Jason, 115
Elisha, Dave, 70
elitism, 108, 122
Elliot, Jack, 4
Emoff, Ron, 11
English Folk Song Society, 9–10
Erlmann, Veit, xiv, xv, xvii, 9, 16, 134
ethnicity, 54, 56, 67, 143, 148

humor, 40, 107; in newsgroups, 49–50, 54; and race, 55; used by folk artists, 2, 32, 36–37, 60, 117

Hurt, Mississippi John, 15, 126–27, 131

Hutchinson, Lydia, 86–87

hybridity, 77, 161, 163

Ian, Janis, 60–61, 86

idealism, folk: in conflict with modern realities, xii–xiii, xxi, 18, 43, 67, 105; construction of, 18, 23; and egalitarianism, xxiii, 131, 162–63; and the folk festival, xxiii, 108, 114, 123, 131, 163; and nostalgia, 28, 117; and populism, xxi, 23, 42

identities: anonymous Internet, 49; construction of folk, 2, 15, 18, 166; collective, 67, 92; cultural, xix, 138; and the Other, 135, 149; public, 13, 142; sameness and alterity in formation of, 128, 144; sexual, 157

image, 25–26, 35, 39, 59; construction of, 114, 162, 166; of folk, 13, 59, 68, 114; of the folk singer, 21, 80, 99; politics of, xvii, 34, 86–87, 105, 135, 145; public, 82, 152; and race, 55, 135–37; of rural America, 26, 28; and signification, xv, xvi, 143

imagery, folk, 26, 32, 33, 34, 35, 40, 107

imaginary, xvii, 23, 27, 38–39; American popular, 6, 19, 21–22; and the Other, 142

imperialism, cultural, xix, 129, 134, 144

International Folk Music Council, 10

isicathamiya, 16, 144

Jackson, Michael, 65

James, Steve, 88

Jameson, Fredric, xvi, 34–35, 142

jazz, Kansas City, 69

Jensen, Jolie, 24, 26

Jerling, Michael, 1

Johnathan, Michael, 12–13

Jones, Mr. See Bichlmeier, Jürgen

Kansas City jazz, 69

Kaplan, Caren, xvi

Kaplansky, Lucy, 79, 82

Katz, Sharon, 135–38

Keb' Mo', 88

Keil, Charles, xviii, 12–14, 166

Kennedy, Rod, 98, 117

Kennedys, the (musical group), 113

Kerrville Folk Festival, xxiii, 15, 26, 51, 83, 86, 88; campgrounds at, 114, 118, 121–23, 125; fieldwork at, 111–23; land rush at, 115–16; Mr. Jones at, 138, 140; power hierarchies at, 121–23, 148; and Rod Kennedy, 98, 117; workshops at, 89

Kingston Trio, 20–21

Kinscherff, Jamie, 51

Krauss, Alison, 78

Ladysmith Black Mambazo, 136, 144

Laing, Dave, 129

Lang, Jeff, 79, 144

Larkin, Patti, 17, 78

Lavin, Christine, 36–37, 78, 117, 148

Leadbelly, xx, 16, 29, 60, 77, 127, 131

Levine, Lawrence, 22, 65, 102

Linda, Solomon, 133–34, 144

Lipscomb, Mance, 15, 131

listserv, 48–49, 52, 56–57, 63

localism, xvi, 83

Lomax, Alan, 21, 23, 116, 134; and Leadbelly, 127; and recording technology, 42–44, 58, 66; and search for authentic folk, 5, 23, 131

Lomax, John, 23, 29, 42, 116, 134; and Leadbelly, 127; and recording technology, 42–43; and search for authentic folk, 23, 131

Lornell, Kip, xx, 127

Lott, Eric, 128, 131

Lumer, Robert, 4

Malan, Rian, 134
Malone, Bill, 21, 30
manager, personal, 66, 74, 81, 84–85
Manning, Jacquie. *See* Small Potatoes
Manuel, Peter, xxi, 44, 47, 62
Marsh, Dave, 70
"Mbube/Wimoweh/The Lion Sleeps Tonight," 133–34, 138, 144
McClary, Susan, 129–30, 158
McLuhan, Marshall, 44
mediation, 14, 144; mass, xxi, 16–17, 55
Melena, Mary, 13, 51
Middleton, Richard, 10, 12, 18, 165
mimesis, 127–29, 138–39, 141
minstrelsy, blackface, 55, 126, 128–29
Mitchell, Joni, 41, 60
modernity vs. past, 16
mouth music (canntaireachd), 142
Musselman, Jim, 70–71
mythology: of authenticity, 96; of constant progress, 146; of the folk, 5–6, 18, 23, 71, 165; and history, 134, 161; and the 1960s folk revival, 15, 59; racial, 55–56; and Ray Wylie Hubbard, 31; of the star, xx, 65, 73; of Woody Guthrie, 124

nationalism, 7
National Socialism, xvii, 7
Neff, Maryl, 85, 90, 125, 148
Nelson, Paul, 4
Newport Folk Festival, 15, 20, 111; Bob Dylan's 1965 performance at, 42, 59
newsgroups, 48–54, 63, 147
nostalgia, xx, xvi, 23, 35, 70, 140; and dialectic of past and modernity, 16, 23; and folk idealism, xvii, 12, 28, 116–17; for lost youth, 32–33; and preservationism, 67; and race, 56; rural, 25–26, 28–29, 40; used in marketing, 90; and Walter Benjamin, 44

Olivia Records, 149
open mic, 51, 95

oral tradition, xviii, 8, 10, 14–16
Ordinary, the, xv, xviii, 35–36, 119, 155; authenticity of, 37; politics of, 147; spectacle of, 131
Orientalism, 30–31
Osiel, Marianne, 117
Other, the, 55, 142, 149; and race, 163–64. *See also* difference

Palieri, Rik, 68
Parry, Hubert, 9–10
pastiche, xv, 60, 69, 117, 125
past vs. modernity, 16
Pattis, Larry, 53–54
Paul, Ellis, 78, 82–83
Peraino, Judith, 149–50
performing rights organizations, 7
Performing Songwriter, 86–87
persona, 2–4, 33; and the Other, 142, 143; and race, 38; and representation, 80, 85; rural, 2, 28, 32; and sexuality, 151–52
phallocentrism, 155
Philadelphia Folk Festival, 15, 42, 110–11
Phillips, U. Utah, 68
Philo Records, 77–78
Pilant, Glen, 97–98
Pilant, LaJeanna, 97–98
Poole, Charlie, 30–31
popular, the, vs. folk, 9–12
postmodernism, xv–xvi
power broker, 110, 163; Alan Rowoth as, 57; in early folk, 6, 58–59, 127, 131; and gender, 149; the presenter as, 97, 103, 107
Prasada-Rao, Tom, 126, 143
preservationism: and the Lomaxes, 42–44, 58, 67, 128, 130; musical, 11, 17–18, 26
Presley, Elvis, 65, 152
Prezioso, Rich. *See* Small Potatoes
Prine, John, 158
Pronger, Brian, 155
Purpose, Darryl, 35–36

Urban Campfires, 98, 100
usergroups, 18, 48, 50, 56–57, 147

ventriloquism, cultural, 43, 145
voice, as subjective property, 7, 43
volk, 7, 165

Wallerstein, Immanuel, xix
Waterbug Records, 13, 78
Waterman, Christopher, 8–9, 129, 144
Weavers, the, 68, 133–34
Weber, Max, 100
Weeks, Jeffrey, 155
Weigle, Mark, 156–57
Weissman, Richard, 21, 64, 68, 70, 95
Wentworth, Wendy, 115
Werner, Susan, 82
Wheeler, Cheryl, 78, 82–83, 101
White, Josh, 15
Whitney, Alan, 76, 160, 166
Wilgus, D. K., 5, 37

Williams, Jack, 28–29, 79, 140
Williams, Patrick. *See* Farm Couple, the
Wilson, Junius Pop, 135
Wind River Records, 28, 72, 78–79
Wolfe, Charles, xx, 127
Wood, Jayne, 98
Wood, Steve, 98
workshops, 70–71, 89–90
world music, xv, xx, xxiii, 70; folk
    associations with, 88, 132, 145,
    160, 163; and record companies,
    75, 77; and Sharon Katz, 135–36,
    138
World Wide Web, 47

Yarrow, Bethany, 76–77
Yarrow, Peter, 76
Young, Faron, 24
Young/Hunter Management, 84–85

Zollo, Paul, 86